The Myth of an Irish Cinema

Irish Studies

James MacKillop, *Series Editor*

The Myth
of an Irish Cinema

Approaching Irish-Themed Films

Michael Patrick Gillespie

Syracuse University Press

This book is published with the assistance of a grant from the Klinger College of Arts and Sciences, Marquette University.

The paper used in this publication meets the minimum requirements of American National Standard for Information Sciences—Permanence of Paper for Printed Library Materials, ANSI Z39.48–1984.∞™

Permission to reprint the following film stills is gratefully acknowledged: The Irish Film Institute for stills from *The Lad from Old Ireland*, *Rory O'More*, and *Irish Destiny*; Redmond Morris for a still from *The Rising of the Moon*; David Collins and Samson Films for a still from *Pigs*; John Boorman for a still from *The General*; Catherine Tiernan and Ocean Films for a still from *The Fifth Province*; Speers Film/Element Films and photographer Jonathan Hession for stills from *Adam and Paul* and *Garage*; Barry Lyons for a still from *Exposure*; Tom Hall and Fionan O'Connell for stills from *November Afternoon*; Liz Gill and Goldfish Films for stills from *Goldfish Memory*; Margo Harkin for stills from *Hush-a-Bye Baby*; Donna Walsh and Little Bird Productions for a still from *December Bride*; Cathal Black for stills from *Our Boys*; Perry Ogden for a still from *Pavee Lackeen*; Ed Guiney for a still from *Disco Pigs*; and Pat Murphy for stills from *Maeve* and *Anne Devlin*.

For a listing of books published and distributed by Syracuse University Press, visit our Web site at SyracuseUniversityPress.syr.edu.

ISBN-13: 978-0-8156-3168-2 (hardcover); ISBN-10: 0-8156-3168-5
ISBN-13: 978-0-8156-3193-4 (paperback); ISBN-10: 0-8156-3193-6

Library of Congress Cataloging-in-Publication Data

Gillespie, Michael Patrick.

The myth of an Irish cinema : approaching Irish-themed films / Michael Patrick Gillespie. — 1st ed.

p. cm. — (Irish studies)

Includes bibliographical references and index.

ISBN 978-0-8156-3168-2 (hardcover : alk. paper) — ISBN 978-0-8156-3193-4 (pbk. : alk. paper)

1. Motion pictures—Ireland. I. Title.

PN1993.5.I85G55 2008

791.4309417—dc22

2008037770

Manufactured in the United States of America

To BRIAN DWYER
a wonderful nephew
and
an excellent golf instructor

Michael Patrick Gillespie is the Louise Edna Goeden Professor of English at Marquette University. He is the author or editor of numerous books on Irish, British, and Irish American literature and film, including *Reading William Kennedy,* also published by Syracuse University Press.

Contents

Illustrations

Preface

What's the Point?

A number of highly acclaimed examinations of the cinema in Ireland by well-known scholars such as Lance Pettitt, Martin McLoone, and Ruth Barton already exist.[1] Consequently, before proceeding it seems appropriate to speak to the subject of the need for another work in this area. I think one finds the answer reflected in the dynamics of the current cinematic environment. The books I have cited have laid useful foundations and offered valuable insights into fundamental aspects of Irish filmmaking. However, none is, nor would claim to be, the final word on the subject, and indeed collectively the works of these writers have raised as many questions as they have answered. My study addresses some of these queries and introduces other issues as well. It expands on previous efforts by extending the viewer's sense of the interpretive possibilities for Irish-themed films, and it offers an alternative approach that encompasses recent cultural changes in the national milieu from which these motion pictures have emerged.

Like the examinations mentioned above, much of this book presents close readings of Irish-themed films, yet several important concepts distinguish my interpretations from those works preceding it.[2] Most significantly, I challenge the central supposition of the other works about the nature of the topic under consideration. I feel that Irish cinema, a term that contemporary critics freely apply, evokes a concept more misleading than illuminating. Despite assumptions to the contrary, it has no stable denotation, and its application creates ambiguities rather than establishes unwavering conceptions. In consequence, viewing all Irish-themed films as

xi

part of the unitary entity that this label implies reduces their significance and circumscribes our ability to understand them.

As I will detail in the Introduction, the problem with discussions about the nature of a national cinema, Irish or otherwise, lies in the presumed constancy of notions that underlie it. To begin with, ontological disputes have led to the erosion of any fixed idea of nation. Among historians and social scientists no consensus exists on whether one should view a nation as a political or a cultural body or whether it stands as the product of modern social alignments or an entity continuing from the premodern past. Thus, merely invoking the term destabilizes the analytic process by putting into play a wide range of possible denotations.

Critics have acknowledged a similar slipperiness obtaining in the received sense of the phrase *national cinema*. Alan Williams sums it up succinctly in his introduction to a collection of essays on the topic, saying that "cinema and nation have always had shifting, problematic functions with regard to one another and to the larger arena of world culture."[3] As I will discuss in greater detail in the Introduction, not only the contributors to his volume but a wide range of film scholars express a variety of views on the concept of national cinemas, and through it all their most convincing, if often unintentional, gesture establishes the subjectivity of the term, both as critics apply it and as filmgoers understand it.

The diverse responses that one can expect readers legitimately to make to the ideas of nation and of national cinema raise important issues about the acknowledgment of the role of subjectivity in forming impressions of Irish-themed films. Just as *Irish cinema* stands as a term too often accepted without question, many film scholars still generate criticism based on the conception of Irish identity as a monolithic temperament, even when Irishness as a stable category finds itself under assault. Rapidly changing demographics, emerging social concerns, and shifting economic assets often make the most accurate representations of contemporary Irish life the ones that are least dependent on conventional Irish cultural markers. (See Appendix A for a survey of individual opinions on the subjectivity of Irish identity.) To complicate circumstances, the institutions that have traditionally defined "Irishness" are changing or becoming obsolete. This condition of flux does not mean that viewers should cease to take Irishness into consideration when interpreting specific films, but it does demand a refinement of one's point of view. Recognizing that mutability, fragmentation, and pluralism have led to a range of diverse entities, all valid representations of Irishness, negates the impulse for a monolithic perception and calls for an acknowledgment of multiple perspectives applicable to the term.

Part of the interpretive problem lies in the fact that long-established analytic habits have impeded any reconfigurations of traditional conceptions. Until now, commentators have tended to embody Irish identity as a fixed concept because the linear, exclusionary methods common to critical responses aim at deducing rigid, narrow, and often reductive assessments.[4] This approach uses cause-and-effect logic to discern in the most direct fashion the elements that produce a particular condition. However, in a postmodern world, analyses perfected with the certitude of Enlightenment thinking do not speak to the contingencies that now confront us. Quite simply, generalizations founded on either-or logic no longer have the efficacy that they enjoyed in times of a more homogeneous society.[5]

A further element, inherent in the cinematic process, complicates assumptions about reading features of an Irish identity in specific motion pictures. From the inception of filmmaking in Ireland, a wide array of individuals from vastly different backgrounds—indigenous and nonindigenous—have made legitimate Irish-themed films, and this demographic variety further undermines the concept of a single entity or a specific vision capturing the essence of Irishness on film. Conversely, a number of individuals in the Irish film industry as often as not have worked credibly on American or British projects, raising questions as to what conditions define an Irish actor or director and how those conditions apply. (See Appendix C for further comments on this situation.) This combination of diverse contributors to the production of Irish-themed motion pictures and the chameleon-like ability of Irish film professionals to work effectively in movies set in other countries and cultures rebuts any assumptions about the existence of an essential Irishness, a term that many scholars already deride even as they speak broadly of Irish identity in an implicitly essentialist fashion.

Although I do feel that Irish-themed films demand multiple approaches significantly different from the singular perspectives commonly followed by critics interested in the national cinemas of other countries, I do not intend to deny the value of looking at Irish-themed motion pictures from the points of view of communal identities. Indeed, the history of filmmaking in Ireland affirms the need for cultural sensitivity. The first stage of cinematic productions, films from the 1910s to the 1940s, clearly lays out the necessity for interpretations inflected by a sense of Irishness, and John Ford's *The Quiet Man,* made in the following decade, demonstrates in a masterful fashion just what one can achieve with a sophisticated appraisal of the power of cultural markers. However, as the conditions and institutions delineating Irishness—class structure, surroundings, the family, the church, and nationalism, to name some of the most prominent entities— have become less stable, less interdependent, and more idiosyncratic, such viewings require a flexible interpretive approach that focuses on immediate circumstances without feeling the need to apply an overarching theory of unified causes.

Modes of perception exacerbate the problem. Culture stands at the center of any discussion of a national cinema. One finds the concept grounded on material referents—social conditions, historical events, geographic dispositions, economic advantages—yet efforts to provide a gauge of the impact of its defining features from individual to individual prove paradoxically elusive.[6] In consequence, no matter how ardently one argues for the applicability of the term, it remains necessary also to recognize the wide-ranging imaginative responses to familiar cultural markers. To speak of films with an ethnic identification (itself a loaded term) like Irishness, one needs to sustain oscillating perspectives that recognize the evocative communal power of cultural references while acknowledging their ongoing mutability.

To address this heterogeneous environment, interpretations of contemporary Irish-themed films need to emphasize a series of new protocols that accommodate both subjectivity and multiplicity. As I will elaborate over the course of this study, Irish identity has emerged as a manifold, fragmented condition. A series of separate entities sustain a variety of idiosyncratic attitudes, impulses, and values. Each element references features of Irish culture even as it undermines an overarching sense of Irishness. Consequently, for each of these features critics need to adopt a perspective that maintains rather than eliminates alternative points of view. In every case, one must focus on the diverse situations that manifest different instances of Irishness rather than attempt a generalizing view of all Irish-themed motion pictures.

Grouping films according to categories or genres allows one to give specific attention to the unique and often unstable features of each while retaining a sense of the consistent manifestations of one aspect of Irishness that the category reflects.[7] Though by no means arbitrary, the categories highlighted in this study are more representative than exhaustive. The genres examined here reflect important cultural markers, but they do not presume to articulate all options for interpretation. Rather, they suggest starting points that will foster additional analytic points of view.

The urban middle-class motion picture, for example, a highly popular category in contemporary Irish filmmaking, provides an enormous overt challenge to interpretation from an Irish perspective. The material changes in the Irish economy over the past sixteen years have had a profound cultural impact on the middle class. The features that had highlighted Irishness for them are becoming as anachronistic as their impulse to celebrate an Irish identity. As the middle class in Ireland increasingly identifies as European, representations of it on film often have little more than a nodding acquaintance with the national culture from which the group has emerged. In consequence, as I will discuss in Chapter 2, understanding Irishness in contemporary motion pictures in this category requires an explanation of absence rather than of presence.

Quite the opposite proves true of the working-class Irish-themed films that I examine in Chapter 3. As a group, the working class retains the most overt signs of Irishness because its members are the least touched by economic development and hence have changed demographically far less than the middle class. Consequently, seeing Irishness in working-class motion pictures demands a sense of local custom that also maintains a detachment that can identify the self-awareness of the genre. These affinities with the Irish milieu of a generation ago contribute to working-class isolation from the rest of the country, and viewers need to hold this contrast in tension as they come to an understanding of motion pictures in this genre.[8]

Rural films, highlighted in Chapter 4, embody a feature increasingly prevalent in, and to a degree threatening to, a number of the categories considered here. Though I have identified *The Quiet Man* as a paradigm of Irish-themed films, the same recent material changes that have reconfigured the Irish middle class have, thanks to generous subsidies from the European Union, erased much of the distinctiveness of country life. Unlike the urban middle class, however, instead of focusing on an easy transition to a more cosmopolitan existence, motion pictures set in the country consistently return to a sense of the ethos that has been lost. In consequence, the most emphatically unique rural films emphasize a retrospective point of view that stresses traditional attitudes, in a manner similar to the prescriptive structure of American westerns.[9] Effective interpretations of these motion pictures resist slipping into formulaic responses, and focus on how adeptly a director can both work within the form and offer imaginative innovations that play off viewer expectations.

As detailed in Chapter 5, films of families and of childhood invite an approach strikingly different from the ones applied to previous genres. These motion pictures tend to be the most introspective, emphasizing the impact of selected elements of Irishness on the individual. Consequently, they often critique one or more of the standard Irish institutions. In some instances this critique can produce heavy-handed didacticism, but more thoughtful efforts compel viewers to examine inherent environmental contradictions that obtain in the process of coming to maturity in Ireland and to read the films in a manner that sustains the emotional, cultural, and social inconsistencies and emphasizes their contribution to meaning. Additionally, the same pressures that have obtained in a number of other categories put the Irishness of the family under erasure in many instances, leaving the best examples of a national character evident in the most marginalized of groups.

Even more than films involving families, motion pictures that feature religion and religious institutions present highly charged individual accounts. At the same time, perhaps reflective of the more regimented framework of religious life, movies in this category show a tendency to take a programmatic approach in describing the experience. Such accounts often include a fierce didacticism that reflects the need to settle scores rather than illuminate conditions. This genre enjoys a great potential for representing cultural nuances, given the traditional importance of religion in Ireland. It is also an area where the most reductive opinions can emerge. As detailed in Chapter 6 the challenge to viewers is to retain a sense of both the strictly delineated manifestations of ritual and dogma and the contrasting individuality that permeates even the most closely controlled organizations. Added to this difficulty is the imperative to refuse to accept stereotyping as a valid representation of experiences within this category. (The recent clergy scandals that have produced a good deal of righteous outrage make it all the more important that one resists reductive views.)

Nationalism, like religion, has a pervasive impact on Irish life, but, as elaborated in Chapter 7, attitudes surrounding it stand as much more diffuse and frankly more ephemeral than the slogans of political parties suggest. The struggles of the War of Independence and the Civil War would seem to have presented clear-cut perspective dichotomies. However, as the most skillful of filmmakers have shown, glaring contradictions often arise between the broad ideologies articulated by various nationalist movements and the ethical issues that surface in implementing the policies associated with those beliefs. The treatment of violence and the shaping influence of brutality have grown to become the characterizing features of films in this category.

In consequence, colonialism and its legacy dominate films of political sensibilities, but these issues also threaten to truncate examinations. Specifically, this emphasis narrows considerations to a perspective of seeing Ireland always in relation to Britain. Although the impact of British imperialism cannot and should not be denied, this tendency toward foregrounding a sweeping, linear application of Ireland as a wounded postcolonial entity can elide important concerns. Instead, one needs to address the vexed question of whether Irish nationalism can exist without the institution of colonialism to struggle against. Analogously, one needs to ask whether the absence of a colonial entity, including its vestiges in the North, and the subsequent removal of the need for confrontation, violent or otherwise, put the Irish political identity under erasure.

Admittedly, despite the qualifications I have outlined for interpreting each of the genres noted above, at first glance this approach may seem little different from the kinds of close readings that have dominated studies of Irish-themed films for the past two decades. However, the effect of emphasizing diverse key elements in the interpretation of distinct genres creates a significant cumulative contrast. Like two objects that leave the same point on slightly dissimilar trajectories, as the readings within various genres accumulate, conceptions of Irish identities emerge significantly divergent from those understandings articulated in earlier film studies. Indeed, over the course of examining a range of representations of identity in contemporary Irish-themed films, one comes to see a movement toward the suppression of a conventional sense of Irishness. I will lay out this approach more specifically in Chapter 1.

I have already intimated the limitations I see in current studies, and before proceeding I think it only fair to acknowledge the boundaries that circumscribe my examination. From the start, my argument concerns itself with the process of interpreting feature-length fictional films. Shorts, amateur films, and documentaries fall outside the scope of my study.[10] I freely admit that one encounters some of the most innovative examples of filmmaking in Ireland among these groups. However, one often finds accessibility both for critics and for general viewers so limited as to render these motion pictures coterie films. As I note in the Introduction, in dealing with Irish culture as a basis for evaluating films, I feel it important to focus on the motion pictures seen by the majority of the Irish. Thus, I direct attention to mass-market, commercial, feature-length fiction movies. (For additional comments on commercial films, see Appendix D.)

I also want to address the analytic thrust of my examinations. I present here an unabashedly thematic study that offers representative examples of Irish-themed films rather than one that undertakes an exhaustive survey. Further, because I have fixed my attention on manifestations of identity, I have followed an approach that emphasizes close readings rather than one that pursues broad concepts of film studies or pays detailed attention to the techniques involved in creating motion pictures. I have adopted this perspective not because I do not value film history, film theory, and filmmaking. Indeed, I will refer to all of these areas at various points in my study. However, the topic of cultural influence manifests itself most clearly through the scrutiny of narratives of the films under consideration here, and thematic readings provide the best interpretive perspective of that issue.[11]

Finally, I offer an apology to readers already well familiar with the Irish-themed films examined here. I have in a number of instances rendered detailed summaries of these works that will be repetitive for seasoned film scholars. I hope, however, that this approach will make these motion pictures more accessible to readers with an interest in Irish studies but without the resources to view these movies. In a related gesture, I have referenced a great many Irish-themed films that I have not examined in detail. Many do not, in fact, merit sustained scrutiny, but acknowledging them helps to trace the stages of development within the various genres under consideration.

What follows, then, is an examination of the cultural narratives of Irish-themed films based on the concept of multiple identities and the need to apply different interpretive approaches to each. The social, economic, and psychological fragmentation of the contemporary Irish ethos means that filmmakers can no longer present Irishness as a monolithic entity. Instead, viewers encounter assorted films offering diverse perspectives of elements defining national character, each arguably as valid as the next. Commentaries on Irish-themed films need to recognize this condition and to offer new strategies for interpretation that accommodates it. My hope is that this study makes a useful start on that project.

Acknowledgments

I would like to thank all of the individuals whose encouragement, enthusiasm, and criticisms did much to enhance the shape of this text. They did not universally endorse the ideas in this study, but they all contributed to making them more coherent: Lenny Abrahamson, Ruth Barton, Maureen Buggy, Sean Crossman, Colin Downey, Fidelma Farley, Eugene Finn, David Gardiner, Luke Gibbons, Liz Gill, Margo Harkin, Cheryl Herr, Jarrod Hurlbert, Ivan Kavanagh, Lir Mac Cárthaigh, Tim Machan, Jim MacKillop, Frank Manista, Linden McBride, Brian McIlroy, Michael McKinney, Manus McManus, Barry Monohan, Diog O'Connell, Kasandra O'Connell, Sunniva O'Flynn, Joy E. Palmer, Valerie Palmieri, Bob Quinn, Orna Roche, James Rogers, Sarah Schepis, Abby Vande Walle, Annette Wenda, Jerry White, and Glenn Wright.

I am particularly grateful to Zachow Home Plumbing, the company that installed our whirlpool. Some of the best ideas I had came during lavender-scented bubble baths.

The Myth of an Irish Cinema

Introduction

The State of Irish Film

—But do you know what a nation means? says John Wyse.

—Yes, says Bloom.

—What is it? says John Wyse.

—A nation? says Bloom. A nation is the same people living in the same
  place.

—By God, then, says Ned, laughing, if that's so I'm a nation for I'm living in the same place for the past five years.

—So of course everyone had the laugh at Bloom and says he, trying to
  muck out of it:

—Or also living in different places.

—That covers my case, says Joe.

—What is your nation if I may ask? says the citizen.

—Ireland, says Bloom. I was born here. Ireland.

                    —James Joyce, *Ulysses*

For the past seventy years the discipline of film studies has widely invoked
the term *national cinema*. However, the ongoing debate over the meaning
of nation, and its corollary, nationalism, has made thoughtful readers
aware of the problematic nature of any application of the concept.[1] Consequently, before taking up the specific issue of the accuracy of the phrase
Irish national cinema, it makes sense first to touch on some of the alternative
conceptions of nation and nationalism and to examine the diverse forma-
tions of national cinemas affected by the range of these views.

Contemporary debate on the varied ideas of a nation began a quarter
century ago with the appearance of several works that laid out the primary
alternatives for perception. Ernest Gellner's study *Nations and Nationalism*

1

emphasizes industrial development, links the rise of nations to the evolution of feelings of nationalism, and most significantly sees nationalism as a distinctly modern phenomenon.[2] Using an approach that highlights the constructed quality of the process, Gellner posits the need for a specific cultural hegemony to facilitate economic progress, and that relationship comes about through the creation of nations. Though his approach seems to present a model of progressive development, when looked at in light of subsequent work, it has the effect of making us profoundly aware of the relativity and even instability of both terms: *nation* and *nationalism*. Indeed, the rise of the postindustrial society that has garnered close scrutiny since Gellner's original publication has only increased the sense of ambivalence surrounding these ideas.

An alternative that emphasizes sociology over economics appears in Benedict Anderson's *Imagined Communities,* a book first published in the same year as Gellner's work and revised since then. Anderson writes in what he calls "an anthropological spirit" to explore the way that socially constructed "imagined political communities" coalesce as nations. He contrasts those individuals viewing nationalism as a product of national reality with those seeing nationalism as a myth and a cause rather than a product of nationality. "What I am proposing is that Nationalism has to be understood, by aligning it not with self-consciously held political ideologies, but with large cultural systems that preceded it, out of which—as well as against which—it came into being." Although this understanding does highlight the metaphysical aspect of nation, for Anderson the term remains one characterized by a leveling, and at times fatal, homogeneous belief. "Ultimately it is this fraternity that makes it possible, over the past two centuries, for so many millions of people, not so much to kill, as willingly to die for such limited imaginings."[3]

The views of Gellner and Anderson have themselves come under scrutiny by critics combining postcolonial and postmodern concepts. Anthony Smith takes the position that positing the abrupt appearance of the nationalist impulse in the modernist context follows a simplistic approach. Though conceding that nationalism per se might be a modern concept, Smith feels that premodern ethnicities had definite influences on concepts of modern nations.[4]

In addition to wide-ranging debates over the general nature of nations and nationalism—reality versus myth, political versus cultural, modern and modernists versus continuity and ethnosymbolists—scholars simultaneously initiated a profound reappraisal of First and Third World perceptions. Edward Said's *Orientalism* stands as a watershed study in this area. Said's work concentrates attention on the distortions that arise from a Eurocentric point of view when applied to perceptions of nations outside that geographic area, but beyond that position, drawing on Michel Foucault's ideas, it takes a fluid approach to the concept of "imagined communities" as it seeks to understand the relativity of national identity.

Homi Bhabha follows Said's pioneering work on postcolonialism by attacking essentialist concepts of nation and nationalism.[5] Bhabha's examinations show, to an even greater degree than Said's, the influence of poststructuralist criticism as he struggles with conflicting notions of nationalism, postmodernism, and postcolonialism. Bhabha extends Said's views on the subjectivity of concepts of nation and nationalism even as he seems to draw back from the consequences. "Nations, like narrative, lose their origins in the myths of time and only fully realize their horizons in the mind's eye. Such an image of the nation—or narration—might seem impossibly romantic and excessively metaphorical, but it is from those traditions of political thought and literary language that the nation emerges as a powerful historical idea in the west."[6] No matter what the individual positions are, however, as scholars continue to apply postmodern views to concepts of identity, subjectivity has become increasingly prominent in discourses on nations and nationalism.

My point remains quite simple. All of these commentators recognize the complexity of ideas about nations and nationalism, and they offer divergent approaches to comprehending these conditions. This range of opinion makes it quickly clear that the lines of demarcation prove difficult to pin down and that mutability stands as a characterizing feature. As Alan Williams noted in an extended examination of Anderson's work, "Nationhood . . . is not merely established, it must be *maintained;* its definition therefore will inevitably shift over time."[7] What Williams does not say is that shifts in definition are not governed by a narrow process of linear evolution but rather are subject to a range of at times conflicting perspectives that inevitably lead to multiple impressions. Inevitably, a diversity of views obtains when commentators invoke the terms *nation* and *nationalism*. This ambivalence over definitive meanings necessarily makes mutability a dominant feature of the term *national cinema*.

In a valuable examination of the problem Valentina Vitali and Paul Willemen open their collection of essays with a survey of the literature of national cinema that reminds readers of the provisionality of the term.[8] In many ways their assessments echo the concerns voiced by scholars wrestling with issues of nation and nationalism, and the responses they have collected underscore the relativity of the labels employed. Indeed, though most of the publications in this book "address questions of national cultural formation," using Gellner as a template, they also demonstrate an ongoing awareness of the limitations of Gellner's views and of the delineations made by alternative positions.[9]

Vitali and Willemen begin with an examination of economic factors, focusing on the way the growth of a film industry as it arose in the United States can propel political decisions that lead to a national monopoly. This analysis produces their assertion that "when considering the question of national cinema, it is necessary to distinguish between two understandings of cinema: as an industry and as a cluster of cultural images." Vitali and Willemen go on to elaborate the problems that arise from a conflation of the two concepts, when countries like Germany and the United States "rewrite the history of cinema" as national narratives in works such as Oscar Kalbus's *Vom Werden Deutsches Filmkunst* (1936) and Lewis Jacobs's *Rise of American Film: A Critical History* (1939). Particularly as a result of Jacobs's work, "the writing of film histories in terms of some intuited national ethos that determines both the industrial arrangements and the films produced has become the norm." However, as Vitali and Willemen note, the technological, cultural, and political changes that have reconfigured the industry from the mid-1970s onward have led critics to see these conventional concepts of national cinemas as inhibiting understanding of "a film's actual mode of functioning."[10] Vitali and Willemen go on to invoke a series of "seminal essays" from the 1980s and 1990s in which intellectuals attempted to reinvent the idea of a national cinema.

Although a Marxist trajectory channels the direction of their inquiry into predictable positions, Vitali and Willemen in their introduction and the contributors in the essays that follow provide an excellent sense of the evolving and provisional condition of the term *national cinema,* and articulate valid concerns over the way that many critics continue to apply it in an undifferentiated, generalized fashion. This collection most effectively underscores the need to acknowledge the impact of diverse cultural forces shaping film interpretation from particular regions and to resist the impulse to impose a monolithic meaning on the term *national cinema.* "The point of departure for this collection of essays is that cinema can be thought of as pertaining to a national configuration because films, far from offering cinematic accounts of 'the nation' as seen by the coalition that sustains the forces of capital within any given nation, are clusters of historically specific cultural forms the semantic modulations of which are orchestrated and contended over by each of the forces at play in a given geographic territory."[11]

Part of the impetus for a shifting sense of the term emerges from the writings of theorists from countries striving to engage the postcolonial experience. One of the earliest and still one of the most radical challenges to conventional notions of a national cinema came from the Argentinean filmmaker Fernando Solanas and his Spanish collaborator Octavio Gettino in their essay "Towards a Third Cinema."[12] In what seems more a manifesto than a critical disquisition, Solanas and Gettino adopt a frankly revolutionary approach to filmmaking: "In this long war, with the camera as our rifle, we do in fact move into a guerilla activity." Their conception of Third Cinema rests on the tension that arises from opposition to institutions that represent a dominant and dominating culture: "Real alternatives differing from those offered by the System are only possible if one of two requirements is fulfilled: *making films that the System cannot assimilate and which are foreign to its needs, or making films that directly and explicitly set out to fight the system.*" Although Solanas and Gettino repeatedly assert that they are not equating their concept of a Third Cinema with Third World filmmaking, in fact the nature of their advocacy of motion pictures as a critique of economic and political exploitation in postcolonial conditions often makes their distinction difficult to perceive.[13] For Solanas and Gettino, Third Cinema responds to the hegemonic force of First Cinema in an aggressive confrontational fashion that foregrounds an agenda of political change.

The concept of Third Cinema has proved popular among many film theorists, and some have suggested this approach as a useful way of coming to grips with the complex features of a national cinema. However, conjoining the elements of the Third Cinema with a practical definition of a national cinema has proved to be difficult not the least because of the occasionally strained relationship between academics and activist filmmakers. (This friction also underscores without actually resolving the problematic relationship between Third Cinema and Third World nations.) The issue came to prominence at the 1986 Edinburgh conference on Third Cinema. There a number of filmmakers questioned the role of academic critics, seeing them as Eurocentric and part of the neocolonial process, particularly in their decisions to publish in languages and venues inaccessible to most Third Cinema practitioners.

Homi Bhabha attempts to address this matter in a sprawling essay titled "The Commitment to Theory."[14] Unfortunately, Bhabha's efforts to cover a topic much broader than the question of academic elitism cause him to slip into generalizations, inflated language, and sinuous arguments that reinforce rather than rebut these criticisms. To a degree, one can understand or at least sympathize with the conflicted nature of Bhabha's response, for the evolving conditions that shape views on nationhood and national cinema raise such a range of diverse issues that any specificity becomes open to charges of reductionism.

Subsequent analyses have noted this tendency and have attempted to overcome this obstacle through modified accounts of the Third Cinema concept. However, more often than not, these efforts merely highlight the narrowness of the term's applicability. Paul Willemen, who has written widely on the topic, outlines a Third Cinema that takes an activist approach, reiterating the argument that a Third Cinema stands as distinct from a Third World cinema.[15] With a subtle sense of his subject, his assessment offers a clear view of an evolved form of Third Cinema, and he demonstrates, far more convincingly than does Bhabha, the relevance of academic criticism in responding to films in this category.[16] At the same time, Willemen presents an approach that functions not as a mode of film criticism (a key feature in my view of the applicability of the term *national cinema*) but rather as a theoretical projection, a prescription for creating a new form of cinema. That position is perfectly defensible, but it emphasizes a broad view of film studies rather than the more narrowly focused aim of film interpretation that I am pursuing.

Julianne Burton explores the interpretive difficulties that arise in coming to a clear sense of Third Cinema through an extended response to Teshome Gabriel's *Third Cinema in the Third World: The Aesthetics of Liberation*. In the process, Burton touches on a problem that will resurface in examinations of national cinemas: "The very proliferation of names which have been used to designate Third World film-making—new cinema, alternative cinema, revolutionary cinema, imperfect cinema, anti-imperialistic cinema, among others—testifies to a certain elusive indefiniteness in the object itself."[17]

Michael Chanan takes up the same topic, and offers an equally thoughtful analysis of Third Cinema, but he too foregrounds issues that go well beyond the goals of interpretation. Chanan aims at theoretical accommodation, endeavoring to expand the idea of Third Cinema beyond associations with a militant Third World view to see a broad subversiveness in the texts of Third Cinema productions. Chanan invokes the by now familiar distinctions between First, Second, and Third Cinema, but then identifies "a certain slippage . . . between the categories of Second and Third Cinema" as a way of pointing out affinities with First and Third World filmmakers.[18] However, he never elaborates that argument, and over the course of the essay, in seeking to give the concept a broader application—like Burton he examines the views of Teshome Gabriel and comments on the "Eurocentric" reaction of some critics to the 1986 Edinburgh Third Cinema conference—Chanan in fact strengthens one's sense of the association between the Third World and Third Cinema.

Before proceeding, I need to clarify the point of my criticism of Willemen, Chanan, and others. Because these writers have done a great deal to make the study of international cinema more theoretically nuanced, my opposition to elements of their approaches may seem misplaced. In fact, I do not question the epistemological validity of any of their assertions. Rather, I emphasize the pointed difference in perspectives among this range of theorists as a means of illustrating that in contemporary film studies, anything other than sharply qualified applications of the term *national cinema* produces an extremely problematic analytic exercise.

This slippage in praxis stands as a central concern for my study. I intend to explore options for interpreting a variety of markedly distinctive Irish-themed films. Although my research acknowledges the importance of diverse elements in shaping the tradition of filmmaking in Ireland and engages the central issues of a film studies agenda, my examination primarily seeks to apply concepts from history and theory as they relate to particular works and to concentrate attention on the responses viewers can make to specific films. Consequently, I am interested in the way the idea of a national cinema can or cannot illuminate specific interpretive enterprises, and the diverse feedback that one encounters in seeking a definition of the terms *nation* and *national cinema* strikes me as an important consideration to address before proceeding.

One of the most detailed examinations of the current state of the problem comes from Stephen Crofts, who begins his study by noting what most national cinemas are not: "National cinema production is usually defined against Hollywood. This extends to such a point that in Western discussions, Hollywood is hardly ever spoken of as a national cinema, perhaps indicating its transnational reach." Crofts then delineates seven "varieties of 'national cinema,'" primarily along economic lines:

> 1) cinemas which differ from Hollywood, but do not compete directly, by targeting a distinct, specialist market sector; 2) those which differ, do not compete directly, *but* do directly *critique* Hollywood; 3) European and Third World entertainment cinemas which struggle against Hollywood with limited or no success; 4) cinemas which ignore Hollywood, an accomplishment managed by few; 5) anglophone cinemas which try to beat Hollywood at its own game; 6) cinemas which work within a wholly state-controlled and often substantially state-subsidized industry; and 7) regional or national cinemas whose culture and/or language take their distance from the nation-states which enclose them.[19]

Crofts goes on to identify the various national cinemas that fall into each category. Overall, the points that become most clear are the relativity of the term and the implicit obligation of critics to adjust their views to that relativity. (As I will explore in greater detail below, the impulse among some Irish film critics to stake out a position "defined against Hollywood" also demonstrates problematic qualities for the very reason that Crofts notes: "its transnational reach.")

In this regard, the closer Crofts's views seem to come to the Irish condition, the more difficult it becomes to apply them specifically. Although he mentions Third Cinema and Anglophone countries, in neither of these instances, nor in any other for that matter, does Crofts refer to an Irish cinema. Rather, in the end he very neatly summarizes a problem facing all who deal with the inherently self-reflective character of a national cinema: "National cinematic self-definition, like *national* self-definition, likes to pride itself on its distinctiveness, on its standing apart from other(s). Such a transcendental concept of an ego repressing its other(s) urges abandonment of the self/other model as an adequate means of thinking national cinemas. For this dualist model authorizes only two political stances: imperial aggression and defiant national chauvinism."[20] The multiplicity inherent in Crofts's approach deftly avoids the either-or reductiveness he condemns. However, he also never engages the consequences of the fragmentation that comes from the qualifying tone inherent in his categorizations.

Whereas Crofts's essay lays out alternative perspectives of a national cinema, its emphasis stresses a perspective oriented toward the process of filmmaking. Andrew Higson points to equally significant demographic features for defining a national cinema when he declares that "the parameters of a national cinema should be drawn at the site of consumption as much as at the site of production of films." In a deft gesture that offers specific points of view without becoming prescriptive, Higson expands his area of concern, summarizing alternative approaches, both inter- and extratextual, to defining a national cinema: economic, text based, consumption based, and criticism led. In delineating these options, Higson touches on a key difficulty, a condition in fact that informs my emphasis on close readings over broader theoretical assessments, that comes as a direct consequence of the process of defining: "Very often the concept of national cinema is used prescriptively rather than descriptively, citing what ought to be the national cinema, rather that describing the actual cinematic experiences of popular audiences."[21]

Higson's remarks highlight the problem that arises in the writings, already referenced, of a number of the theorists on national cinema.

Their assertions have a great deal of validity in any discussion of how a national cinema might evolve. However, applying their ideas to a body of work already part of the film heritage of a particular country can distort rather than clarify the impact of indigenous features on specific motion pictures.

Although I will contest the use of the term *national cinema* in applications to films relating to Ireland, Higson does invoke it in an approach that touches on many of the issues I find key to understanding Irish-themed films: "What I have suggested is a more *inward-looking* means, constituting a national cinema not so much in terms of its difference from other cinemas, but in terms of its relationship to an already existing national, political, economic and cultural identity (insofar as a single coherent identity can be established) and set of traditions."[22] Higson here summarizes the central elements that engage the critic examining Irish-themed films—the need to view these works in terms of the social context from which they have emerged—but he also points to a vexing problem, the instability of national identity in a country undergoing rapid social, cultural, and economic changes.

Along these lines, Susan Hayward rightly calls a nation "a social cultural community," and her understanding of the slipperiness of the term *national cinema* neatly summarizes the issues that have coalesced from the essays surveyed above: the requirement for precision in articulating the attributes that one assumes this label to manifest and the daunting challenges that imperative presents. What one needs is a concept open to the evolving qualities encompassed within a nation yet founded on consistent analytical values. Hayward sums up this problem in assessing Tom O'Regan's examination of Australian national cinema: "O'Regan suggests that rather than talk about nationalism and national cinema as exclusive terms we should seek to investigate the way in which society as a national whole is problematized and the kind of nation that has been projected *through* such problematisation."[23] Hayward asserts a key point here: concepts of a national cinema best emerge from a dialectic that encourages multiplicity. At the same time, there remains an unspoken assumption of some form of homogeneity when referring to "society as a national whole," and, as I will elaborate in the next chapter, the makeup of the Irish nation and of filmmaking in Ireland resists such a totalizing categorization. Instead, one needs an approach that acknowledges the value of cultural markers even as it explores the subjectivity of their applications.

Philip French touches on another issue that makes the study of Irish-themed films a unique experience and one that requires a measure of elaboration. He has noted that a national cinema needs not just material support but also a creative heritage and an ongoing indigenous commitment to producing narratives that record on film aspects of the country's character and identity. Without "the tradition of movie-making associated with a place or area, a body of work expressing, directly and obliquely, the spirit of its inhabitants, their character, aspirations, hopes and anxieties," that country lacks a national cinema.[24] His position carries the implicit assumption that engagement with a national cinema requires a unique understanding of the cultural context from which it emerged. A local perspective, both for filmmakers and audiences, seems crucial.

Even given the diverse approaches to national cinema cited above, French's requirements seem fairly applicable within a range of contexts. However, that condition proves a bit difficult to apply to filmmaking in Ireland. Whereas most concepts of a national cinema assume links to an indigenous creative force, a very different relationship has obtained in Ireland.

For nearly one hundred years, foreign motion picture production companies, particularly from the United States and Great Britain, have contributed palpable advances to the development of cinema in Ireland. Early in the process Americans demonstrated the viability of filmmaking in Ireland with the production of many of the first fiction films shot there. Sidney Olcott's *Lad from Old Ireland* (1910), made by the U.S.-based Kalem Company with a predominantly American cast and a Canadian director, began the process. Over the next four years, Olcott directed more than a dozen fiction and documentary films in Ireland, and, had not World War I disrupted his plans, he would have established a studio near Killarney in Beaufort, County Kerry.[25]

By the time political events prohibited Kalem from continuing to produce motion pictures in Ireland, indigenous filmmakers had begun to demonstrate their own abilities in a convincing fashion with films such as *Knocknagow, In the Days of St. Patrick,* and *Willy Reilly and His Colleen Bawn*

The Lad from Old Ireland: Contemporary poster advertising the film. Courtesy of the Irish Film Institute.

being well received by local audiences. As Brian McIlroy notes, "The enthusiasm for [native Irish] film production ran in tandem with Olcott's activities." Between 1915 and 1922, according to Kevin Rockett's tally, thirty-five indigenous motion pictures were made, many by the Film Company of Ireland, along the same lines as the Kalem films.[26] Indeed, one would be hard-pressed to find significant formal differences between any of these motion pictures.

In any case, just as a cinematic industry seemed to be taking hold, political conditions again inhibited development. Within a few years, the War of Independence and the Civil War combined with the 1923 Censorship of Films Act to curtail both native and foreign productions. These events had long-term consequences, for filmmaking in Ireland would not again experience such a strong output for sixty-five years. Nonetheless, throughout the twentieth century, both native and foreign companies continued a range of projects, albeit to a lesser extent than during the early years of development, delineating the evolution of filmmaking in Ireland as a hybrid production.[27]

After the political upheavals of the 1920s subsided, a trickle of native motion pictures appeared, and a number of foreign filmmakers released Irish-themed movies as well. For several decades, the hostilities leading up to and surrounding the establishment of the Irish Free State dominated the imaginative consciousnesses of both groups. Indigenous companies examined the War of Independence in *Irish Destiny* (1926), *The Dawn* (1935), and *Guests of the Nation* (1935). At the same time, British director Alfred Hitchcock and American director John Ford proved equally adept at chronicling the Troubles, offering films like *Juno and the Paycock* (1930), *The Informer* (1935), and *The Plow and the Stars* (1936).

Throughout the years between the world wars, foreign talent, technicians, and financing continued to play crucial roles in defining the parameters of what many viewers chose to call Irish cinema, while simultaneously putting stress on what delimited that term. Whether it was the British-based Gainsbough Pictures, Ltd., sending the American documentary maker Robert Flaherty to Ireland to make the tightly orchestrated *The Man of Aran* (1934) or Samuel Goldwyn producing a highly fictionalized version of the life of Michael Collins, *Beloved Enemy* (1936), with a predominantly English cast, including stars Brian Aherne and Merle Oberon, a great many seemingly Irish films were at the very least an amalgamation of domestic and nonindigenous resources.

Irish and Proud of It (1936) wonderfully illustrates the easy mixture of foreign and native talent. It was produced by Fox British Studios. It had a cast drawn from the Belfast Repertory Company. And shooting alternated between English and Ireland, with interiors shot at the Wembley Studios in London and exteriors filmed in County Antrim.

This trend of near-indistinguishable approaches in both foreign and domestic productions continued and even increased after World War II. Likewise, an interest remained in the conflicts that had divided Ireland over the first decades of its emergence as a nation. The British motion picture *Odd Man Out* (1947), detailing the efforts of Johnny McQueen (James Mason) to escape from Belfast after a bungled Irish Republican Army (IRA) payroll robbery, carried on the pattern of foreign interpretations of political division in Ireland. A decade later, another British film, *Shake Hands with the Devil* (1959), focused on the conflicted feelings of an Irish American caught up in the War of Independence. And eleven years afterward, *Ryan's Daughter* reiterated the British inclination to offer a romanticized view of the Troubles. Nonetheless, a significant change was already in the works.

For the first fifty years of motion picture production in Ireland, the thematic narrowness of the topics chosen by filmmakers—both foreign and native—put little pressure on defining the term *national cinema*. From the explorations of Ireland's past undertaken by the Kalem Company to the examinations of more recent political upheavals by filmmakers in the 1920s, '30s, and '40s, to the periodic representations across those decades of stage Irishmen, the predominant impulse was to present a homogeneous image of Irishness, and filmmakers made little effort to scrutinize the impact of diverse elements of an Irish identity on characterization or story line. However, in 1952, a truly momentous challenge to the concept of an Irish national cinema emerged. American director John Ford came to Cong and its surrounding countryside, and made *The Quiet Man.*

Ford arrived with solid credentials supporting his ability to depict the Irish ethos on film. Nearly twenty years earlier, in a motion picture unique for its time in its reflection of diverse and complex attitudes, Ford's movie *The Informer,* based on the novel of the same name by Liam O'Flaherty, wonderfully captured the tension between national and personal loyalties during the War of Independence. Further, it laid out a pattern of ambivalence that would be featured in the best of the subsequent Irish-themed film.

Ford had strong family ties in Spiddal. He had visited relatives there during the War of Independence, and in fact initially had hoped to shoot *The Quiet Man* in that area.[28] Combined with this intimate cultural engagement, Ford applied a detached American perspective to create this particularly keen portrait of rural Irish life. Over the course of the motion picture, this duality enabled Ford to present a multilayered representation, particularly through the framework of the film, classic Hollywood cinema, which provided viewers with a familiar structure by which to follow the narrative.[29] Indeed, knowing the audience's awareness of common Hollywood filmmaking techniques allowed Ford to take creative chances, particularly in his provocative use of stereotypes, which move viewers toward a subjective sense of Irishness without undermining the integrity of the concept.[30]

Thus, throughout the motion picture, John Wayne's character, Sean Thornton, can look and behave like a stage Irishman without turning the movie into a gigantic cliché. Near the film's opening, for example, Thornton's extended revery directed toward White o' Morn, the cottage where he was born, offers simplistic contrasts of Ireland and America through a cloyingly sentimental voice-over recollection of Thornton's mother inculcating in him a romanticized conception of his birthplace. At the same time, cinematographic techniques challenge unquestioning acceptance of Thornton's nostalgia. Ford has clearly shot the close-ups of Thornton in this scene on a soundstage, with only the establishing shots filmed on location. This decision to make the backdrop to Thornton's reminiscences overtly artificial neatly metatextualizes the discourse. It heightens our awareness of the subjectivity of Thornton's sense of Ireland, and it sets up conditions in which that view will compete with the highly individualized conceptions of others.

Later, more obvious examples of the disparity between Sean's ideas of village life and actual practice underscore the conflicting points of view that inform the narrative. Thornton's awkward efforts to join the community at Cohan's pub meet with disdain from the clannish locals until one of the patrons makes the connection between the man standing before them and his father and grandfather. Those ties to the village legitimate Thornton's presence, even as they undermine the hegemony of his perceptions regarding the protocols of rural social life.

Finally, the narrative insistently demonstrates the disparity between actions and aspirations. In the climactic scene at White o' Morn, for example, a drunken Sean Thornton brings home an equally inebriated Will Danaher after the two had fought one another to a standstill. Thornton shows no remorse for, or even recollection of, his broken vow never to fight another man. He seems equally unaware of or at least unconcerned about the physical abuse to which he had subjected his wife, Mary Kate, earlier in the day. And his alcoholic stupor is taken simply as a matter of course.

This performance stands as a powerful portrayal not simply because of Thornton's assumption of the role of caricature but through his innocence in doing so before viewers who cannot fail to judge him harshly. This representation marks a significant cinematic risk, particularly in conventional filmmaking, yet Ford has the courage to trust the interpretive skills of his audience, conditioned by exposure to years of classic Hollywood cinema, to bring the enterprise to fruition by balancing the subtle aspects of the discourse in a complex equilibrium. However, the film does more than evoke familiar narrative patterns.

Ford relies on sophisticated moviegoers to see the organizing feature of *The Quiet Man* as a problem of finding an identity, but he also invites them to engage the multiplicity inherent in the story. Thornton may take on the role of a caricature, but it does not inhibit the complex metamorphosis he endures. He has come to Ireland yearning for a Rousseau-like redemption through exposure to simple rural virtues. Instead, the corrosive cynicism of the villagers of Innisfree reshapes him into their image without his realization. Thornton can choose to ignore the authentic, unromantic Ireland that surrounds him and to suppress recognition of the extent to which his own actions conform to that harsher world. However, that choice in itself cannot reverse or even slow the changes taking place in him. Nor can it prevent perceptive viewers from reading that adaptation into his nature. Delineating that transformation, however, requires an alternative to exclusionary cause-and-effect analysis.

Throughout its narrative, *The Quiet Man* sustains the duality of innocence and degradation in Sean Thornton's nature. Whatever his attitude and whatever his behavior, an insistent irony critiques all that Thornton does and observes. The denizens of Innisfree constantly offer glosses of the action for the audience. Whether commenting in direct discourse, by means of voice-overs, or through simple gestures and postures, they persistently convey their assessments of Thornton's mawkish behavior. At the same time, the narrative calls their credibility into question by making little effort to conceal their venality, displaying it in small-minded gossiping, petty grudge bearing, unrepentant avarice, or aggressive narrow-mindedness. In a film obsessed with the idea of becoming Irish, no character can speak with authority on the topic because every point of view is occluded by naïveté or corruption or both.

Even the carefully constructed ethos of the village points toward indeterminacy rather than resolution. A veneer of conviviality runs through Ford's film. At the same time, a scathing portrait of rural violence, domestic abuse, chronic alcoholism, and religious hypocrisy flows as an undercurrent through the narrative. As one sees in the scene in which Father Lonergin and his Catholic parishioners take up the role of loyal Protestants, mutability stands as an inherent feature of life in Innisfree. *The Quiet Man* celebrates the complexity and contradictions of the Irish identity, and its ability to resist domination by either the sentimentality of Thornton or the cynicism of the villagers establishes it as a preeminently Irish film.[31]

In *The Quiet Man,* Ford has redefined the nature of the Irish-themed film, and has replaced a monolithic sense of Irishness with an awareness of uncertainty. In the process, Ford has privileged the local over the general. He has acknowledged the value of introducing national types if only for the opportunity to undermine them. And he has relentlessly invoked the central institutions of Irish identity—the Family, the Church, and the Nation—only to highlight the provisional nature of one's understanding of each. The release of *The Quiet Man* made it extremely difficult for subsequent directors to make a genuine Irish film in the sense that the term had been understood for decades and much easier to make a motion picture with elements of Irishness. Even more significantly, Ford's problematic representation of national character in *The Quiet Man* challenged subsequent filmmakers to eschew stereotypes and explore the impact of multiplicity and indeterminacy on national character.

Certainly, many found the standards set by *The Quiet Man* daunting, and in fact, in a subsequent motion picture made by Ford himself, broad farce and wide-reaching melodrama replace the tightly focused cultural sophistication of the earlier film. *The Rising of the Moon,* brought out in 1957 by Four Provinces Productions, in reality presents three unrelated shorts, all directed by Ford—*The Majesty of the Law,* an adaptation of a Frank O'Connor story; *A Minute's Wait,* based on a 1914 Abbey play by Martin J. McHugh; and *1921,* taken from Lady Gregory's play *The Rising of the*

The Rising of the Moon: A scene from *1921*, the third film in the trilogy. Courtesy of Redmond Morris.

Moon. With Irish stories, an Irish cast, and a proven director, *The Rising of the Moon* has the fundamental features of a prototypical Irish-themed film. Unfortunately, in a project that could have offered three defining presentations of different perspectives of Irishness, Ford loses his sense of complexity, and never troubles to develop the communal identities of any of the characters.

In each narrative, a simple plotline founders on predictable, linear development. *The Majesty of the Law* portrays the behavior of a stiff-necked man without offering any interesting exploration of his intransigence. *A Minute's Wait* unfolds like a bad music hall joke that goes on long after everyone guesses the punch line. And *1921* manages to make Lady Gregory's political fervor seem little more than a melodramatic impulse. These results seem all the more painful because each short film has a strong Irish cast, but the directing of John Ford highlights a tendency for stereotyping without the counterbalancing irony found in *The Quiet Man*. Although *The Rising of the Moon* may have made greater use of local actors, technicians, and facilities than did *The Quiet Man*, it shows remarkable timidity in its representation of Irishness.

At the same time, other movies attempted to foreground Irish connections, engage complexity, and eschew closure. *This Other Eden* (1959) presents the story of a rural Irish community attempting to deal with the conflicted legacy, both public and private, of the War of Independence. The narrative introduces a range of volatile issues well worth exploring: attitudes toward illegitimacy, divergent expressions of nationalism, and an insistent concern for revisionist history. It suffers at times from what Fidelma Farley, in her excellent assessment of the work, terms the conventional directing of Muriel Box, the stiffness of some of the acting, and the limitations of the script.[32] Nonetheless, despite a predictable happy ending, at numerous points the narrative highlights conflicted elements of Irish identity in much the same fashion as did *The Quiet Man*.

At its most successful, *This Other Eden* interrogates generalizations about the Irish identity from a local perspective that illuminates its contradictions. Further, it builds on the viewers' familiarity with *The Quiet Man* to address directly the inherent mutability of Irishness. Two people share the role of the outsider who comes to Ballymorgan, the enthusiastic Englishman Crispin Brown (Leslie Phillips), who speaks Irish and wishes to immerse himself in the culture, and the embittered returning emigrant Maire McRoarty (Audrey Dalton), who cannot think of living in Ballymorgan without breaking into tears. Although the two leading characters in *This Other Eden* fail to project the sophisticated dialectic between romanticism and cynicism evident in *The Quiet Man*'s Sean Thornton, the narrative nonetheless uses them to assault conventional generalizations about identity. Nationalism becomes as much an affliction as a virtue, and the nuanced representation of Carberry (the Michael Collins–like figure murdered at the close of the War of Independence) through the recollections of various individuals opens questions about the nature of the veneration afforded the men of 1916. *This Other Eden* was adapted from a play, and the film's representation of the clergy in the persons of Canon Moyle (Hilton

Edwards) and the Mother Superior (Ria Mooney) blunts the harshness of their stage characters without removing elements of cynicism in their natures. The interplay of idealism and pragmatism foregrounds a sense of their duality. In script, characterization, and acting, *This Other Eden* falls short of *The Quiet Man*, but it nonetheless affirms the cinematic power of a narrative willing to eschew linearity to highlight complexities and contradictions in elements of Irish identity.[33]

Coincidental to the production of *This Other Eden*, Walter Macken starred in an indigenous adaptation of his play, which premiered in 1952 at the Abbey Theatre, *Home Is the Hero* (a film that I will examine in greater detail in Chapter 2), the story of a brutal ex-convict reuniting with his family. Ruth Barton offers a good summary of the narrative in which she perceptively highlights the film's willingness to engage characters as complex individuals.[34] Again, like *The Quiet Man*, this film shows an ability to play off stereotypes by exploring contradictory aspects in the nature of the central characters—the brutish father who comes to see violence as a threat to his nature, the devoted mother who also seems open to the temptation of alcohol, and the ambivalently independent son and daughter who simultaneous seek acceptance and freedom from the community. This polymor- phic approach in turn reflects the same confidence that Ford's *Quiet Man* had shown in the viewers' ability to deal with conflicted identities that arise in a local environment and to appreciate the effects of a film that initiates and then plays against common expectations.

The 1950s marked a sea change for filmmaking in Ireland. With the example of Ford's *Quiet Man*, indigenous and nonindigenous filmmakers had the paradigm for expanding the scope of their narratives by paradoxically focusing on the complexity and contradictions of highly particular situations. Unfortunately, the 1960s produced few Irish-themed motion pictures, either foreign or domestic, and the ones that did appear in the early 1970s, such as *Quackser Fortune Has a Cousin in the Bronx* or *Ryan's Daughter*, made scant efforts to explore Irishness beyond the invocation of predictable types. However, from the mid-1970s through the mid-1980s, a number of directors emerged. Following the example of Ford in *The Quiet Man*, they committed themselves to exploring the range of unique experiences of life in Ireland.

Keeping the impact of *The Quiet Man* in mind remains an important element in understanding the cinematic achievements of the mid-1970s and early 1980s. The critic Martin McLoone rightly singles out this time as a period of immense creativity in Irish film, but the term he uses to identify it, *first wave,* itself can create a bit of confusion given the body of work produced by Irish filmmakers over the sixty some years that preceded it and the ongoing multinational efforts that make up a substantial portion of the canon.[35] McLoone's label does effectively highlight a phase of intense activity among indigenous filmmakers. Their output certainly justified hopes for the immanent emergence of a national cinema. However, the changing nature of both the motion picture industry and the Irish cultural environment has made the designation of a "second wave" of Irish filmmakers a much problematic project.

These new conditions do not, of course, diminish the achievements of the native filmmakers of this period. Bob Quinn contrasts English and Irish interpretations of the Celtic past in *Coineadh Airt Uí Laoire* (Lament for Art O'Leary) (1975). He examines the harshness of rural existence in *Poitín* (1978), and explores the isolation of the clerical life in *Budawanny* (1987) and *The Bishop's Story* (1994). Joe Comerford shows the powerful narrative that one can produce from marginalized communities. His *Down the Corner* (1977) portrays with gritty aplomb the working-class youth in Dublin, while his *Traveller* (1981) sensitively examines the often chaotic life of the Traveller community. Yet even as these films demonstrate the power of depictions of highly individualized representations of Irishness, they also assert the fragmented aspects of a society in which the concept of an identity changes radically from group to group. All of the characters in these motion pictures stand at the very margins of traditional Irish society, and the dominant social order comes to be characterized more by its absence than by a presence.

Each of these films has a clannish quality to it that demands interpretive approaches that acknowledge the uniqueness of their experiences. Identity emerges as the crucial concern, and the community's tolerance for individuality comes under the greatest scrutiny. This impulse to explore a variable Irishness that transcends simple causal relationships signifies a renewal of the cinematic impulses that informed *The Quiet Man* rather than the initiation of a broader, more inclusive social vision.[36] These directors share with Ford an interest in examining antinomies in Irish life. Individual examples of Irishness occupy significant positions in their narratives. At the same time, their refusal to generalize ensures that an audience's interpretations of Irishness will remain highly subjective and even at times idiosyncratic.

Many of these films center on conflicted impulses, and a number of directors offered powerful explorations of the range of frustrations of Irish society in the 1980s. Kieran Hickey's *Criminal Conversation* (1980) brilliantly captures the conflicted world of middle-class marital infidelity. Cathal Black's *Our Boys* (1981) blends documentary and fictional styles in an examination of the corrosive and morally ambiguous atmosphere affecting both students and teachers at a Christian Brothers boys' school, whereas his *Pigs* (1984) looks at the degraded and ennobled lives of squatters in the Dublin slums. Joe Comerford's *Reefer and the Model* (1987) depicts the anger and alienation of a former IRA man figuratively (and literally in the final scene) adrift in Irish society. As filmmakers with pronounced imaginative abilities emerged during this decade of intense creativity, Irish-themed motion pictures inevitably reflected more nuanced views of a fragmented society and pushed filmgoers toward more innovative interpretations. At the same time, economic, creative, and cultural conditions made distinctions between indigenous and nonindigenous films more difficult to ascertain, and reinforced the idea that the most Irish of films are the ones concerned with the most marginalized groups or individuals.

Indeed, the interpretive fragility of the notion of the broad concept of a national cinema emerges quite clearly from an examination of these and other efforts, particularly those films using the political upheavals in the North as a metaphor for the conflicted attitudes of Irishness that go well beyond conventional delineations. Pat Murphy directed an "Irish" and a "British" film within the space of three years, yet each motion picture questions the value of sweeping ideological positions while giving the most private gestures a charged political significance. In the process of exploring the personalities of two strong-willed women in social constructions separated by one hundred and eighty years, Murphy nonetheless skillfully

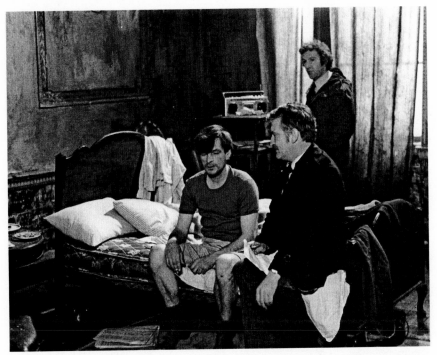

Pigs: The closing confrontation of the film. Courtesy of David Collins and Samson Films.

evokes the presence and the uniqueness of "Irishness" without imposing exclusionary, linear requirements for its delineation.

Her *Anne Devlin* (1984) is the story of a patriotic woman involved in Robert Emmet's abortive attempt at fomenting a rising against English rule. With a predominantly Irish cast and crew, financial assistance from the Irish Film Board and the Arts Council of Ireland, and an association with Radio Telefís Éireann (RTÉ), *Anne Devlin* asserts impeccable Irish credentials extending well beyond its sweeping historic references. The suffering and indignities endured by the title character relate, more than anything else, to the social and sexual status of women in Ireland at the time. It most skillfully affirms the ambiguity of Irish identity through the shifting roles—daughter, patriot, servant, prisoner—assumed by Devlin.[37] In Brid Brennan's masterful performance, one sees an individual whose sense of self never falters even as the various men with whom she interacts continually reflect their reductive sense of her.

Three years earlier Murphy, with John Davies, had directed *Maeve* for the British Film Institute Production Board, an exploration of issues similar to the ones she would take up in *Anne Devlin*, albeit with a sharply different social backdrop. The film examines the gritty and dangerous urban scene of Belfast in the early 1980s. However, despite the dissimilar location and time frame, *Maeve* confronts the same thematic issues that Murphy will later address in *Anne Devlin*. Although the title character of the 1981 film has acquired a greater sense of her rights as an individual, she faces impediments to exercising them as daunting if not as overt as the difficulties Anne Devlin endured. Indeed, Maeve's brief return home after her emigration to England underscores the transitory nature of her Irishness, for the role she can assume in London stands out as starkly different from her Belfast identity.

In these motion pictures, Murphy articulates the powerful conception of a localized "Irishness," fiercely articulated by the colonized community as a highly personalized sense of identity. At the same time, she shows that community denying a full articulation of that identity to at least half of its population. With admirable dexterity, both of her movies shift emphasis from the male-centered world of other films to an extended examination of the female condition under the dual domination of the British colonial government and an equally repressive paternalistic family structure. In each case, the title character comes across as grounded in an unshakable sense of self, though Maeve may seem more outspoken than the taciturn Anne Devlin. Nonetheless, each character raises important issues relating to the role of women in Irish society even as each questions the stability of that role.

Without denying the importance of Murphy's work in exploring female identity, I want to highlight another issue that it introduces without necessarily resolving: the ability of foreign companies to convey Irishness. Despite the heavy English involvement in *Maeve*, Murphy's Irish nationality makes classifying her work as nonindigenous problematic. However, other productions from that period have far more tenuous Irish connections yet can make equally strong claims to Irishness by following the same pattern of exploring the uniqueness of individual experiences within a tightly defined community. Mike Leigh's *Four Days in July* (Great Britain, 1985) contrasts the mundane lives of two young Belfast couples, one Catholic and one Protestant, during the summer marching season. Colin Gregg's *Lamb* (Great Britain, 1985) follows the spiritual struggles of an Irish Christian Brother in a rural home for delinquent boys. John Huston and Tony Huston's *Dead* (USA, 1987) dramatizes James Joyce's short story, a tender yet relentless examination of bourgeois ambition and self-delusion, and Matt Clark's *Da* (USA, 1988) brings Hugh Leonard's representation of a young man's struggle for identity in de Valera's Ireland to the screen.

The purpose of this inventory is not to denigrate the individual achievements of either foreign or native directors and production companies. Rather, I wish to emphasize the fact that even during a period that a number of film critics see as the high point of indigenous Irish output, nonindigenous companies produced films of the same type and of the same quality. My point is not that one mode of production deserves more consideration than the other but that, if similar results accrue from filmmakers with sharply divergent backgrounds, then the interpretive assumptions that one makes about how the cultural identity informs films need reconsideration.

In the 1990s foreign productions continued to offer Irish-themed films indistinguishable from local efforts. For example, Irish director Cathal Black's 1995 film *Korea* (the first feature-length film he made since *Pigs* in 1984), examining the pettiness and claustrophobia of rural Ireland, reflects a broad narrative plan similar to the one in Gillies MacKinnon's British production *The Playboys* (1992) or Paul Quinn's American film *This Is My Father* (1999). Within a year of Paddy Breathnach's indigenous gangster film *I Went Down* (1997), English director John Boorman released *The General* (1998). Brendan Gleeson stars in both, and in *The General* American actor Jon Voight turns in a strong supporting-role performance. One could offer a much longer list, but doing so would simply belabor the point that the more successful Irish-themed films prove to be, the more a variety of filmmakers show themselves to be adept at making them.

Of course, given current conditions and practices in the motion picture industry, any national cinema will experience at some level the influence

The General: Martin Cahill (Brendan Gleeson) and Noel Curley (Adrian Dunbar) on Cahill's Harley-Davidson motorcycle. Courtesy of John Boorman.

of U.S. filmmaking. By the same token, one cannot ignore the special relationship between Hollywood and Ireland. Indeed, both the depth and the breadth of integration of American influence on the Irish film scene reflect a unique environment: American production techniques shape the way films are made in Ireland, U.S. motion pictures dominate the Irish market, and Irish directors, screenwriters, and actors are active in the U.S. industry. (See Appendix C for a more detailed account.) Perhaps most strikingly, middle-class urban Irish films are taking on American values or at least an ethos as familiar to Chicagoans, Bostonians, or New Yorkers as to Dubliners.

A number of commentators place the blame for this homogenization on Hollywood, but complaining about this condition misses the point. Undeniably, a degree of competition obtains between American and Irish filmmaking, but the complementary relationship that has also existed for nearly a century makes the laments by Kevin Rockett and others regarding the "Los Angelesation of Ireland" simply too reductive to capture the complexity of the association. Rockett, for example, points to "the national celebration which greeted the success of *My Left Foot* at the [1990] Academy Awards" as illustrative of a disturbing internationalizing trend. He sees in that motion picture narrative priorities reflecting

> the sea change in national ideology during the past three decades. [*My Left Foot*'s] universalist sensibility helps confirm the replacement of the earlier inward-looking cultural and political nationalism with an outward-looking liberal humanist ideology. This allows, as in so many aspects of Irish life in recent decades, for a displacement of what is particular to the Irish social formation on to a non-specific universalism. As a result, with British and American investment in Irish films replacing Irish money, we are likely to see more sanitized or neutral versions of Ireland produced for cinema and television.[38]

Rockett published this criticism at the beginning of the 1990s, with the widely respected films of Bob Quinn, Kieran Hickey, Pat Murphy, and Cathal Black still relatively recent releases, and the achievements of these directors must have made the Hollywood threat to their independence seem even more serious. To compound this feeling, the early 1990s marked a time when those individuals involved in Irish film—particularly actors and directors—were becoming more aware of the opportunities offered by Hollywood.[39] Consequently, with pluralism asserting itself as an integral feature of filmmaking in Ireland, by singling out Jim Sheridan's highly commercial effort, *My Left Foot,* and resisting all things American, Rockett attempts to conduct a battle that has already been decided. When Britney Spears performs at the RDS arena and the McDonald's in Tralee has become the luncheon destination of choice, Ireland has moved well past the point of worrying about resisting the infusion of American culture. Indeed, as I will discuss in the next chapter, the country has welcomed it.

In point of fact, local filmmaking has grown out of the proliferation of worldwide technological advances, and, as noted already with reference to *The Quiet Man,* a common narrative form—classic Hollywood cinema—has characterized filmmaking from the Edison era to the present. Its prevalence has led Thomas Elsaesser to note the inherent contradiction of efforts to exclude Hollywood from the discourse on national cinema: "Hollywood can hardly be conceived in the context of a 'national' cinema as totally other, since so much of any nation's film culture is implicitly 'Hollywood.'"[40]

The challenge now facing commentators on Irish film tests their abilities to accommodate and reconfigure evolving conceptions of the term. Numerous elements in Irish society have rapidly embraced an international perspective. Filmmaking in Ireland has long seen a mixture of indigenous and nonindigenous talent. Recognizing the impact of these conditions means that understanding Irish-themed films can no longer rest on tendencies to apply unvarying, linear assumptions to every interpretation. Instead, one needs to pursue particularized, nonexclusionary approaches that both acknowledge the elements associated with Irishness in each film and that accommodate their idiosyncratic manifestations from motion picture to motion picture. As internationalism becomes an increasingly prominent feature in Irish lives, representations of the contemporary environment are marked by a progressive diminution of what most viewers traditionally think of as Irishness.

What I propose is a close examination of alternative approaches to the idea of a national cinema, a summary of the unique tradition of filmmaking in Ireland, and a view of how prominent Irish film critics have engaged the topic. From this analysis, I want to derive an alternate approach to interpreting Irish-themed films, one that rejects the hegemonic implications of a national cinema without ignoring the importance of Irish identity. The key to this view lies in understanding the simultaneous qualities of affirmation and subversion in the most effective Irish-themed films and in resisting the exclusionary impulse to impose narrow, linear conceptions.

1

What Is to Be Done?

Although many critics of Irish-themed films acknowledge the influence of Hollywood as a threat to national cinematic integrity, a great diversity obtains in the sense of what the term *Irish motion picture* means. Few in Ireland have defined Irish film according to concepts as precisely delineated as the theories generally applied to other national cinemas. Four years prior to Kevin Rockett's "Los Angelesation" essay, in their pioneering book, *Cinema and Ireland,* Kevin Rockett, Luke Gibbons, and John Hill seem to acknowledge, admittedly without overtly stating the fact, that references to an Irish cinema can encompass anything from a narrowly focused emphasis on indigenous films (an Irish cast, an Irish crew, and Irish backing) to the broadest possible view that includes any Irish-themed motion picture. Brian McIlroy's very useful history, *Irish Cinema,* follows an equally broad-minded course of inquiry with a classification system characterized by an avowedly "liberal policy" of categorization: "I believe one should consider not only films directed by Irish people on Ireland but also films directed by foreigners on Ireland, provided their images have been regarded as influential." Rockett, in his monumental reference book, *The Irish Filmography,* chooses not to engage the question beyond announcing his wide-ranging intention to document "fiction films made in Ireland and about Ireland and the Irish."[1] (For an overview of indigenous film criticism, see Appendix B.)

Foreign critics have advanced similarly broad propositions with the same emphasis on a thematic view of the material that Irish critics followed. In the introductory paragraph to a filmography that appears in *Contemporary Irish Cinema,* Anthony Kirby and James MacKillop begin their gloss of the term by offering a very precise set of criteria for defining an

Irish film, and then conclude with a qualification that provides them a great deal of leeway in categorizing specific motion pictures. An Irish film must be "(a) one made in Ireland, with (b) an Irish director, (c) produced or backed by an Irish company, and (d) based on a text by an Irish writer, or a compelling minority of those four elements." Lance Pettitt's *Screening Ireland* presents the most detailed assessment of the problem. He links Irish film to a national cinema, and then goes on to acknowledge the difficulty of defining the idea of nation: "In Ireland, where the nation-state remains a matter of dispute and the 'people-nation' has (with few exceptions) been serially depleted, defining a national cinema is particularly problematic." Ultimately, because he recognizes the multinational component of most feature-film productions, Pettitt sets Irish film in a broad context close to McIlroy's approach: "a national cinema may be identified by the narratives that occur in the films themselves."[2]

Back among Irish critics, Martin McLoone's *Irish Film* also endorses thematic delineations and adds economic criteria to a view that moves, though perhaps not intentionally, toward putting Irishness under erasure. Certainly, McLoone follows the impulse of many theorists by privileging intricacy and experimentation. He highlights "medium- and low-budget films [as representing] an emerging national cinema defined, not by an essentialist conception of Irishness, but by a desire to explore the contradictions and complexities of Irish identity as it looks inwards and backwards at its own history and outwards and forwards to its European future." He goes on to "schematize . . . recurring themes" in the following manner:

> —an interrogation of the rural mythology which underpinned cultural nationalism and is encapsulated in the used of landscape;
>
> —a new concern to represent urban experience which was largely submerged and ignored by this rural mythology, especially the urban experience of the rapidly modernising contemporary Ireland;
>
> —a consequent desire to reveal the social and political failures of independent Ireland and latterly to probe the failures and contradictions of the Irish "economic miracle";
>
> —an interrogation of religion in Ireland, especially in relation to education, sexuality, and gender;

—the question of women in Ireland, especially in relation to nationalism, Catholic teaching and imagery, and the discourse around women's bodies engendered by the abortion debate in Ireland;

—an interrogation of Irish history and Irish tradition and the conflict between tradition and modernity (often rendered as a generational conflict);

—the question of Northern Ireland, political violence and the disputed notions of identity which form the crux of the conflict;

—a new concern to imagine the nation differently, sometimes in its European context and sometimes probing its "special relationship" to the USA and American culture, especially through diasporic Irishness;

—a concern with film form itself, especially the desire to work through existing forms in the search for a new or more characteristic aesthetic.[3]

McLoone does an excellent job delineating the various issues that manifest Irishness in feature-length motion pictures, and his checklist underscores the importance of taking a context-driven approach to Irish-themed films. However, the linearity of his categories undercuts his gesture toward "the contradictions and complexities of Irish identity," presuming an interrelatedness not always sustained by films meeting his criteria. At the same time, McLoone's categories have the potential for outlining alternative forms of Irishness if one sees them not as highlighting an overarching Irish consciousness but as expressing the range of identities that coexist within Ireland.

Ruth Barton comes closer to engaging this individuality overtly when she expands the range of thematic possibilities to incorporate the way others see the Irish cinematic tradition. "If we are to talk of a national cinema, or a national film text even, we have to engage in a series of acts of creative bricolage; that is, to see how an image of Ireland on screen emerged out of the national industries of other countries. . . . An Irish national cinema is thus defined here firstly as a body of films made inside and outside of Ireland that addresses both the local and diasporic cultures."[4] I agree with what Barton says as long as one resists the implication that a gesture toward "bricolage" or the application of any other interpretive strategy with linear assumptions can produce an overview applicable to any Irish-themed motion picture.

All of the authors whom I quote enjoy deservedly strong reputations as sophisticated commentators. This fact makes it all the more telling that the more these critics attempt to pin down the definition of an Irish cinema, the more nebulous that definition becomes.[5] Their efforts in fact underscore my central assumption: filmmaking in Ireland has always been a fragmented process, depending as much on foreign involvement as on domestic participation, making a national cinema, when seen as an entity whose products can be viewed from a single perspective, an impossible dream.

Nonetheless, the works of these critics lay down important guidelines for understanding motion pictures in Ireland. Most significantly, their approaches to Irish-themed films underscore the need for sensitivity to narrative structure if one hopes to come to a full comprehension of the impact of cultural markers on the discourse. Irish-themed films have a much more diffuse, much more subjective quality than the films of other nations. They rely on localized customs and attitudes that define specific points of view far more effectively than broad nationalistic assumptions. In this situation, the imperative to articulate the aesthetic impact of cultural markers remains strong, but the stability of those markers from film to film and even within a particular motion picture always stands in doubt.

Since *The Quiet Man,* the most effective view of an Irish experience avoids the straitjacket of monolithic nationalism and accepts the uneasy blend that arises from culturally inflected discourses. It is a form of analysis that rejects the drive for closure. Instead, it privileges the importance of sustaining multiple, often contradictory, points of view. And it categorizes understanding as a process that, though logical, must resist the Cartesian worldview that dominated perceptions until the early twentieth century.

At the same time, simply evoking the most recent critical theory does not ensure an approach that will accommodate the complexity of national identity. Dudley Andrew illustrates how difficult it is to pin down the concept of Irishness in the cinema in his essay "The Theater of Irish Cinema." Andrew, in identifying what he calls "fluid binarism," adopts a both-and view that simultaneously tries to define and to avoid being held to a definition of Irishness. In seeing Irishness as "a habit of response," Andrew suggests the subjectivity to which I have alluded already, but he does not present a specific approach to engaging that subjectivity as part of the interpretive process. Instead, he focuses on the agents of Irishness, "the habits by which actors and directors respond to the (post)modernity of their medium." Andrew also highlights "demi-emigration," the phenomenon of Irish actors and directors working both at home and abroad as "a situation that may ironically promote Ireland to the cultural avant-garde."[6] (He obviously has not seen Brendan Gleeson as Hank Keough, a rural Maine sheriff, in the 1999 release *Lake Placid*.)

The result is a rather long and roundabout disquisition that, without specifically saying so, leaves the reader with a subjective concept identified by an objective label. Although Andrew offers an insightful overview of the problem, he comes no closer to resolving it than someone who simply says, "I don't know." I by no means object to Andrew's methodology. Indeed, I am advocating similar techniques. However, as is the case with a great deal of poststructuralist writing, Andrew cannot overcome the Cartesian impulse to move toward closure, and that inability undermines his argument. Instead, what these films require from viewers is what Kenneth Burke terms "a compensation for disunity."[7]

The problem of constructing this sort of reconciliation has long been an issue in Irish film studies. In particular, the diverse features of Irish filmmaking already touched on have made commentators, from the earliest writers, conscious of the need to privilege the designation "Irish films" even as they struggled to articulate what that meant. In a January 1922 column in the *Irish Times*, for example, an anonymous author writing on filmmaking attempted to address this issue by highlighting ethos. "We must start by being Irish in our point of view, and when our work is finished it must be of such a character that there will be no doubt in anyone's mind that the result attained is all the time Irish. This does not necessarily preconceive narrowness of treatment; it merely means that the only picture worth making in Ireland is an Irish picture."[8]

"Being Irish in our point of view" privileges any motion picture—indigenous or nonindigenous—that demands a unique understanding of some aspect of national culture, particularly as it has evolved and continues to evolve. In addition, both the all-inclusive "our" and the unintended subjectivity it confers upon the statement enforce an equally profound point.

Although "Irishness" is often proposed as a generalized perspective, its application ultimately stands within the province of the viewer. It remains the critic's task to avoid essentialism by holding in suspension both the putatively objective and subjective assumptions of the term.

For the first half century of filmmaking in Ireland, the homogenization of the cinematic output and the static nature of Irish society made this approach, whether it captured the full sense of a motion picture or not, relatively easy to sustain. The cumulative overt changes in film and society that have arisen since *The Quiet Man,* however, now have reached a critical mass, and they insistently assert the need for new approaches. As already noted, John Ford's film illustrates the profound effect of a narrative that accommodates nonlinearity and a denial of closure. Effective readings of Irishness in subsequent films need to adopt the same perspective with an even greater sense of the shifting features of identity.

Although definitions of cultural distinctiveness have always involved the application of subjective impressions to generalized conditions, the instability of those generalizations has grown more pronounced with the recent rapid changes experienced by Irish society, which in turn is reflected in Irish-themed films. For example, as will be explored in detail in the next chapter, both *Criminal Conversation* (1980) and *About Adam* (2000) present comprehensive examinations of the sexual mores of Dubliners of the periods they depict, yet the grimness of the former and the blitheness of the latter could not provide a greater contrast in the reactions each would evoke in contemporaneous audiences. In the first instance, viewers a quarter century ago would have seen the conflicted attitudes preying upon characters, but, given prevailing standards regulating marriage and sexuality, they would also have had a relatively homogeneous understanding of those frustrations. By the time the second film appeared, the actions and attitudes of its central figures unfold in the context of an Ireland where gay rights are now (sometimes grudgingly) recognized, divorce has become at least a possibility, and the practice of living with a partner to whom one is not married is taken for granted. At the same time, a good many Irish remain at the very least uncomfortable with these changes, and the reactions of a cinema full of viewers of this film would be much less predictable.

Without the particular social and legal restrictions that caught the characters of *Criminal Conversation* in a claustrophobic system from which escape did not seem possible, the blithe sexuality of *About Adam*, though much more insistent, seems considerably less significant. With a population that now articulates very diverse attitudes toward divorce and marriage, the uniquely identifiable Irish atmosphere of the former motion picture has vanished from the latter. Rather than defining the cultural identity of the narrative, sexual behavior stands as a contributing feature in a romantic comedy that could credibly be set anywhere in the world. Given the social context presumed to delineate an Irish-themed motion picture, this difference represents much more than simply opposing interpretations of a familiar topic. It testifies to the striking diminution of what features now legitimately constitute an Irish film.

The erosion of traditional Irish mores is by no means a new discovery, and the sense of the fragmentation of the concept of Irishness has become a particularly popular topic in motion pictures. Martin McLoone, writing near the end of the 1990s in a *Cineaste* special issue on contemporary Irish films, seems on the point of acknowledging this condition even as he offers a very exuberant view of the thematic evolution of Irish filmmaking:

> Contemporary Ireland, on the other hand, is now on the cusp of European modernity with the fastest growing economy in the European Union as well as the youngest population and together these have given rise to a cinema which offers a challenge, not only to the *"cinéma de papa"* but also to the laws of the father and the embraces of both Mother Ireland and Mother Church. Even the new orthodoxy in Ireland, built on modernization and secular liberalism, is subject to interrogation and challenge. In this way, contemporary Irish cinema is beginning to emerge as a cinema of national questioning, one that seeks to re-imagine the nation in excitingly different and profoundly challenging ways.[9]

McLoone is quite right about the radical social changes taking place in Ireland since the early 1990s, and I agree that these changes are reflected in the narrative discourses of the films made since then. His optimism about the new direction of Irish film, however, does not translate into a new approach to understanding it. In this statement, McLoone is outlining a move away from Irishness in films made in Ireland, a position with which I heartily agree. In his book-length study of Irish motion pictures, McLoone has gone from staking out a cosmopolitan point of view to articulating a series of parochial thematic criteria (quoted above) that establish the authenticity of a film claiming to be Irish.

Although I note the seeming contradiction, I am not simply dismissing McLoone's cataloging impulse. Indeed, as I noted earlier, his list makes a good start on narrative features to keep in mind, and the method that I follow through this study has a similar categorizing inclination. Unfortunately, an either-or quality remains the prevalent tone of McLoone's approach. The consequent programmatic interpretive attitude this approach produces still does not fully take into account the kind of subjectivity inevitably heightened by the scenario McLoone describes in the above quotation. Perhaps more to the point, McLoone does not see that the shifting milieu and fragmented nature of Irish life make it extremely difficult to set up stable overarching criteria to address every manifestation of Irishness.

Uncertainty surrounding identity makes it far easier for commentators to lay out what no longer represents a national ethos in an Irish film, and no group proves to be more attuned to this problem than filmmakers. A portion of dialogue from the motion picture *The Fifth Province* (1997) neatly illustrates how growing consumer sophistication and a shift in public taste have complicated the choice of topics for Irish films. In a scene presented as a farcical depiction of a script-writing seminar, the workshop leader, Diana de Brie (played by Lia Williams), sums up the industry's current conception of a viable script for an Irish movie by telling her audience: "When it comes to the story, I'll tell you what we don't want. We do not want any more stories about Irish mothers, priests, sexual repression and the miseries of the rural life. We want stories that are upbeat, that are urban, that have a pace and verve and are going somewhere."[10]

Despite the avowedly satirical aims of de Brie's disquisition, her prohibitions summarize the implicit guidelines followed by many of the Irish-themed middle-class motion pictures released over the past decade. With an insistent undertone of material satisfaction, a tendency to privilege global culture, and a lack of interest in national identity punctuating their narratives, these recent efforts move toward the erasure of features traditionally

The Fifth Province: Literally and metaphorically afloat in the film. Courtesy of Catherine Tiernan and Ocean Films.

associated with an Irish cinema. Certainly, one still finds a uniquely Irish ethos in the grit and desolation in working-class-oriented films such as *Last Days in Dublin* (2000), *Disco Pigs* (2001), *Intermission* (2003), and *Adam and Paul* (2004) that evoke the seamy side of the Celtic Tiger. At the same time, there are an even greater number of movies, including *When Brendan Met Trudy* (2000), *Wild about Harry* (2000), *The Most Fertile Man in Ireland* (2001), and *Goldfish Memory* (2003), that, through comedy or drama, endorse a less ethnic, more cosmopolitan worldview. This tendency underscores my point about the need for multiple modes of interpretation.

Common social features, albeit in forms significantly different from what was in evidence even a half century ago, continue to influence the narrative structure of the Irish cinematic landscape. However, their stability as uniquely Irish elements has changed radically. The challenge for contemporary film critics is to adopt a methodology that allows one to understand how this new Irishness informs cinematic interpretations.

In offering an analytic strategy in response to these conditions, I have traced the evolution of Irish identity in films in a number of broad cultural

Adam and Paul: Adam (Mark O'Halloran) and Paul (Tom Murphy) in search of a fix. Courtesy of Speers Film/Element Films and photographer Jonathan Hession.

categories and have examined these motion pictures from the perspective of whatever identifiable cultural markers each chooses to emphasize: city life, the country environment, the family, religion, and Irish political beliefs. In engaging these institutions, however, I emphasize the mutability of individuals' perceptions of each. This method rejects the essentialism arising from seeing these establishments causally. Instead, it develops the idea of Irish identity as an increasingly idiosyncratic concept. It acknowledges the erosion of the distinctive Irish nature of the cultural markers that define each of the categories into which films can be grouped. And it addresses the inevitability of increasingly less predictable individual responses to each. The key to understanding these new conditions lies in sustaining multiplicity, which is best achieved through a nonlinear perspective.

Admittedly, one faces formidable challenges in making the transition from linear analysis. A continuing adherence, in formal interpretation, to Enlightenment thinking has embedded in the consciousness of most viewers a critical method that runs contrary to such efforts at multiple perceptions. Based on Cartesian assumptions, this conventional approach reifies the need for closure and resolution. This type of scrutiny works with ruth-less efficiency as it progressively narrows alternatives until one can form a clear picture of a cause-and-effect relationship from the selected elements that remain under consideration. At the same time, its narrowing impulse continually runs the risk of a reductive conclusion.

In contrast to this programmatic form of expression, most human observation and comprehension follow expansive, nonlinear patterns of thought. We regularly hold numerous images in interpretive hypostasis, and we feel no compulsion to exclude conflicting or extraneous views. How-ever, under the influence of a Cartesian-based system, we often articulate our opinions in a truncated fashion.[11] To convey fullness of one's impres-sions, particularly a subjective engagement with a piece of art—which owes its creation to the artist's equally subjective engagement with the creative process and with the environment from which it emerges—one needs a system free of the exclusionary inhibitions of current critical intercourse.

To illustrate how this goal can be achieved and lay out the method I will follow throughout this study, I propose to examine the diverse ways that concepts of Irishness impact viewers' interpretations of *Waking Ned Devine*. My aim at this point is not to argue for its worth as an aesthetic project, though defending its Irishness may seem analogous to such a posi-tion. Nor do I want to advocate reading all Irish-themed motion pictures in precisely this fashion. Rather, I seek to highlight features within *Waking Ned Devine* that establish it as a prime example of the recently evolved Irish-themed motion pictures that are particularly receptive to the nonlinear approach that I advocate.

A Paradigmatic Reading: *Waking Ned Devine*

My defense of the film's Irishness begins with some observations about the interpretive flaws that result from some viewers assuming a determinedly Cartesian mode of analysis of *Waking Ned Devine*. (I will end subsequent chapters with similar detailed analyses of a single motion picture.[12] In this case, however, I am also addressing in some detail its critical reception as a way of illustrating how an expanded view of identity markedly changes one's sense of a work.) In an essay written in 1999 titled "Myth, Mammon, and Mediocrity: The Trouble with Recent Irish Cinema," Hugh Linehan questions the legitimacy of categorizing this brand of film as Irish. With a harsh opening that dismisses a range of movies that strike him as little more than stereotypes, Linehan uses sweeping generalizations to brush aside the notion that an entire category of films does anything more than ridicule the concept of Irish identity.

> Despite rumors to the contrary, stage Irishness is alive and kicking. Films such as *The Matchmaker* (1997) and, most recently, *Waking Ned Devine* play on the sort of awful whimsy that sets Irish teeth on edge. Most of these films have been written, directed, and produced by non-Irish filmmakers (and, in the case of *Waking Ned Devine*, weren't even filmed in this country). They present an arch, cutesy image of this country that has its roots in Victorian stereotypes and has been well charted by Irish film historian Kevin Rockett.[13]

Certainly, Linehan's remarks raise a problem of identity that critics need to address: what specific elements legitimate a motion picture as Irish? At the same time, his views betray just the sort of linear, exclusionary tendency toward classification that oversimplifies the function of identity in cinematic narrations. He presupposes a single overarching definition of Irishness, and then, without enunciating that definition, dismisses a work as outside the pale by simply relying on vague generalizations in lieu of reasoned arguments. As I affirm in Appendix D, neither rigid classification nor elitist bias should influence the debate on identity, and certainly neither public acclaim nor commercial success should call the credentials of an Irish film into question.

By invoking the term *non-Irish*, Linehan follows a familiar tactic of associating perceived flaws in a film like *Waking Ned Devine* with a presumed tendency of nonindigenous filmmakers to travesty Irish subjects in a way that indigenous artists would never dream of doing—"the sort of awful whimsy that sets Irish teeth on edge"—though that point of view strikes me as simply another form of stereotyping. (Curiously, for a writer condemning foreign influence, Linehan identifies it by the title given it for its U.S. release, *Waking Ned Devine*, rather than the title by which it was known in

Ireland, *Waking Ned.*) If an American film critic, for example, complained that the German-born director Billy Wilder had insulted Americans by a clichéd representation of Sugar Kane (Marilyn Monroe) as a dumb blonde in *Some Like It Hot,* others would be justified in suggesting that critic has at best a very simpleminded understanding of the film. This unsubstantiated judgment too easily establishes a reductive dichotomy between native good–foreign bad without assuming the responsibility of producing proof that supports such a pronouncement.

Linehan does go on to make the telling observation that *I Went Down* succeeds by taking a familiar American genre, the gangster film, and translating it into an Irish context (a concept with which I agree and will take up further in Chapter 3). However, he misses the point in not seeing a similar process at work in *Waking Ned Devine.* Like *The Quiet Man,* though admittedly with less subtlety, *Waking Ned Devine* plays on audience expectations about stereotypical Irishness to set up a searing critique of pieties about rural life and bucolic innocence. (In fairness, in other writing Linehan suggests that he possesses a very good conception of the complexity of the issue of Irish identity, and quite likely this impression of his critique of *Waking Ned Devine* comes from the limited space allotted by *Cineaste,* forcing a truncated consideration of matters. For example, in a 1994 interview with Rod Stoneman, then chief executive officer of the Irish Film Board, Linehan's questions make clear his wider concerns.[14] At the same time, the fact that he asks rather than answers the questions limits one's sense of his views, and their exchange does no more to hint at issues rather than define the problem.)

Admittedly, many Irish critics share Linehan's opinion of the film. In the opening paragraph of a relentlessly acerbic review posted on his Web site, Harvey O'Brien, an instructor at University College–Dublin, ably illustrates the animus that many feel toward *Waking Ned Devine:*

> Worthless comedy shot in the Isle of Man but set in Ireland which attempts to capture the feel of Ealing films from forty years ago, but fails miserably to achieve their tone, pace and humour. This film is transparently desperate in its appeal to sentimentality and it is offensive in assuming that the sight of Ian Bannen and David Kelly romping naked on a motorbike

along the roads of an ersatz Ireland is actually funny. Its makers seem to presume that audiences will allow any amount of bad dialogue, poor plotting and mawkish drivel to pass for entertainment in the name of "old fashioned" comedy, and that playing the Irish card will excuse the absence of any kind of intelligence.[15]

Neil Jackson, writing the Kirk Jones entry for *Contemporary British and Irish Film Directors*, offers a slightly less vitriolic perspective of *Waking Ned Devine*, calling it "not as saccharine as it might have been," with "a strain of black humour that provides a welcome relief."[16] And in his book *Irish Film*, Martin McLoone, though marginally less splenetic than O'Brien, proves far less forgiving of the movie than does Jackson. In concluding, he makes an unfavorable comparison to *The Quiet Man* that I believe a less linear perspective would refute:

> The problem with a film like *Waking Ned* is that it lacks any degree of self-consciousness or internal subversion that might rescue it from the charge of "paddywhakery." The mythical rural community that is created, with its wily and resourceful inhabitants, stands unproblematically for an authentic organic community that outfoxes the po-faced representative of urban modernity. The film's celebrated leads, two old men on an outrageous scam to defraud the national lottery, certainly add an original element to the story (no doubt achieving in the process a significant blow against the ageism of much contemporary cinema). However, the set of oppositions that the film sets up—between tradition and modernity, between Tullymore and Dublin—are almost exactly the same as those we located in *The Quiet Man*, but without the latter's ironic self-subversion as compensation.[17]

All of the points raised challenging authenticity and worth merit response, and I will address them over the course of this analysis. However, the most serious question remains how one determines whether *Waking Ned Devine* can legitimately be considered an Irish film. Sweeping dismissals of its claims to an Irish identity, without concomitant evidence to support them, seem to assume that an objective approach to thematic analysis— a standard for determining the Irishness of a motion picture that many commentators, including McLoone, have championed—can offer clear and unambiguous conclusions to the issue. (Because I see the film as subverting stage Irishness, I do not deny that, like *The Quiet Man,* it evokes and then manipulates stereotypes. However, a critic who invokes the term *paddywhakery,* without any detailed examination of what transpires, simply truncates the interpretive process.) It is my contention that Irishness, by its very nature, projects unclear and ambiguous features, and interpretations that seek to grasp its influence must accommodate these features. However, as I will demonstrate below, even if one feels committed to linearity, *Waking Ned Devine* meets many of the criteria for Irishness employed by critics who dismiss it.

In particular, *Waking Ned Devine* illustrates what one can accomplish by playing on conventional expectations to offer a scathing critique of specific social conditions. In the tradition of American slapstick films, though without their breakneck pace, the narrative contrasts slapstick and cynicism, the naked motorbike ride that seems to be little more than innocuous buffoonery comes hard on the heals of a scene in which Jackie O'Shea (Ian Bannen) manipulates the innocent Michael O'Sullivan (David Kelly), using him as a pawn for fooling the lottery man. This approach of presenting a broadly comic scene and then undermining its presumed harmlessness by a much more skeptical one, though perhaps not as skillful as the strategy employed in *The Quiet Man,* demonstrates the same subversive impulse for representations of fundamental aspects of Irish identity, in this case sentimental suppositions about rural Ireland.[18] Indeed, the nonlinear complexity of *Waking Ned Devine* comes closer to the corrosive self-examinations of *The Quiet Man* than McLoone and others believe. Further, in its combination of Irish themes and international issues, *Waking Ned Devine* assumes a paradigmatic role in outlining central concerns of contemporary Irish cinema.

Finally, before going into nonlinear ways of responding to *Waking Ned Devine,* let me address some of the more persistent linear complaints about the film's authenticity as an Irish motion picture. Although I have spoken broadly in the Preface and the Introduction about the range of features that legitimately distinguish an Irish-themed film, I think it important to rebut specific attacks on this motion picture. A number of commentators have grumbled because filming of *Waking Ned Devine* took place on the Isle of Man and because it has an English director (Kirk Jones) and a Scot (Ian Bannen) in a starring role. This critique simply reinforces the standard of privileging indigenous over nonindigenous Irish-themed films without fully articulating an argument for this point of view. I have seen no similar assertions that *Cold Mountain*—filmed in Romania with an English (Jude Law) and an Australian (Nicole Kidman) actor in each of the leading roles and a Brit, born of Italian parents, as its director (Anthony Minghella)—falls into any category other than an American film. In fact, a long cinematic tradition exists of integrating actors and filmmakers of various national backgrounds into films that nonetheless retain their national flavor. More to the point, actors have become so mobile that when Fionnula Flanagan (who plays Annie O'Shea in *Waking Ned*) convincingly takes the role of a woman of the American South, Teensy Melissa Whitman, in *Divine Secrets of the Ya-Ya Sisterhood* (2002), and a Detroit foster mother, Evelyn Mercer, in *Four Brothers* (2005), it becomes meaningless to classify her performances in those films as the work of an Irish actor. (See Appendix E for additional comments on transnational efforts.) Surely, one can follow the same protocols for accepting Ian Bannen's performance.

Waking Ned Devine has also been criticized for its British and French financial backing. Given the fact that multinational funding has become a way of life for feature-length productions, this observation seems at best a questionable complaint, and a condition often overlooked in assessments of other Irish-themed motion pictures with foreign investors. Indeed, in the rancorous debate over the merits of *Michael Collins* as an Irish film, for example, the fact that a large American studio bankrolled its production never entered into consideration.[19]

It seems much more to the point, particularly given the tradition of context-driven interpretations of Irish-themed films, to question whether the thematic choices in *Waking Ned Devine* affirm its Irishness. As I have already asserted, interpretive criteria, like the list outlined by Martin McLoone, require refinement to accommodate the complexities of fragmented, nonlinear, Irish identities. Nonetheless, the topics themselves provide a very useful start for determining the legitimacy of McLoone's dismissal of the film's claim to an Irish connection. *Waking Ned Devine* does not address every criterion that McLoone lays out, and in fact I doubt that any motion picture could. However, I have listed below the relevant categories that have an active role in its narrative:

(1) An interrogation of the rural mythology that underpinned cultural nationalism and is encapsulated in the use of landscape. Director Kirk Jones and cinematographer Henry Braham deftly integrate lush scenery and rural types that evoke standard expectations of rural Ireland while using their narrative to confront the audience with repeated and insistent evidence of the venality and mendacity that underlie these images and subvert the impulse to valorize their depiction of country life.

(2) A consequent desire to reveal the social and political failures of independent Ireland and latterly to probe the failures and contradictions of the Irish "economic miracle." Waking Ned Devine presents the issue of collecting the lottery winnings in slapstick comedic perspective that highlights the mendacity of everyone living in Tullymore, and offers the fanciful opinion of the child Maurice (Robert Hickey) that no one would leave the village since their only ambition would be to spend the money in the pub. At the heart of the narrative, however, a grimmer view emerges of a stagnant social life dominated by gossip and alcohol in a village with only one child in evidence and a mere handful of people under the age of sixty. That is to say, beneath its veneer of charm, Tullymore embodies a portion of the country that has found itself marginalized and embittered by the achievements of the Celtic Tiger.

(3) An interrogation of religion in Ireland. Despite the pieties of Annie in praying for the soul of Ned Devine (Jimmy Keogh), a cynical sense of the way that religion functions in the lives of the villagers permeates the film. This point becomes particularly evident in Annie's decision to participate in the swindle and in the willingness of the visiting priest not only to look the other way as the villagers defraud the lottery commission but also to allow Jackie O'Shea to travesty Ned Devine's eulogy funeral to fool the lottery man.

And (4) the question of women in Ireland.[20] Though the narrative gives relatively little direct attention to Irish women, it does offer a muted and admittedly breezily optimistic picture of single motherhood. Although the subplot of the romance between Maggie (Susan Lynch) and Pig Finn (James

Nesbitt) may seem predictable in its resolution, the conflict acknowledges complex social and economic considerations. Maggie takes a practical view of providing for herself and her fatherless son, initially dismissing Pig for hygienic reasons while considering Pat Mulligan (Fintan McKeown) for financial ones and later reversing the order of preference when the lotto money alleviates financial and insalubrious impediments.

I do not intend this application of McLoone's criteria to establish the cultural worth of *Waking Ned Devine.* I will take up that issue in subsequent paragraphs. I do mean to show, however, that if one lays down standards for measuring Irishness in films, one cannot simply override these principles by introducing sweeping charges of *faux* Irishness. An Irish-themed film might be imaginatively lacking, but such a failure does not change its fundamental character, particularly if it conforms to the critic's own criteria.

By all this explication I do not mean to dismiss the question of the film's artistic quality, also an issue for McLoone and others, but a full appraisal of its merit will not come from a linear approach. One needs to accommodate its self-consciously contradictory perspectives. *The Quiet Man* has already shown that a narrative can introduce stereotypical views of Irish identity and retain its integrity if it properly interrogates those stereotypes. I want to make the argument that by seeing *Waking Ned Devine* from a nonexclusionary attitude, a position lacking in the criticisms of the film that I have cited, one can find it introducing and subverting stereotypes in a manner that gives it paradigmatic value for assessing contemporary Irish films.

A fair interpretation of *Waking Ned Devine* begins with an acknowledgment of its imaginative context. The motion picture foregrounds its credentials as a slapstick comedy, but that fact in itself does not prescribe narrow, predictable interpretations. The opening scene, with Annie's brisk smack to Jackie's cheek in response to his trickery, announces the physical dimension of the film's humor, even as, through Jackie's manipulation, it subtly signals a strong counterforce to the surface narrative. In subsequent scenes—Jackie replacing Ned's upper plate, Michael O'Sullivan's naked motorbike ride and Jackie's similar journey in briefs, the removal of Ned's remains in a post office van, and Lizzy Quinn's (Eileen Dromey) spectacular fall from a cliff inside a telephone booth, to name the most obvious examples—the film relies on the same broad physical humor that the Marx brothers made famous in their films of the 1930s and remains a staple in movies such as *Animal House, Raising Arizona,* and *Analyze This.* Irish movies such as *The Snapper, Puckroon,* and *Everlasting Piece* echo this tradition as well. In every motion picture of this type, the story line follows a familiar narrative arc, and the action often plays on the viewer's emotions. What creates a distinguished film is the ability to add complexity to these expectations, an element that I will take up below.

The slapstick mode can easily lead to the complaint, mentioned by McLoone though not with the same ferocity that O'Brien displays, that the dialogue is weak and the characterization facile. Like any interpretative judgment, *weak* and *facile* function as subjective terms. Applying them in an exclusionary fashion, however, produces a reductive impression. In this case, one can grant a superficial predictability to the language of the film, and still see a complexity in its application. For example, the transparent discourse of romantic subplots—like the courtship of Maggie O'Toole by Pig Finn—highlights a common feature of motion pictures of this sort, and it represents a banal domestic alternative to the chaotic lives of the central figures. More to the point, however, in slapstick films it is the slipperiness of meaning in the seemingly ordinary exchanges between characters and the promise of imaginative complexity beneath the surface of mundane behavior that carry the narrative.

When Jackie and Michael go to the pub with Pig Finn, for example, their conversation plays on an intentionally banal tone. The animating force of the action comes from the audience's awareness of the subtext of the discourse. Talk that may initially appear superficial, even stereotypical, can in fact have a more profound imaginative effect once one becomes attentive to the cynicism and ambivalence that underlie the exchange. As I will note below, one can take little of what Jackie O'Shea says at face value, and the quotidian tone of his statements masks his complex approach to the world that surrounds him.

As in so many slapstick movies, much of the film's humor turns on the interaction of a comedic pair—in this case the sweet-natured straight man, Michael O'Sullivan, and his conniving partner, Jackie O'Shea. Michael projects the nature of a guileless creature whose simpleminded generosity makes him an easy foil. Jackie readily assumes the part of trickster, but remains very much the country fellow, as Annie pointedly reminds him at several points in the narrative. In consequence, these roles could easily degenerate into stereotypes. However, two key features in Jackie's personality prevent this deterioration.

From the start, *Waking Ned Devine* invites us to see an alternative side to Jackie's seemingly genial nature. The narrative hints that the ruthlessness of a natural predator informs his behavior. In matters grand and small, time and again Jackie moves determinedly to gain an advantage and to forestall the success of others. His life seems informed by a zero-sum game philosophy that characterizes every interaction as a challenge to get the better of the situation, and the narrative presses us to reconcile these acts with the stereotype that he seems to project. (In this fashion, beneath a veneer of bumptiousness he displays the same callous, single-minded determination that one finds in Michil, the rural whiskey maker in Bob Quinn's determinedly Irish film *Poitín*.) A number of events in the first portion of the film alert viewers to this aspect of his nature.

The first instance, tricking Annie into bringing his apple tart into the parlor so that he does not have to leave his chair, seems a small gesture of connubial deception and one that would be familiar to many long-married couples. Nonetheless, it signals the presence of traits that will drive the action in matters great and small: a sharply focused, cunning resolve and a relentless desire to best the other fellow. The tart itself means little, and the slap Annie administers in response means less. What remains important is that the scene highlights Jackie's ability to manipulate, to get another to do his will whether she wishes to do so or not.

The series of equally small gestures following this interchange neatly reinforce the impression of a more complex, and perhaps darker, side to Jackie than a viewer might initially suppose. Once he deduces that someone from Tullymore has won the national lottery, a gesture that in itself testifies to Jackie's continual watchfulness for opportunities to exploit, he seizes on the idea of finding the winner and, as he tells Michael, "making sure we are their best friends when they cash the jackpot." (Enlisting Michael O'Sullivan to help him may not seem to fit the pattern of a self-absorbed conniver until one considers Jackie's near complete control of Michael.)

After a fruitless night of buying drinks for the village, Jackie takes another turn at finding the winner of the lottery with his scheme to invite the eighteen regular lottery players to a chicken dinner so he can interrogate each more closely. He reproduces the same pattern of inquisitive behavior that he followed in the pub, but iteration gives us a starker view of his nature. As the camera makes clear, Jackie displays an adept skill at turning the conversation toward winnings and at making himself seem the most openhanded of men. However, this routine unfolds as more than a broad portrayal of a good-natured if canny country fellow. A mirthlessness informs his actions. His preoccupation reveals not a man who enjoys the company of others but rather one who, when in a group, always remains a bit aloof, on the lookout for an advantage. Jackie stands out as a hybrid rural figure, a descendant of Sean Thornton no longer charmed by the narrowness of options and not content to accept society as it comes.

The actual discovery of the ticket underlines Jackie's relentless self-absorption. After Annie points out that someone failed to attend the dinner, Jackie realizes that Ned Devine was not present. He cannot contain himself, but sets out late at night in the middle of a storm with a dinner for Ned. When he discovers the body of Ned in front of a flickering television with the lottery ticket clasped in his hand, Jackie does not hesitate for a moment. In a wonderful bit of cinematography, the camera moves to a close shot of Ned holding the ticket, and then shows Jackie's hand, shark-like, snapping it up.

Certainly, none of these scenes reveals Jackie to be a debased and depraved individual on the level of Hannibal Lector or Jack the Ripper, but that's not the point of slapstick comedy, a genre founded on the often convoluted struggles of an individual determined to overcome the circumscription of the quotidian. As with the films of W. C. Fields, Peter Sellers, Robin Williams, Steve Martin, Jim Carey, and Will Ferrell, scene after scene alert us to an underlying complexity in Jackie's character. Though he shows himself adept at self-deprecation and at seemingly straightforward selfishness (and this deftness is where some critics detect stage Irishness), in fact there is much more to his temperament. He has an animal cunning and a consistent need to triumph over others that lurk just beneath the surface, but, even more arresting, an ambiguity inherent in his nature makes it difficult even for the audience, seemingly aware of his goals and motivations, to understand completely what he intends. These traits do not so much blacken his character as suggest a multiplicity to it that his easygoing demeanor and supposed stage Irishness belie.

Like any con game, the film takes great pains to set up the circumstances for tricking its victim. For the first half of the movie, *Waking Ned Devine* shows us what Jackie plans to do to get the lottery money, but, as evident in the examples already adduced, it also provides numerous opportunities to see Jackie as more than the village character willing to run great risks for the thrill of the game. Jackie certainly plays that role, but he also appears as an isolated, predatory individual. He has a keen sense of his environment because he makes it his business to stalk anyone who inhabits it. His conviviality stands as camouflage, at once part of his nature and at the same time screening his deeper impulses. In the end, recognizing the paradoxical quality of the ambiguity inherent in the relatively straightforward elements of Jackie's character keeps us from being taken in by the simplistic figure that he presents to the public, and it invites us to see much broader opportunities for interpreting the film's commentary on the environment from which Jackie emerges.

This ambiguity about motivations in key situations informs the action. Jackie's desire for the money always emerges clearly, but only gradually do we come to realize that money may be of less significance than the pleasure that he derives from manipulating others. One of the first suggestions that Jackie's roughish nature might not be as transparent as it seems comes in his recruitment of Michael as an accomplice. As they discuss their plans, Michael says something about his half of the winnings. Jackie immediately replies, "We agreed on half, did we?" Though the conversation goes no further and Jackie's teasing nature makes it easy to dismiss his remark as banter, the suggestion of an edginess beneath the amiability remains.

After the lottery man (Brendan Dempsey) announces his intention to return to Tullymore to verify Ned's identity, it becomes clear to Michael and Jackie that they cannot keep the secret of the winning ticket from the rest of the village. Rather than give up the plan, however, Jackie determines to repeat it on a larger scale by enlisting everyone in the village in the plot. He does so in a speech that mixes exhortation and confession, telling all assembled that he realizes that he was wrong to keep the secret from them and that Ned wants them all to share the good fortune. The very simplicity of Jackie's remarks clashes with the cunningness of his nature already displayed, and it begs the question of whether his dream of Ned becomes a convenient excuse to make his behavior palatable to others. (He first invokes it to convince a skeptical Annie of the rightness of keeping the lottery ticket.)

The eulogy that Jackie delivers in the church stands as one of the most sentimental moments of the film, but it also challenges viewers to reconcile alternative interpretations. On the one hand, it expresses quite poignantly the power and satisfaction of a lifelong and intimate friendship. It charms both the lottery man who witnesses it and, if the transfixed expressions on the faces of the congregation serve as accurate reflections, the villagers who know the irony of Jackie speaking of the man, Michael O'Sullivan, sitting in the pews with them.

At the same time, the very power of the scene turns on the ambiguity created by the repetition of familiar sentiments. After all, the eulogy as Jackie delivers it acts as a self-conscious, if extemporaneous, performance undertaken to fool the lottery man. Although it may seem delightful to viewers to think that in telling the truth Jackie is succeeding in his deception, there is no reason to believe that he feels any more sincere in what he says here than he did when he told the villagers at the chicken dinner that if he ever came into money he would simply "take what I need, and then share the rest with my friends."

What seems to be his most generous and straightforward gesture comes near the end of the film when, during the final celebration in the pub, Maggie comes to him for advice. "Would you say Maurice needs a father more than seven million pounds?" She goes on to reveal, admittedly somewhat improbably given the differences in age (though in the slapstick genre such illogic is often part of the narrative), that Ned Devine is Maurice's father. Jackie gallantly urges Maggie to take all the money, but one might reasonably see that gesture as nothing more than a calculated risk. Maggie has already indicated an inclination to give up a complete claim, and, by seeming to urge her toward the greatest material benefit, Jackie provides her with the opportunity to feel that she has made the right decision on her own. A true con man would know that maneuver was the best way to play a mark.

The possibility of cynicism informing Jackie's nature becomes more believable as one observes its replication in the atmosphere of the village of Tullymore. Although, like Jackie, the inhabitants seem to fall into familiar types, a persistent sense of widespread venality and greed makes them more complicated. Annie, Jackie's putative moral compass, proves to be as quick to go off in search of the lottery winner as is he. Though the harridan, Lizzy Quinn, stands out as the fiercest embodiment of grasping self-interest, all of the villagers show themselves quick to assess a situation in terms of its benefit for them. Time and again, as Jackie uses openhandedness to facilitate his search for the winner, wary people ask him, "Have you come into some money?" Indeed, chicanery emerges as second nature to nearly all the characters. Given the opportunity to profit from participating in defrauding the lottery, the villagers line up at dawn in front of Jackie's door, and as the scheme progresses the publican, Dennis Fitzgerald (James Ryland), proves canny enough to advise on arranging an offshore bank account to collect the winnings. Even the visiting priest finds himself swept into the scheme with very little persuasion.

In the end Jackie O'Shea stands out as a cunning, ruthless, and determined rural character not too distant from those individuals whom we see in motion pictures such as *Traveller* or *The Field*. The fact that he appears in a comedy seems superficially to soften his nature. However, the overt sentimentalism of the film is as cynical as any technique that Jackie himself would use: it shows how an unscrupulous manipulator can play on emotions to gain his ends.

At the same time, despite the length of my explication, I have offered only one perspective of Jackie O'Shea, and it reflects my cynicism as much as what I suggest is his. My aim has been, after establishing the Irishness of the film, to emphasize the possibility of this stance as one reading of his nature. However, if one displaces an alternative, more sentimental view with this analysis, one falls into the same linear trap of the commentators whom I have critiqued. Multiplicity makes Jackie engaging, with the possibility of redeeming generosity always counterbalancing the seeming chicanery of his nature. To limit him to a particular role, be it trickster, stereotype, or sentimentalist, reductively limits one's sense of him.

Waking Ned Devine, like so many slapstick comedies, winks at the viewers. It flaunts a superficial sentimentality that, as some critics have complained, comes very close to stage Irishness. It can in fact be seen to insinuate a much darker view. By evoking and then undermining the stereotypes of Irish identity, *Waking Ned Devine* implies that a truly sophisticated audience will understand the send-up, appreciate the irony, and incorporate this range of natures into its impression of him. In the process the film critiques both the simpleminded view of the Irish nature that those stereotypes play to and the humorless insecurities of critics who cannot see beneath superficial representations. Indeed, Jackie's multiplicity may prove more familiar to the Irish sense of themselves than some would wish to admit. Although this film may not stand out as the kind of production that Irish cinema critics would prefer to reference to define the medium, it shows itself more in keeping with the multiplicity inherent in the national filmmaking tradition than many would acknowledge.[21]

2

Latent Metrosexuality

The Erasure of Irish Identity in Middle-Class Cinema

As I note throughout my Introduction, representations of Irishness have become increasingly nuanced in all film genres. However, nowhere does one find the challenge to define representations of national identity more evident than in films about the Irish middle class. As economic development creates record numbers of Irish who fall into that category, the visible traits that signal elements unique to their national nature are diminishing exponentially, and increasingly the middle class defines it character more through cultural absences—often directly related to institutions like the family, the church, or the state—than through presences. (For a selection of subjective views on Irish identity, see Appendix A.) Readings of contemporary films need to approach the middle-class genre with this special condition in mind.

Though one can decry the circumstances for any number of reasons, during the decades of political conservatism and economic stagnation from the founding of the Free State through the 1960s, assumptions about the features of Irish identity remained relatively stable, just as middle-class life stood outside the experience of most of the country's inhabitants.[1] As a consequence, when Irish-themed films were not taking up political issues or presenting historical dramas, examinations of ordinary behavior meant movies that highlighted the routines of country existence or the trials for the working class struggling to survive in the city. From *The Lad from Old Ireland* (1910) to *The Quiet Man* (1952), motion pictures reflected an Irish ethos in which the majority of the population, either through their own experiences or through the lives of their immediate families, identified

54

with life on farms or in rural towns. When middle-class figures appeared in political films such as *The Dawn* (1935) or *This Other Eden* (1959), their roles were always inflected by monumental social changes. It was not until the revival of filmmaking in the 1970s, coinciding with a movement out of the economic stagnation of the de Valera period, that the seemingly mundane lives of middle-class urbanites held sustained cinematic interest.

The shift in aesthetic and creative attention coincided with Ireland's efforts to move from an agricultural- to an industrial- and ultimately to a postindustrial-based economy. After some unforeseen political struggles and a series of temporary economic setbacks in the 1970s and 1980s, the Celtic Tiger brought a surge of prosperity that has propelled the majority of the population into the financially secure realm of the middle class.[2] With newfound material well-being came a self-conscious movement away from what was seen as the provincialism of Irishness, as economic transformation fueled a concomitant incorporation of the broad social and cultural markers of the Western way of life. Internet cafés in Bray, high-rise office blocks designed in generic Euro-ugly architecture dotting the west country, Virgin megastores in places like Newbridge and County Kildare—all of these aggressive assertions of internationalism have pushed aside many of the uniquely Irish features of the environment. Whether one sees this as progress or as a sellout to consumerism, this rapid metamorphosis remains a condition more striking in Ireland than in other postindustrial countries because of the long-standing homogeneity of its society.[3]

At the same time, the clear-cut shifts in the cultural, social, and economic landscapes have not produced a similarly easily definable internationalization of values and attitudes. As established in several recent surveys, in fact, the Irish feel a sense of nationalism markedly higher than any of their European counterparts.[4] Although this point of view initially may seem a refutation of the significance of the cosmopolitanism so evident in Irish cities, in fact such dispositions underscore the complexities and contradictions characterizing a great deal of Irish life. Even as many Irish are acutely aware of and perhaps made self-conscious by their rural, Catholic, conservative heritage, they simultaneously have an insecure sense of the diverse attributes of Western culture that would have been unknown and even unimagined by their parents. Though one finds this condition applicable in varying degrees across all segments of society, for the newly affluent middle class—having greater access to ways of seeing the world, patterns of behavior, and material comforts very different from the parochial environment of their parents—Irishness has become a concept grounded on antinomies.[5]

Unsurprisingly, the contradictory elements pervading middle-class life have made depictions of its Irishness increasingly problematic for filmmakers.[6] As a result, manifestations of cultural identity in motion pictures dealing with the middle class have become more and more nebulous and ephemeral. Over the past decade a number of movies featuring middle-class characters have been released, but in these narratives their lives, their problems, and their concerns seem interchangeable with the experiences of their counterparts in other countries in Europe and North America. For the films considered under this rubric, Irishness has taken on a much more muted quality, indeed at times asserted through its nonappearance, and its apprehension demands more diversified and far less linear thinking. To implement successful national readings of these motion pictures, one needs an approach that reconciles the range of conflicted features characterizing contemporary middle-class life.

The difficulty of establishing a clear middle-class Irish identity has not always been so great for filmmakers. A quarter century ago, two of Kieran Hickey's films—*Exposure* (1978) and *Criminal Conversation* (1980)—accomplished exactly what directors in other countries continue to achieve: in deft narrative styles, Hickey's motion pictures caught the angst peculiar to Irish middle-class life in the late 1970s and early 1980s without becoming analytically prescriptive. These movies served as declarations of cultural independence from the tradition of rural or political motion pictures that had dominated filmmaking in Ireland up to that time, and they seemed to point to a rich narrative territory that other filmmakers could explore. Ultimately, larger cultural events made such emulation more difficult than anyone might have anticipated at the time, but Hickey's achievement of capturing that moment when the middle class had a uniquely Irish identity nonetheless demands examination.

Hickey's motion picture *Exposure* works powerfully because it offers a seemingly straightforward narrative that in fact invites viewers to engage

Exposure: The three surveyors before the film's disruptive confrontation.
Courtesy of Barry Lyons.

the complex, but recognizable, cultural motivations behind its characters'
behavior. The film recounts an experience that begins as an innocuous
episode in the lives of three ordinary men, ranging in age from young
adulthood to late middle age, and ends with a profoundly disturbing,
though unvoiced, insight for each. The three are employed by the government to do a land survey in the West of Ireland, and are staying at a rural
hotel on the coast.

Although the action takes place in the hotel and the surrounding countryside, the men's conversations with one another and phone calls home
offer glimpses of their domestic situations in Dublin. Dan (T. P. McKenna)
is an older man with an unhappy marriage and bothersome domestic
upheavals. Middle-aged Eugene (Bosco Hogan) feels bored with his wife.
And the youngest, Oliver (Niall O'Brien), is unmarried and, initially at
least, offers viewers no clear sense of his attitude toward relationships with

women. To varying degrees, each man conveys restlessness and frustration with the life prescribed by his role, though Hickey's narrative, by simply sketching these attitudes, leaves viewers to decide the measure of sympathy that any deserves.

A catalyst to release their pent-up tension appears in the form of Caroline (Catherine Schell), a French photographer who is also staying at the hotel. From the start she represents Otherness—foreign, female, and independent—that sets her in stark contrast to the surveyors and makes viewers aware of the men's culturally inhibited world. All three pay attention to her, and in a short time she and Oliver begin an affair. One night, after Caroline and Oliver have gone out, a drunken Dan and Eugene go into Caroline's room and rummage through her underwear. She and Oliver come back, and catch the other two in the act. All four are clearly embarrassed, but no one says anything. The next day Caroline leaves, and the men act as if nothing has occurred. In the closing scene, Caroline develops a photo that she had taken of the three men, but allows it to fade in its chemical bath.

Without polemics or moralizing, *Exposure* invites viewers to examine the sexual and social dissatisfaction of the men as they interact, ultimately ineffectually, with one another, with their families back home, and with an attractive stranger. On the surface the narrative seems to lay out straightforward sexual competition, frustration, and retribution. Although that tension is undeniably present, making that response the exclusive reading too quickly truncates the range of attitudes enriching the narrative's complexity. By leaving the men's motivations vague and their own articulations circumscribed, the film invites viewers to derive their own sense of the environment that produced such behavior.

This kind of elaboration is by no means uncommon in Irish art. Indeed, the awkward silences at the film's end evoke the same sense of paralysis permeating the short stories in James Joyce's *Dubliners*, and, as with Joyce's stories, they suggest without specifying the catalytic potential of social claustrophobia. Hickey, like Joyce, gives the Irish the opportunity to see themselves "in my nicely polished glass."[7] In Joyce-like epiphanies, Dan, Eugene, Oliver, and, to a degree, Caroline have come away from the experiences at the hotel with new but not necessarily shared insights.

Indeed, as the viewer achieves an understanding of what has transpired, it would be reductive to see any sort of a resolution. *Exposure,* as the title suggests, underscores instead a full representation of the contradictions that inform the lives and natures of its middle-class characters.

A key feature of the film is the tenuous awareness that the male characters have of the power of environment to shape them. Despite the protagonists' lack of introspection, viewers become gradually aware of the insecurities and ambivalences in the men's natures that make them seem childish and emotionally stunted in comparison to their continental counterparts. Dan and Eugene's invasion of Caroline's room and their sullen silence when caught conflate images of social immaturity and truculent aggression, making evident without explaining a pathetic insecurity. At the same time, in the very ordinariness of their natures, they delineate the implicit argument that they are representations rather than aberrations of middle-class Irish manhood. The film leaves viewers with a disturbing image of the products of Irish middle-class life, but, like Joyce, it self-consciously refuses to impose meaning. Rather, it gives filmgoers the task of discerning what the "finely polished glass" reveals.

Caroline's gesture of effacement in the last scene underscores the challenge confronting viewers seeking to fix the natures of the other figures in the film. A full sense of the distinctiveness of the male characters demands acknowledgment of both their coarseness and their vulnerability, and it puts the burden of constructing their identities clearly on the audience's ability to sustain these contrasting traits. Simply excusing or condemning their actions becomes a reductive gesture. Rather, one must accommodate both responses to come to a full sense of the experience.

Exposure works so powerfully because it plays on the domestic turmoil inherent in the middle-class Irish world that the men inhabit. Hints of a puritanical Catholicism and an impotent patriarchy highlight the conflicted experience, and provoke but do not prescribe judgment. Rather, the film draws viewers into completing the meaning of the cultural implications without denying the Irish characters' ambivalent attitudes or dispelling the ambiguities surrounding their engagement with the world. *Exposure* successfully establishes the sense of a stable but complex environment from which these men emerge. Thus, Caroline's equally stable and equally complex Gallic consternation underscores the Irishness of their behavior even as it avoids articulating narrow perspectives for understanding it.

Two years later, Hickey followed this bittersweet project with the release of a less muted and much more complex examination of Irish bourgeois betrayal and emotional stagnation, *Criminal Conversation*.[8] This film focuses attention on the upwardly mobile, urban middle class, a group to that point that had rarely been examined by Irish filmmakers. Again, without imposing a prescriptive interpretation, Hickey's motion picture highlights the social unrest and personal frustration that punctuate the lives of modern Irish city dwellers. Specifically, *Criminal Conversation* captures the tension between the permissiveness of affluent middle-class Dubliners and the claustrophobic limitations surrounding marriage in a country where at that time divorce was unthinkable, abortion was a taboo topic, and society tacitly accepted the right of religion to shape civil law. Over the course of its narration, the movie offers a stunning condemnation of materialism, hypocrisy, and solipsism as corrosive influences on middle-class life. At the same time, it deftly avoids simplistic judgments of any of the central characters.

The narrative begins with Frank Murray (Emmet Bergin), a Dublin estate agent, hosting a Christmas party in his office. Successive scenes establish him as extremely flirtatious, and strongly suggest an element of promiscuity in his nature. When he returns home, the chilly relations he has with his wife, Margaret (Deirdre Donnelly), convey the sense that although she puts up with his behavior, it disgusts her. Nonetheless, they go to dinner at the house of longtime friends, advertising executive Charlie (Peter Caffrey) and his wife, Bernadette (Leslie Lalor). The couples reminisce about their younger days, and recall the trips that they have taken together. Over the course of the evening, they smoke hashish and get progressively drunker. Eventually, Margaret reveals that she has had an affair with Charlie, and she becomes enraged when she realizes that he has had a number of other liaisons. In sharp contrast, Frank discloses that he has never been unfaithful to Margaret. However, his statement increases rather than meliorates the tension. Bernadette tries to ignore the deteriorating situation, though it is clear that she has long been aware of Charlie's philandering. As his anger boils over, Frank strikes Charlie, and stalks off. He returns home alone to find the babysitter (Kate Thompson) and her boyfriend (Garrett Keogh) about to have sexual intercourse. After an uncomfortable exchange with Frank, the boyfriend leaves, and Charlie and Margaret come in on the half-naked babysitter and Frank. The film ends with Margaret in the bathroom compulsively banging her head against the wall and turning the light on and off.

Although *Criminal Conversation* uses twists in the plot to catch the viewer's attention—the seemingly long-suffering Margaret in fact has committed adultery, whereas her apparently lascivious husband, Frank, has not—Hickey does not present simple role reversals any more than he offers unambiguous standards for evaluating the characters. Contextualizing each individual, in a manner more detailed than in *Exposure,* gives the audience background without prescribing opinions. The concreteness of the complexities distinguishes both films from projects of the previous decade. Despite a sense of the contradictory urges informing behavior, the sources for those impulses stand as relatively clear.

Certainly, Hickey captures a time of cultural flux that eschews straightforward explanations. Given the evolving Irishness of these characters, touched by the New Europe but still constrained by tradition, terms like *innocence* and *guilt* quickly lose their absolutist qualities, and become not so much relative as unstable. Indeed, as the narrative unfolds, it shows the inadequacy of a single perspective. Either-or views of Frank or Margaret or for that matter of Charlie or Bernadette cannot suffice to sum up their natures or capture a full response to them. Indeed, no steady, unwavering guidelines for judgments seem to exist in this world. As a result, once the film suggests instability, though not complete speciousness, in the institutions that seem to set the parameters for the characters' existence, linear, objective analyses no longer obtain. Instead, one must come to a subjective sense of how to define these figures within the environment that surrounds them. With deft understatement, Hickey sets up the situation that critiques Irish society in highly individualistic fashion, for it compels each member of the audience to recognize how that society exists in his or her mind.

Criminal Conversation unfolds in its own right as a stunning narrative, but it also marks an important achievement for narratives in this genre.

Hickey's film takes an unblinking view that neither meliorates nor over-simplifies contemporary social conditions. It captures a moment in Irish middle-class life as surely as Cathal Black's near-contemporaneous *Pigs* (1984), a film discussed in the next chapter, represents the hardscrabble world of Dublin squatters as it existed in the 1980s. *Criminal Conversation* simultaneously evokes sympathy, aversion, and even confusion. Most significantly, it foregrounds a discernible, if complex, Irishness as the basis for understanding its narrative.

In light of all these achievements, viewers do well to remember that *Criminal Conversation* very much reflects the ephemeral qualities of a particular time and place. The Dubliners who are its main characters came to maturity at a time when the country was still feeling the optimism engendered by the economic boom of the 1960s and before the spike in oil prices and the crippling inflation of the late 1970s and early 1980s took full effect. They could enjoy the benefit of broadening economic opportunities, encapsulated in the first infusion of funds from the European Economic Community. At the same time, whatever their personal disposition, they continued to live in an aggressively homogeneous, almost stifling, environment in which the Catholic Church and conservative political views exercised an overriding control of daily life in Ireland.

The predictable qualities of many contemporary motion pictures examining middle-class life might lead one to assume that, despite the achievements of *Exposure* and *Criminal Conversation*, subsequent work has done little to extend the narrative lines delineated in Hickey's pioneering work. Such a view is not completely fair, because emerging Irish filmmakers face creative challenges that Hickey could not have foreseen. In just over a decade after the appearance of *Criminal Conversation*, the social, emotional, and spiritual atmosphere of Ireland developed in such a radical fashion that the subtle political, cultural, and intellectual markers that provided such provocative signifiers in Hickey's films had lost their catalytic reliability. Divorce laws changed. New arrangements for marriages and different relationships with partners evolved. Public attitudes toward contraception, abortion, and sexual identity shifted markedly. In short, the certitudes that informed and circumscribed the lives of characters in *Exposure* and *Criminal Conversation*, the societal anchors against which they

could strain, no longer obtained, and features that formerly sharply delineated Irish middle-class identities had become blurred and indistinct.

In conjunction with social changes, and often perhaps as an engine
for them, the aforementioned economic boom of the 1990s brought the
cultural insularity of Ireland to an abrupt end. Petit bourgeois, Catholic
homogeneity gave way to affluent, secular multinationalism. As already
noted, icons of American consumer culture—Kentucky Fried Chicken,
MTV, and Abercrombie and Fitch—became as prevalent in Tralee as in
Topeka. Irish families found themselves more likely to vacation in Tenerife
or Orlando than on Achill Island. The middle class in Ireland developed
greater affinities with people in Europe and America in the same economic
category than with working-class or rural Irish.

That being said, prosperity has not precluded the possibility of making
finely crafted Irish-themed films about the middle class, but it has sharply
reconfigured the defining features of the genre. The emotional insecurities
that Hickey traced so marvelously have become intensified by the erosion
of comfortable social biases and traditional habits of behavior. Absences—
cultural, moral, emotional—increasingly became the defining feature of
cinematic representations of the Irish middle class. Although absence, particularly in the determinedly narcissistic atmosphere of a number of the
more recently released films, does not always equate with loss, it does often
signal a radical shift in the nature of identity. Insightful directors have
explored such alterations, particularly in terms of traditional expectations,
and their work demands new modes of analysis to facilitate one's grasp of
their achievements.

In 1994 Paddy Breathnach released *Ailsa*, a tense and sensitive examination of lives of quiet desperation, which already signaled a shift away
from the distinctive cultural markers of middle-class identity that distinguished Hickey's films. It also signaled the start of a series of increasingly
universalized representations of the Irish middle class in films. Myles But-
ler (Brendan Coyle) and Sara (Andrea Irvine) lead an uneventful existence in a suburban flat in a converted villa. Myles enters one of the other
flats while it is being redecorated, and finds a box, full of money and a gun,
which he keeps. An American lodger moves in, Campbell Rourke (Juliette
Gruber), and Myles slowly becomes obsessed with her. He begins stealing

her mail to learn about her and paying her bills so she will not discover what he is doing. Campbell becomes concerned about the strange conditions in the villa, and eventually goes to Myles and Sara for help. She also tells them she is having a baby. The news of Campbell's pregnancy accelerates Myles's unstable behavior, and as a consequence he is fired from his job. He subsequently has a physical confrontation with Sara, but after staying with their downstairs neighbor for a few days he appears to recover himself. Myles renews his relationship with Sara, and things seem back on an even keel. They receive a letter from Campbell, who has left the villa, saying that she has had the baby, which she named Ailsa, and that she, the baby, and her new husband are returning soon.[9] Myles records a farewell message on Campbell's answering machine and then shoots himself.

Like the middle-class lives it chronicles, *Ailsa* derives its narrative arc from the force generated by the juxtaposition of random events in a quotidian world. Myles strives to construct an identity in an environment nearly devoid of the institutional character that might guide him. At the same time, the viewer remains conscious of a system, not readily evident, that shapes his surroundings. Myles's powerful compulsion at first seems disproportionate to the events that surround it. As each element interacts with the next, however, force builds incrementally. The violence at the end of the film is certainly not causally predictable at the movie's outset, but it becomes comprehensible from a nonlinear perspective as one sees how mundane, unrelated conditions interact to build toward significant consequences.

Through all these events, Breathnach's film shows a wonderful trust in its viewers. Although the narrative painstakingly reveals the details of Myles's life, its tone remains dispassionate, like the manner of the ideal scientific observer. It represents but does not judge Myles's mental degeneration. Each audience member interprets why Myles behaves as he does and what one should think of it. At the same time, a Beckett-like opaqueness pervades the action. *Ailsa* has no real cultural markers beyond those generic features common to contemporary Western urban life. The film teases out representations of the rootlessness invading the Irish middle class, even as it grounds Myles in a perverse domesticity. Inclusiveness without endorsement becomes the motion picture's hallmark. In a Derrida-like gesture, *Ailsa* puts this group under erasure, and it leaves the viewer the task of integrating a sense of identity into an interpretation of a narrative that works to suppress that condition.

The need for sustaining a nonlinear interpretive perspective increases for films made in the mid-1990s, when opaqueness becomes a defining feature of depictions of the Irish middle class. *November Afternoon,* released in 1996 and directed by John Carney and Tom Hall, illustrates the difference a decade and a half has made in representing the consequences of intimacy. It takes up the issues of infidelity and sexual responsibility explored by Hickey, presenting a similarly charged sexual situation in an equally conflicted emotional world of urban middle-class Irish. At the same time, in a society that has just gone through the divorce referendum and has evolved very different attitudes toward the bounds of marriage, one finds the consequences of such behavior as significantly different.

The film begins with Rob (Michael McElhatton) picking up his sister Karen (Jayne Snow) and brother-in-law John (Mark Doherty), who have flown into Dublin Airport from London for a weekend visit. At Rob's flat, where they are staying, John is determined to have a good time and is drinking heavily. Karen seems tolerant of this behavior, while Rob appears a bit disgusted. Rob's girlfriend, Kathy (Tristan Gribbin), arrives to complete the party. Within a short time, the narrative reveals that Rob and Karen have been having sexual intercourse since Rob was fifteen. The narrative then contrasts a weekend of going to lunches, a dinner with Rob and Karen's parents, a visit to a jazz club, and walks around the neighborhood with a series of conversations between Rob and Karen, Rob and Kathy, and John and Karen endeavoring to come to grips with the brother and sister's incestuous relationship.

The choice of black-and-white film stock, the reliance on cramped interior shots, and the evocation of intense, conflicted sexuality raise the viewers' sense of crisis similar to what one sees in *Criminal Conversation*. At the same time, contemporary social mores—divorce certainly stands as an option, cohabitation has become common—enforce a very different conception of that world. Like Kieran Hickey's films, Carney and Hall's *November Afternoon* presents a marvelous study of relationships that have gone well beyond the control of the parties involved. However, the attitudes of

November Afternoon: John (Michael McElhatton) and
Karen (Jayne Snow) in a moment of intimacy. Courtesy
of Tom Hall and Fionan O'Connell.

the characters and the consequences of their behavior are no longer held
in check by predictable Irish social conditions and values. As a result, this
motion picture stands not simply as a reflection of middle-class alienation
but as a measure of how that feeling has taken on a cosmopolitan tone.

The directors' decision to occlude motivations undermines linear
approaches to this work. Instead, one has the option of imposing a range of
interpretations on the narrative. However, those views come out of a generalized sense of modern life rather than from the imposition of exclusively Irish

November Afternoon: Robert (Mark Doherty) coming to a sense of the complexity of his relationship with his wife. Courtesy of Tom Hall and Fionan O'Connell.

values. Irish mores are not so much ignored as missed. (The brief appearance of Rob and Karen's parents evokes a world to which the main characters no longer have access.) Viewers construct their understanding of the film at least in part by engaging an Irish environment devoid of Irishness.

A less bleak ethos, but one still one grounded in an exploration of the diminution of bourgeois sensibilities, characterizes Trish McAdams's film *Snakes and Ladders,* also released in 1996. Though set in Dublin, it projects a world seemingly detached from the lives of most of the people who live in that city. Nonetheless, in a fashion that highlights a pattern established in *November Afternoon* and still followed by contemporary middle-class motion pictures, the audience's sense of Irishness, though muted and even arguably inauthentic or at least retrograde, plays a key role in evoking a viewer's responses to the environment of the film.

The perpetually angry Jean (Pom Boyd) stands at the center of a group of thirtysomething women on the fringe of the music scene. She lives in a flat in the central city with her friend Kate (Gina Moxley), though her doggedly suburban mother, Nora (Rosaleen Linehan), reminds Jean of her conventional childhood. When Martin (Sean Hughes), her musician boy-friend, proposes marriage one night in a ladies toilet, Jean accepts, seemingly on a whim. Then, in no small part owing to her mother's enthusiasm over the engagement, Jean becomes increasingly disaffected with the idea of marriage. A series of pointless arguments with Martin lead to a breakup, and shortly afterward Jean begins an affair with a TV producer (Padgue Behan), and lands a job in television. Meanwhile, after a night of drinking together, Kate and Martin have intercourse, and she gets pregnant. Jean, who has become disillusioned with TV work, subsequently reconciles with Martin, whose band, the Lost Souls, has suddenly become famous. Steadfastly refusing to name the father, Kate gives birth to the baby, and Martin and Jean marry. The film ends at the wedding with a scene that conveys the implicit sense that Martin and Jean realize that Martin is the father of Kate's baby.

Although Jean, Kate, and Martin seem to lead a bohemian life, in fact their minor rebellions do more to underscore the nondescript middle-class world that surrounds them than illuminate their own condition. Indeed, although the film chronicles the lives of the young people, the parallel story of the women in Jean's mother's crowd stands as equally compelling. It contextualizes her daughter's behavior and makes the justification for Jean's rebellion problematic.

In fleeting glimpses—such as the appearance of Joe Dolan, a singer who became popular in the 1960s, or the news that Nora and her friends have formed a communal bond through the Dead Husbands Club—the narrative deftly evokes a poignant view of how the social fabric of Ireland has altered over their lifetimes, exchanging its distinctive parochialism for a vapid cosmopolitanism. The rootedness of Nora and her friends lies in their memories. As the narrative progresses, it gradually becomes clear that to understand Jean, viewers must reconstruct the world from which she has emerged, one that no longer asserts its hegemony but nonetheless stands in continuing tension with Jean's surroundings.

To a degree, that construct becomes the point of the film. Jean is angry with an Ireland that is quickly slipping away. She and her friends, for all their impetus toward independence, are in fact becoming generic Europeans.

What cultural power the film exerts comes from Nora and her aging friends, and the narrative leaves it to the viewer to determine how this fast-disappearing identity informs Jean and the others through the consequences, whether the characters feel an awareness of them or not, of its loss.

Snakes and Ladders foregrounds the impact of transitions on the intra- and extratextual levels, for it acknowledges changes in society more overtly than the claustrophobic narratives of *Ailsa* and *November Afternoon*. However, all of these motion pictures draw the viewers' attention to the value of local cultural markers by underscoring what an individual misses without them. This perspective stands on one side of the boundary, marking a shift in the creative attention of filmmakers. In subsequent motion pictures, middle-class anonymity rapidly ceases to be a condition producing anger or indifference. Instead, the absence of cultural identity becomes a cause for celebration.

By the beginning of the twenty-first century, with the release of motion pictures such as *Saltwater, When Brendan Met Trudy, About Adam, Goldfish Memory,* or *Wild about Harry,* the pronounced changes in the material and psychological landscape of Ireland had taken on a fixed quality. The differences had been absorbed, and a much less distinctly Irish social milieu had evolved. Movies began to portray this reconfigured society, but a distinctly Irish nature was difficult to discern.

A quick survey of recent motion pictures shows a determinedly superficial trend in representations of Irishness. Such films assert a slick, clever, and charming tone. At the same time, none comes close to evoking the overt impact of the Irish ethos on the individual identity the way that *Criminal Conversation* succeeded in doing. Nor is there the sense of absence and loss that one finds in *Ailsa* and *Snakes and Ladders*. Instead, these movies have the look of Bord Fáilte (Irish Tourist Board) promotions, using familiar landmarks as if in themselves these locations establish a national identity, incorporated into the motion pictures to spur the viewers' conceptions of Ireland without burdening the characters with the features of uniquely Irish traits.

Conor McPherson's *Saltwater,* released in 2000, offers a plot that reads like any American television soap opera or sitcom. An eccentric Irish-Italian family owns a snack shop in an unnamed seaside town north of

Dublin. The narrative, organized around days of the week, centers on how all of the family members deal with unsettling events in their lives. The father, George (Brian Cox), endeavors to pay off a loan secured at exorbitant rates and to thwart a gangster, Simple Simon (Brendan Gleeson), who is trying to take over the family business. The daughter, Carmel (Valerie Spelman), copes with her pretentious and insecure philosophy teacher–boyfriend, Ray (Conor Mullen). The younger son, Joe (Laurance Kinlan), is trying to adjust to school, but falls under the influence of a thuggish new student who assaults a teacher and rapes a drunken girl. The elder son, Frank (Peter McDonald), plans and carries out in slapstick fashion a robbery of Simple Simon's bookmaking shop to get money to pay off his father's loan. The philandering boyfriend humiliates himself at a philosophy lecture, much to Carmel's chagrin. Joe is accused of rape by the rapist, but in the end is exonerated, and Frank leaves home.

Like so many motion pictures made in Ireland over the past decade, a generic story line propels the action, and locale becomes its most Irish feature. The cinematography captures the beauty of the seaside north of Dublin and the generic charm of the surrounding towns. Given the limitations of the script, the film's stellar Irish cast turns in strong performances. However, the narrative offers no interpretive challenges, and its ethos remains nondescript. Even the approaches that one could apply to the transitional films examined above—playing with the chimera-like features of a tradition of which the characters are aware but cannot readily invoke—no longer produce satisfactory interpretations. Instead, a cultural nihilism unconsciously pervades the film and challenges the legitimacy of assuming a collective national identity in any contemporary motion picture dealing with the Irish middle class.

Kieran Walsh's 2000 film, *When Brendan Met Trudy*, takes the tendency toward erasure to the level of parody. Though set in the country's capital, its tone adopts a mimicry that aligns it more directly with Hollywood than Dublin. Its title invites viewers to associate the film with the Billy Crystal and Meg Ryan American romantic comedy, *When Harry Met Sally* (1989), and throughout the narrative *When Brendan Met Trudy* repeatedly and unself-consciously quotes from a number of other Hollywood movies. It begins with a send-up of the opening of *Sunset Boulevard*. Brendan (Peter

McDonald) is lying face-down in a gutter with rain pouring down on him, and his voice-over narrative references a swimming pool (just to be sure we get the connection) before beginning to unfold his story. Like *Sunset Boulevard*, the film jumps back six months to a scene showing Brendan watching Sean Thornton's first kiss of Mary Kate Danaher in a television broadcast of *The Quiet Man*. Paradoxically, throughout *When Brendan Met Trudy*, Brendan's obsession with movies facilitates the sense of cultural abnegation previously mentioned and evokes a metacritique of the narrative.

From the start, the film presents itself as hip and clever. It deftly evokes the American screwball comedies of the 1930s and 1940s, and it consistently rewards film buffs with its offhand references to classic scenes, as when Brendan stands framed in a doorway in a pose similar to one assumed by John Wayne as Ethan Edwards in *The Searchers*. At the same time, this gimmicky feature turns viewing into a game of Trivial Pursuit. It places all its emphasis on knowledge of classic Hollywood cinema, and it puts no requirement on the audience to understand a more complex discourse, let alone engage the Irish ambiance. Indeed, despite the film's Dublin setting, Ireland cannot even assert itself as a recognizable absence. Rather, it holds no position within the interpretative demands of the movie. This is not to say that *When Brendan Met Trudy* possesses no imaginative appeal but rather to note the growing irrelevance of viewers evoking Irishness to understand middle-class films set in Ireland.

Wild about Harry, released in 2000, proves itself similarly devoid of national character, and lacks even the cleverness of parody to give complexity to its narrative. The film ostensively endeavors to go beyond sexual activity to an examination of its title character's motives, but in fact the narrative cannot get past tired jokes about his libidinous appetites. Harry McKee (Brendan Gleeson) is a TV chef going through a divorce brought when his wife, Ruth (Amanda Donohue), finally grows tired of his philandering. After thugs severely beat Harry one night while he is going out for cigarettes, he begins to act out of character, and collapses in the middle of the divorce proceedings. He goes into a coma, and, when he revives, he thinks he is eighteen years old. Ruth takes him back to their home to recuperate, and, as he learns of his past, Harry comes to realize how badly he has been behaving. Feeling genuine remorse, he tries to win his wife back.

As he is on the point of convincing her of his reformation, he seems to relapse into his old ways with a reprise of the hedonism that characterized the unregenerate Harry. A confrontation on TV with a crazed politician (James Nesbitt) adds a bit of slapstick diversion, and the film ends with the promise of reconciliation between Harry and his family confirming its programmatic structure.

As was the case with *Saltwater*, a number of problems plague *Wild about Harry*. However, foremost is its inability to avoid squandering the talents of a very fine cast. This film has the framework of motion pictures that Cary Grant and Katharine Hepburn made delightful in the 1940s, but they did so with dialogue that set a hectic pace and revealed nuances in their natures. A weak script ensures that scenes in *Wild about Harry* never develop the story line or present any character as engaging. Individuals behave more like types or even caricatures than like well-rounded figures. More to the point, despite the motion picture's setting in Belfast, the insulated lives of its characters present one of the most nationalistic of Irish cities as socially, culturally, and historically nondescript. Although the intention of making a Belfast motion picture without reference to "the Troubles" is admirable, the more sophisticated the film attempts to be, the less successful it becomes in establishing any sort of identity. Its defining element stands as the completely generic tone that it emits. In the end, neither linear nor nonlinear analysis can bring *Wild about Harry* to life, for it steadfastly avoids any situation that would require interpretation.

In the absence of clear affiliation with other cultural markers, a series of films have recently appeared that seemed determined to define the Irish middle class through examinations of its sexual predilections. The approach itself is certainly not new, with films such as *The Quiet Man*, *Ryan's Daughter*, *Traveller*, and *Criminal Conversation* all providing examples of how one could address such an issue. However, an antiseptic quality to these most recent efforts has stripped them of any cultural definitiveness. In some instances, this trait provides a searing view of contemporary society. In others, it results in formulaic drivel.

Liz Gill's *Goldfish Memory* (2005) stands as an accomplished example of the former. Like a number of other contemporary middle-class films set in Ireland, it offers an ethos uncomplicated by cultural stresses or

Goldfish Memory: Sexual possibilities for young Dubliners. Courtesy of Liz Gill and Goldfish Films.

ambivalent attitudes, and as sociological works cited throughout this chapter attest, such a perspective captures perfectly the solipsism that has come to characterize young middle-class Dubliners. The film's title offers a defiant rejection of introspection. According to one of the central characters, Tom (Sean Campion), a lecherous college professor, goldfish have a three-second memory, and by implication the central characters of this narrative live in the moment without deeper connections to their experiences. The film offers accounts of a series of hetero- and homosexual encounters. Nearly all involve fundamentally shallow individuals just entering adulthood (chronologically if not emotionally). For the most part, they hold marginal jobs or are students, yet inexplicably they enjoy a comfortable upper-middle-class lifestyle. (This backdrop might seem a misstep in terms of verisimilitude, but it works very effectively to underscore the smug self-satisfaction of the characters.) The very good cinematography, particularly a series of stunning cityscapes, emphasizes the presentation as all surface with no substance. Indeed, the film's location in Ireland stands as little more than an accident of geography. The same narrative could play out, with no change and no need of further explanation, in any city in the Western world, but its location exudes a sense of artificiality.

From the start, however, imbedded ambiguities disrupt conventional readings of the narrative. Like the best Restoration comedies, individual shallowness produces sophisticated social commentary. The insistent carnality of the characters may at first seem more evocative of juvenile fantasies than adult interactions, but a paradox obtains. For all its sexual frankness, *Goldfish Memory* turns on the time-honored premise of the importance of love and commitment.[10] The final scene of the film lingers on images of the characters who have found peace and satisfaction in committed, monogamous relationships. Those individuals still dedicated to sexual experimentation simply drop from consideration. Although the narrative arc of the film seems initially to lead toward unbridled hedonism, this unambiguous endorsement of conventional family life, whether for hetero- or homosexual couples, turns the narrative on its head and calls for a reassessment of the uninhibited sexual activity that preceded it.

In consequence, despite the apparent straightforward conclusion of *Goldfish Memory*, linear readings create problematic interpretations of the film. If one sees the final scene as endorsing a return to stability and equilibrium after a period of recklessness, then much of the praise given the film for its sexual daring begins to ring hollow. If one reads that ending as satiric, then it seems to suggest a corrosive bitterness running beneath the narrative surface. In fact, the contradictions that disrupt the choice of either interpretation enhance the narrative when viewed from a nonlinear perspective. Embracing the conflicted feelings within the film's apparent resolution simultaneously enables reading irony and sentiment into the scene, and adds a depth to characters whose apparent shallowness has dominated the narrative. Without distinct cultural markers, the film takes on a universal quality that both celebrates and reviles affluent young Ireland.

This impulse toward universality becomes a subtle but effective investigation of the self-absorption of the characters. Rather than make even a passing reference to the often turbulent events of the gay rights movement or to the sea change in Ireland's acceptance of premarital sex, the

Goldfish Memory: The affection of his former lovers shocks Tom (Sean Campion). Courtesy of Liz Gill and Goldfish Films.

narrative, like the characters it represents, refuses to move beyond its immediate determination to explore the possibilities of sexual license. It would be a mistake, however, to view this strategy as a gesture toward reductive simplicity. True to the nature of the characters it portrays, the film insistently ignores the issue of social friction and elides any wider concern about the consequences of the frenetic sexuality of the characters, but its very silence on all too familiar social issues enforces the audience's sense of the insularity of these individuals.

In this regard, though in a much more oblique fashion, *Goldfish Memory* proves to be as critical of the early-twenty-first-century middle class as *Criminal Conversation* was of its late-twentieth-century counterpart. Both films insinuate a claustrophobic hopelessness into the lives of their characters. Gill's work, however, differs from Hickey's in showing individuals who have suppressed all awareness of their desperation.

Less diffuse, and much less introspective, than *Goldfish Memory* is Fintan Connolly's 2005 *Trouble with Sex*. Also set in contemporary Dublin, it focuses on the relationship of Michelle (Renee Weldon), a successful lawyer who revels in physical intimacy but shies away from emotional commitments, and Conor (Aidan Gillen), who has committed himself to running a pub and caring for his father. Like so many other films I have referenced, the acting is quite good, and the cinematography is well done. However, the story of individuals materially comfortable and emotionally desolate has both a universality and an inevitability that leaves one imaginatively unengaged by the narrative. In motion pictures of this sort, even linear cause-and-effect analysis proves superfluous because the predictability of the plotline requires nothing more than passive apprehension.

Whether any of these recent films of contemporary sexuality succeed or fail aesthetically remains a separate issue (though one often difficult to separate from cultural responses). What strikes me as infinitely more significant is that they all have a nonspecific quality that severs communal affiliations. One finds in each of these motion pictures numerous geographic evocations of modern-day Ireland undercutting national markers by an insistent cosmopolitan tone. A determination to convey a sophisticated approach to physical intimacy does not translate to an inherent narrative flaw, but without further distinguishing features it can lead to an undifferentiated quality infusing the plot and a random familiarity, akin to the ethos of catwalk models, suffusing the characters.

I do not take these features as distortions of contemporary urban middle-class Irish life. Quite the contrary, they seem to capture it quite well, a circumstance that highlights an integral element of the problem of identity. For better or worse, the Irish middle class no longer defines itself according to a national character similar to that force shaping the individuals in *Criminal Conversation*. In consequence, reading contemporary middle-class Irishness in motion pictures requires an awareness of their heightened specificity and an inversion of conventional cultural approaches. The following extended reading illustrates a response to this challenge.

A Paradigmatic Reading: *About Adam*

Clearly, filmmakers have responded to changes in the Irish middle-class ethos in a fashion that reconfigures conventional narratives. For those individuals interested in continuing to discuss Irish-themed films, a significant challenge has arisen. Irish identity no longer asserts itself as a topic of interest for filmmakers examining the middle class. Indeed, any reference to cultural markers seems to have become a source of embarrassment.

About Adam (2000) foregrounds all of the features that exemplify contemporary middle-class films: It deals easily, explicitly, and frequently with a range of sexual situations. It celebrates materialism with no evidence of reflecting on the implications of such a commitment. And it privileges narcissism above all other human motivations. In sum, *About Adam* reflects a ruthlessly cynical sense of contemporary Ireland, even as it underscores in an almost elegiac fashion the profound loss that society has sustained through the triumph of this hedonistic view. (The passage from David McWilliams quoted in Appendix A shows how closely the film matches perceptions of contemporary Irish middle-class life.) It is a film that rigorously erases Irish identity while simultaneously deriving its central significance from the traditions it disdains. In the following pages, I offer a strategy for approaching this conflicted attitude that pervades *About Adam* and other contemporary middle-class films that claim to be Irish themed.

On the surface, *About Adam* seems to' present a very clear response to the assertion of the absence of a discernible middle-class identity in Irish motion pictures. It proposes itself as a sophisticated romantic comedy, featuring numerous recognizable Dublin locations and presenting an updated version of the courtship rituals enacted by Clark Gable, Cary Grant, Henry Fonda, Claudette Colbert, Barbara Stanwyck, and Katharine Hepburn in numerous Hollywood screwball comedies made in the 1940s. One could argue persuasively that *About Adam* foregrounds the changing cultural values of young Dubliners, showing a noteworthy insouciance toward sexuality completely lacking in the tense domestic relations of films made a quarter century earlier. Nonetheless, while an evolved attitude toward sex and sexuality asserts itself throughout this motion picture, the self-absorption that stands as the defining attribute of the narrative of *About Adam* precludes any communal connections. Indeed, extrapolations from individuals' behavior within the film point toward a nihilistic alienation not evident in the seemingly grimmer motion pictures of this type released a generation earlier. *Criminal Conversation,* to cite just one example, remains energized by despair up to its final frame. *About Adam,* in contrast, glibly celebrates a pointless existence with banal aphorisms and smug self-assurances.

At its core *About Adam* evinces elements that make it a profoundly disturbing movie. The film turns not simply on the promiscuity of the central characters but also on the ruthless self-absorption that allows them to commit monumental betrayals without a moment's hesitation or the slightest measure of guilt or remorse or even reflection. It brings to the foreground of the narrative an amoral environment, and it challenges viewers to balance the easygoing selfishness of all its characters with the deeper insinuations of a rapacious, unprincipled society that tolerates this behavior.

Part of the difficulty that arises in efforts to understand the milieu portrayed in *About Adam* can lie in the analytic assumptions that one brings to viewing it. Most moviegoers will feel inclined to apply a logic that presumes the ability to identify cause-and-effect patterns that eliminate ambiguity and highlight the narrative structure. In this film, however, competing forces complicate such a perception and resist its pattern of easy delineation. Viewers can readily understand the overall narrative direction, which simply recapitulates the conventional marriage plot, but a great deal of uncertainty obtains regarding the forces shaping behavior. In essence, the film describes a chaotic system whose governing forces remain undetected by exclusionary determinations and suggest that the Dublin social framework upon which the narrative rests constitutes a much more fragmented and unsettled cosmos than initial impressions indicate.

That condition does not make *About Adam* incomprehensible, but it does demand recourse to the elements of nonlinear analysis that I have been advocating. The motion picture's disruptiveness takes on a wonderfully subversive tone with the title character functioning as a catalyst rather than as the central figure in the action. Indeed, the narrative derives its diegetic force not so much from the escapades of the sybaritic Adam but rather from the far more shocking (if utterly predictable, given the formulaic story) reactions to these impulses by the seemingly more conventional members of the Owens family. I do not mean that observation as a gesture to diminish Adam's importance, for he remains the object toward which all of the others gravitate. However, the film does not highlight Adam's nature as a stable entity. Rather, it focuses on the mutability of his character when seen by other individuals in the film.

This oscillating perspective takes subjectivity to a new level, giving it a transformative power on the environment and implying a salubrious quality to the emotional volatility inherent in each character. When Neil Jordan attempted the same commentary in *The Butcher Boy*, he produced graphic images of an individual's mentally unbalanced condition. In *About Adam*, rather than portraying a character sensitive to his isolation from the community and deeply scarred by extreme self-absorption and aggressive individuality, all of the major characters, in the grip of a similar, though not nearly as violent, solipsistic force, are rewarded by achieving the various manifestations of self-gratification to which each aspires.

With this awareness of how materialistic narcissism dominates individual interactions, viewers need to reconsider the impact of the process of observation within the film. Lucy Owens (Kate Hudson) falls in love with Adam (Stuart Townsend) at the beginning of the motion picture because she projects upon him the persona of the shy, sensitive man that she believes she wants. In short order, however, he proves himself not simply to be the man any woman can have but to be the man that any woman chooses to imagine. Rather quickly, Laura (Frances O'Connor), Lucy's bookish sister, becomes Adam's lover after she sees him as mirroring her sensual appetites reflected (or repressed) through Victorian poetry. Next, Lucy's brother, Davey (Alan Maher), who views Adam as a testosterone-driven mentor, asks for advice on how to get his girlfriend, Karen (Kathleen Bradley), to sleep with him. The narrative does not reveal whether Adam seduces Karen in the process, but, after Adam leaves Karen's flat, she is suddenly not just willing but anxious to have sexual intercourse with Davey. Finally, Adam gets involved with Alice (Charlotte Bradley), the eldest sister in the family. She finds Adam a welcome alternative to the tedium of her married life, and she has intercourse with him just before he goes to the church to wed Lucy.

The key to comprehending each of these events seems at first to be the realization that Adam's chameleon-like nature makes him able to appear to be whatever a woman wishes. In fact, a delineation of reality stands as much more fragmented, and the film makes more sense when one puts the agency for these proceedings on the observers. Like the consequences outlined by the field theory in physics, each person who perceives Adam changes him through the act of observation. Despite what he asserts late in the movie in a conversation with Alice, Adam becomes a different character for each of the Owens family members not so much from a grand plan of acting upon them but because of the way their viewing acts upon him.

This multiplicity makes comprehending Adam's wholesale seduction of the Owens family members, according to linear reasoning at least, a strain in credulity. It is difficult to imagine, following conventional logic, a family, outside of the Borgias or de Medicis, to be so venal as to betray one another's trust with the alacrity displayed by the Owens sisters. Further, the speed with which Adam accomplishes his seductions of Lucy, Laura, Alice, and possibly Karen makes it seem far more complex than would be explained by the linear point of view that either he has an animal magnetism unperceived by most viewers or these women have the libidos of teenage boys and the morals of alley cats. In fact, neither option presents a sufficient sense of what transpires.

As the film's title suggests (though in a deceptively arch fashion), solipsism dominates the action. The instability of the signifier produces multiple signifieds. The near-instantaneous emotional commitment of Lucy reflects the way she wishes to see her situation with Adam. The seemingly radical change in Laura's personality demonstrates feelings that she has always harbored but that required an object upon which to focus them. Even the fawning adulation of Davey and the speedy acquiescence of Alice to adultery become less fantastic, though no less matters for critical interpretation, when one considers their behavior as deriving from each choosing to see Adam as a force that meets long-held needs. With this kind of analysis, the radical changes in all the main characters can be as plausibly attributed to the highly charged, exceedingly sensitive environment in which they exist as to moral deficiencies or amoral solipsism. The sexual success of Adam becomes no less fantastic and the betrayal of Lucy by her sisters no less profound, but alternatives for understanding the forces motivating characters who perform these acts increase exponentially.

Perhaps the clearest demonstration of the power of observation to create a subjective reality comes in the rapid-fire reenactments of the events of the engagement scene. In quick succession the film presents and then re-presents the moment in the restaurant when Lucy, in front of her family, asks Adam to marry her. Each recounting of the scene reflects how one of the central characters has perceived it unfolding. No two accounts are the same, and none gives any clear indication of being the privileged version. Indeed, in a film that highlights solipsism, each stands as a valid representation of what transpired. One cannot fully grasp the narrative without first accepting this condition and sustaining all of the diverse perceptions.

What gives *About Adam* depth as a contemporary middle-class Irish-themed motion picture is its determined frustration of all viewer expectations of Irishness. Despite the narrative's emphasis on personal observation, individual characters emerge from the same cultural context. As a result, it seems reasonable to think that an amalgamation of their attitudes would reflect a good overview of the urban middle-class Irish nature. In this instance, morality, or its absence, stands as a key issue in the formation of our conceptions. Though Adam's sexuality dominates the narrative, other characters shape his attitudes and behavior. In consequence, one needs to decide whether these individuals merit the same judgment if, despite similar actions, their motivations reveal quite different natures. Further, since Adam concentrates his sexual adventures on members of a single family, issues of loyalty to one another cannot fail to emerge. No matter how one judges Adam, how one assesses the characters of sisters who have intercourse with their sibling's boyfriend—one over the course of Adam's developing relationship with Lucy and one on the day of the wedding—remains an issue. What ultimately challenges viewers in this film is how to judge not simply the sexuality of the characters, portrayed as liberating, but how family ties, or the lack thereof, redefine Irishness in postmodern Dublin.

Indeed, the narrative coherence of *About Adam* depends on the moral vacuum in which it exists. In a world defined by cultural mores, no matter what they prove to be, viewers could hardly avoid judging the ethical behavior of the characters in the film. In the value-free world of *About Adam* contextual immediacy justifies all actions, and characters find themselves free from any responsibilities created by adherence to any form of abstract principles.

In this fashion, the film emerges as far more than simply the story of how different people project themselves on an interesting young man. A provocative undercurrent of nihilism drives the narrative forward. It invites viewers to consider whether the self-absorption of the characters in *About Adam* in fact reflects a searing portrait of contemporary attitudes among affluent, narcissistic young adults living in Dublin. (Paul Hogan's series of satirical novels on the life of Ross O'Caroll-Kelly from secondary school to marriage and parenthood offers a parallel approach, though with far more outrageous representations.) If this judgment is the case, then one further needs to consider how this portrayal invites a reconfiguration of our sense of Irish identity. If one accepts the paradigmatic nature of *About Adam*, middle-class Irishness takes on qualities far more profound than simply a Celtic version of Europeanism. It reflects a powerful rejection not only of traditional Irish values but of any communal impulse, and the interpretations test a viewer's ability to sustain perceptions of this attitude in tension with conceptions of the Irish character that it rejects.

3

Urban Legends

The Survival of Working-Class Films

Since the opening chapters, I have argued that rapidly changing economic, social, and cultural conditions across a range of classes, locations, and institutions have accelerated the erosion of a homogeneous contemporary Irish identity. This transformation has fragmented the concept of Irishness into multiple personalities while simultaneously making many of the social features examined in various Irish-themed films distinguishable by their lack of cultural specificity, a condition of which the Irish are themselves acutely aware.[1] However, the Irish working-class motion picture, a genre that only recently has attracted the sustained interest of filmmakers, has proved to be the notable exception to this tendency. Representations of individuals in movies of this group evoke more of the conventional markers of Irishness and impose upon them stability greater than any seen in the other categories considered in this study.

This emphasis facilitates the most direct examination of identity evident in any of the categories, highlighting presence rather than absence. Indeed, this category stands as the exception that proves the rule, tolerating far more conventional approaches to interpretation than any of the other genres. At the same time, given the cultural ambiguities of the world surrounding the working class and their increasing economic and social marginalization, a number of these films still project multiplicity and resist exclusionary, linear interpretations.

A straightforward, if not particularly uplifting, condition explains the continued appearance of conventionally determined Irish features in the working-class character. Over the past decade and a half, rapid economic growth and consequent demographic changes have affected everyone in Ireland.[2] At the same time, with the cost of living expanding and demand for an educated workforce increasing, the experience has not proved to be universally beneficial.

Prosperity has led to rapid reconfiguration of the middle-class world. However, significantly fewer economic benefits have reached the working class, and consequently its environment has experienced fewer alterations.[3] As a result, in the working-class motion pictures considered in this chapter, as often proves the case in everyday Irish life, individuals remain in a stagnated, parochial condition despite the material development going on around them.

As already noted, middle-class figures in contemporary Irish-themed films have the same unself-conscious, cosmopolitan awareness as do their counterparts in motion pictures set in any Westernized urban area of the world. In sharp contrast, characters in working-class Irish-themed movies define themselves through neighborhood rather than global references. They remain keenly aware of their pitch, fiercely loyal to their local, and suspicious of anyone living in Dublin 4. Overall, they retain an abiding sense of their immediate environment because they find themselves trapped within a narrowly defined world whose only change has been the addition of a superficial patina of pop culture and a growing awareness of the disparity between their environment and conditions of their counterparts in the middle class.

In consequence, even with the intrusion of multinational commercialism, films in this category unfold without evidence of the transformative impact of the nonindigenous cultural and economic influences that shape so many other groups in Ireland. Thus, a dual interpretive insistence arises. These motion pictures make strong, overt demands on viewers to apply a sense of popular culture toward understanding this world even as they also privilege the importance of Irish attitudes, customs, and conditions in any interpretations of the films.

This type of motion picture has only recently appeared in significant numbers and consequently commanded widespread attention for its own attributes. Nonetheless, since the late 1950s, at regular intervals, movies emerged demonstrating graphically the powerful dramatic force that one could derive from a narrative that focused on the experiences of ordinary working-class Irish. Films in this category have grown to prominence by delineating the heretofore overlooked complexities of both the living situations and the natures of working-class characters.

Home Is the Hero (1959), Henry Keating's film adaptation of Walter Macken's 1952 Abbey Theatre play directed by Fielder Cook, serves as a prime example of the inherent complexity of an ostensively straightforward representation of the genre. It tells the story of Paddo O'Reilly (Walter Macken), a barroom bully in a small Galway town (though the same atmosphere would obtain in a large urban setting), who accidentally kills a man in a drunken brawl. Paddo is sent away to prison for his crime, while wife Daylia (Eileen Crowe), son Willie (Arthur Kennedy), and daughter Josie (Joan O'Hara) struggle to survive economically, emotionally, and socially.

In a subtle but insistent fashion, their situation acknowledges the narrow parameters of the working-class culture even as their responses to these conditions foreground a significant reordering of the hierarchy and a pronounced reconfiguration of the patterns of life of the family that Paddo has left behind. Without Paddo's wages, the O'Reillys take in as borders Dovetail (Harry Brogan) and Bid (Marie Keane), a husband and wife who had been friends of Paddo's, to help make ends meet, and under their influence Daylia begins to drink. After a great deal of effort, Willie finds work as a shoemaker's apprentice, and eventually he opens his own shop. Josie, though stung by the ostracizing of people her own age, defies the harsh opinion of the town and begins to see the local bookmaker, Manchester Monaghan (Michael C. Hennessy).

After serving five years in prison, Paddo returns home chastened by his experiences and uncomfortable with the recollections he has of the man he once was. He spurns efforts by Dovetail to give him a hero's welcome, and he makes clear his determination to renounce his old way of life. Nonetheless, he finds the alterations that his family has made in their mode of living disconcerting. With a combination of patriarchal arrogance and puritanical intolerance, he condemns Daylia for drinking. He abuses Josie for associating with a bookie. And he forbids Willie to marry the daughter of the man whom he killed.

The world he now inhabits, however, proves much more difficult to control than the one he left, and Paddo responds to this new environment with increasing frustration. In a gesture that parallels the events of the opening scene, he strikes Dovetail in a bar, and briefly fears that he has killed him as well. Dovetail, however, recovers, and this experience and a confrontation with Willie over who has authority in the family cause Paddo to accept the new state of things.

Despite the melodramatic resolution of the plot, *Home Is the Hero* presents a powerful, understated perspective on working-class family life that ultimately resists conventional analysis, even as it echoes themes similar to the ones explored in *The Quiet Man*. Dominant traits distinguish the characterization of the central figures in each film, but other attributes, shaped by the environment, manifest themselves and hint at complexity and even contradiction that the viewer must reconcile.

In *Home Is the Hero* the narrative shows Paddo as a simple, but not simpleminded, individual. He never questions his right to use force until it sends him to prison, and then he emerges as a man no longer sure of the defining features of his world. He seems profoundly ashamed of his past, but nonetheless still feels the pull of impulsive violence.

Daylia remains loyal to Paddo over the course of the film, but also evinces a willingness to act on her own. Freed from patriarchal domination, she indulges her appetites, yet, despite Paddo's subsequent claims, she retains an aura of self-control. (Although Daylia does begin to drink, the film is careful never to show her inebriated.) There is even a hint a sexual energy when she tells Paddo on his return that she has put new sheets and pillowcases on their bed. In contrast, the narrative suggests a conventional prudishness in Paddo when he naps on a cot in an adjacent room rather than in the bed he presumably will share with Daylia.

In fact, representations of all the main characters chronicle individual change while subtly acknowledging the shaping power of communal opinion on identity. Willie, for instance, a character freighted with the community's patronizing view of his lameness from a childhood injury (caused by Paddo's carelessness), takes the length of the motion picture to define the bounds of his nature. In incremental fashion, he shows himself to be neither pathetic nor noble but simply a young man struggling to move out of his father's shadow and determined to define his manhood in a fashion other than what his father has chosen. Paddo finds himself caught in the restrictive identity of the village strongman, lauded by fellow drinkers until he carries the characterization to its tragic if inevitable conclusion when he causes the death of another. He struggles for the rest of the film, not altogether successfully, to find an alternative role. And Josie is as willful as she is courageous in her efforts to live as an ordinary young woman, despite the impediments imposed by a judgmental society. Throughout the motion picture, figures evolve within their context, and the film subtly pushes viewers toward an awareness of the complexity of the characters' world as a means of understanding their development.

Macken's characterizations provide excellent models for films in this category, and stimulate an open approach to their interpretation. They acknowledge the shaping impact of the environment that surrounds figures in the film even as they trace the paths followed by individuals to avoid prescriptive delineations. Characters in *Home Is the Hero* achieve uniqueness by foregrounding their humanity, often combining dignity and venality in equal measures and leaving viewers to articulate the role of specific figures in the film. This condition stands as a central concern for those viewers seeking to understand the range of potential interpretations. Although the overall structure of *Home Is the Hero* appears to conform to cause-and-effect logic, the complexity of the seemingly commonplace individuals who populate the story demands broader analytic options.

Characterizations of Paddo, Daylia, Willie, and Josie go beyond representations of types functioning in a narrowly delineated world. Although a dominant trait—strength, loyalty, respectfulness, chastity—initially identifies each, no characteristic proves sufficient to explain motivation or delineate the identity of any of the figures. Each goes through a process of reformation, struggling with limited communal options to assert individuality. Each takes on new strengths and weaknesses, additional virtues and vices, and the film leaves the viewer to reconcile these features in interpreting the narrative. Ireland has already seen this sort of characterization in *The Quiet Man,* and the narrative of *Home Is the Hero* unfolds with the expectation of an audience capable of responding to the same sort of complexity.

Over the next decade a number of working-class films set in Dublin appeared, though it was not until the mid-1970s that directors began to exploit the complexities of the genre with the sophistication found in the narrative of *Home Is the Hero*. Prior to that period, films such as *Rooney* (1958), *Paddy* (1969), and *Quackser Fortune Has a Cousin in the Bronx* (1970) never rose above the level of melodrama. *Rooney* traces the adventures of the title character, a corporate-dustbin man, as he earns acclaim in hurling and finds love in rented accommodations. A decade later *Paddy* follows the predatory sexual exploits of its title character. And the next year *Quackser Fortune Has a Cousin in the Bronx* gives emphasis to romance over promiscuity, though again the title character finds ample opportunity for the latter as he sells potting manure to Dublin housewives. In all three cases, clichés and stereotypes dominate the narratives' approaches to working-class identity. Although these films fit the category of motion pictures considered in this chapter, they offer little insight into the formative nature of the environment.

Down the Corner, a film released in 1977 and directed by Joe Comerford, initiated a series of motion pictures that insightfully represent working-class life, demonstrating how a seemingly minimalist approach to narration can evoke a powerful sense of a complex urban environment. I will discuss this film in greater detail in Chapter 5 as an example of representations of children in Irish-themed films. For now, I simply note that Comerford has a great sense of the complexity that punctuates the quotidian lives of Dublin working-class families caught up in times of economic depression. In presenting the often tawdry events of the film, Comerford eschews moralizing, and in fact suggests that viewers who take an exclusionary perspective of conditions miss the essential features of the action. Rather, the chaotic system delineated in the film demands the open-ended engagement of nonlinearity.

Along the same lines Cathal Black's 1984 film, *Pigs*, shows what one can derive from a combination of a gritty Dublin cityscape and a narrative that goes beyond predictable types in representations of its characters, not by focusing on development but by highlighting deterioration. The film unfolds in a decaying Georgian mansion on Henrietta Street where a diverse group of misfits lives as squatters. The narrative opens with Jimmy

(Jimmy Brennan) breaking into an abandoned house to assume posses-
sion, but this exertion reflects a rare burst of energy in an otherwise mad-
deningly passive character. In due course, Jimmy's apathy makes it relatively
easy for the other squatters to move in as well.

Initially, each seems more a type than an individual. George (George
Shane) is a failed businessman. Orwell (Kwesi Kay) is a Jamaican pimp,
and Mary (Joan Harpur) is his hooker. Ronnie (Liam Halligan) is a drug
dealer. And Tom (Maurice O'Donoghue) is a paranoiac. They live in
proximity to one another, but with rare exceptions maintain a diligently
enforced separation. Through Black's deft direction viewers find opportunities to probe the individuality of each individual.

The action of the narrative builds slowly until Jimmy, after picking up
a man in a gay bar, is chased by homophobic thugs. When these hooligans
later come to the house to buy drugs from Ronnie, they recognize Jimmy
and beat him. In the aftermath, George is the only one who attempts to
help Jimmy. Perhaps in response to the violence or in revulsion over its
consequences, the others drift away from the squat. George offers to share
his new apartment in Ballymun with Jimmy, but Jimmy declines. (Even for
a 1980s audience, by that time well aware of the degeneration of the Ballymun flats, this offer would have been seen as a painfully ironic gesture.)
Finally, two police officers (Donal McCann and Johnny Murphy) arrive
and force Jimmy to sign an admission that he has been defrauding the
welfare system by claiming his wife, who is in fact living in Scotland, as a
dependent. Wandering around the now deserted house, one of the police-
men declares that the squatters lived like pigs.

Entropy emerges as the dominant impulse within the film, but as a
transformative force it moves at a glacial pace. A sensitive dependence to
change characterizes the environment of the squat, and this condition
invites the viewer to remain attentive to the subtle accumulation of tension. For instance, one misses the full significance of the violent assault on
Jimmy if one focuses exclusively on the beating. In fact, the chilling reactions of the occupants of the squat both immediate and long term have as
much or more interpretive import as the attack itself, and understanding
their responses can come only through a retrospective sense of the ever
increasing pressure that informs all of their lives.

A contrasting motion picture that appeared a decade later helps one come to a better sense of the interpretive options in *Pigs*. Gerard Stembridge's *Guiltrip* (1995) underscores the way a working-class ethos can exacerbate suffering in an already intolerable situation. Set in a small town, *Guiltrip*, through a series of flashbacks, recounts the events of a day in the life of a timid young woman, Tina (Jasmine Russell), and her overbearing husband, Liam (Andrew Connolly), a corporal in the Irish Army intent on running his home in a rigid, patriarchal fashion. Whereas the narrative repeatedly enforces the film's working-class ethos, the environment it traces emphasizes isolation rather than communal support.

Whereas *Guiltrip* shapes its narrative through a series of viscerally painful scenes that trace the rapid degeneration of Tina and Liam's marriage, *Pigs* evolves in a more incremental fashion. From the meal shared by the squatters early in the film to the gradual disappearance of all of the tenants, minute changes punctuate the narrative. Idiosyncrasies emerge and become the basis for self-exclusion. Jimmy takes to going about the house wearing a bath towel as if it were a skirt, announcing his difference from the others. Ronnie and Orwell become fixated on their professions. Tom grows more and more withdrawn, and George tries with increasing desperation to maintain his facade of middle-class respectability. Because of the diversity inherent in a large urban environment and the implicit dependence on cooperation that this milieu creates, the film shows us, even more starkly than *Guiltrip*, the corrosive effects of a lack of community. *Pigs* captures the significance of the ethos of a working-class society by showing the chaos that results when it breaks down.

That is not to say, however, that *Guiltrip* does not make a powerful comment on the mores of the working class. In a fashion analogous to Kieran Hickey's critique of middle-class marriage in *Criminal Conversation*, *Guiltrip* examines flawed characters caught in a stifling atmosphere unrelieved by any possibility of change. It plays on the limited choices available to a working-class married woman in an Ireland just prior to the 1995 divorce referendum, and it hints at the desperation of a working-class male whose world is changing so rapidly that only the regimentation of the army can provide solace.

A combination of cultural rigidity and individual neuroses lead to catastrophic decisions on the part of both individuals. Tina steals a CD player from the electronics shop that Michelle's husband, Ronnie, manages as a gift to placate her mercurial husband. Liam tries to engage in adultery, and then commits murder when his efforts at seduction come to a humiliating end.

The proportional responsibility for events stands unambiguously clear. At the same time, although the actions of both central characters and their consequences appear evident to the most casual observer, the forces motivating them remain occluded. The anger of Liam and the timidity of Tina go unexplained throughout the narrative. Paradoxically, the spareness of the narrative and the directness of the action produce an ambiguous picture of the world these figures inhabit. A viewer's sense of the film will come directly from his or her impression of the impact of environment on the central characters. Interpretation turns on considerations of the balance between individual and ethos, and in this fashion *Guiltrip* provokes a closer scrutiny of the working-class world than many of the more overtly delineated films in this category.

This pattern of straightforward demographic representation offering multifaceted interpretive opportunities becomes even more apparent in two motion pictures that combine expectations related to Hollywood gangster films with strong Irish working-class associations. Paddy Breathnach's *I Went Down* (1997) establishes its Irish credentials with an ease and authority that belie its imaginative complexity. The film draws on the elements of a genre made familiar by countless American movies—the crime drama featuring a man who has just been released from incarceration and is trying with scant success to reform—and reconfigures the narrative direction to accommodate the unique cultural landscape of the clannish working-class world of Dublin. In the process the film both affirms and undermines viewer expectations of genre and identity.

The tension of the narrative rides on antinomies within its central figures. Git Hynes (Peter McDonald) displays a maddening combination of passivity and determination. The film opens with him leaving prison after serving a sentence for a crime that, the audience later learns, was committed by his father. Almost at once, he finds that his friend Anto (David

Wilmot) has formed a romantic relationship with Sabrina (Antoine Byrne), Git's now ex-girlfriend. He nonetheless rescues Anto from a gangland beating, and as a consequence incurs a debt to the local criminal boss, Tom French (Tony Doyle), that can be expunged only by traveling to Cork to pick up another gangster, Frank Grogan (Peter Caffrey).

Bunny Kelly (Brendan Gleeson), teamed with Git to go to Cork, vacillates between a range of types. He is introduced as a hardened ex-convict drawn into the job to ensure its proper execution. However, he quickly shows himself to be an uxorious husband, and demonstrates at best a dubious competence in performing the simplest of crimes. And most tellingly, he suffers quite self-consciously from sexual ambivalence in an environment intolerant of that kind of ambiguity.

As a mismatched pair, Bunny and Git make the trip to Cork, and their adventures seems to follow the pattern of a conventional buddy picture with an element of slapstick not usually seen in gangster films. They rob a gas station with an offhand ineffectualness that disarms any sense of menace in the act. They squabble over a pistol and its bullets like a pair of children arguing over a toy that neither wants. And they generally approach their task of collecting Grogan like two surly teenagers being compelled to visit an aunt whom no one really likes.

The ambivalences in Git and Bunny's natures combine with the ambiguities of the job upon which they have been sent to undermine types, reconfigure perceptions, and give the film a distinct and very particular Irish identity. Bunny's contrasting attitudes, sexual guilt, and aggressive mendacity take significance from the context of the insular working-class society that maintains prescriptive expectations for the role it imposes on him, and this conflicted nature frustrates single-minded interpretations of his behavior. Likewise, Git's maddening devotion to Sabrina combined with a stubborn determination to follow his own course of action reflect an individual unwilling or unable to escape or to conform to his milieu. To comprehend these characters, viewers need to come to a sense of the world that Git and Bunny inhabit and then understand how the pair renegotiates the terms of the roles that they assume.

Though the plot twists of *I Went Down* are clever in themselves, what most engages the audience is the very precisely delineated criminal and working-class ethos that gives meaning to the conflicted world of the central characters. Bunny and Git exist in a complex, dynamic system shaped by both fixed and random influences. They not only evolve over the course of the film but also make apparent the forces that have shaped their identities. A series of vignettes—from Bunny's ineffectual efforts to contact his wife, through Git's bumbling attempts to become a man of violence, to their final confrontation with Tom French—demonstrates without articulating their conflicted values, and viewers are left to balance the impact of a tightly delineated society on the natures of determinedly individualistic characters.

John Boorman's 1998 film, *The General,* offers a similar, though even more understated, approach to the cultural complexities inherent in the nature of a seemingly straightforward, working-class character. Brendan Gleeson stars in a quasi-autobiographical portrayal of Martin Cahill, the leading Irish criminal of the 1980s. Though Boorman makes Cahill's disposition as a thug evident from the start, the narrative also depicts Cahill as a man shaped by intelligence, clannishness, and ferocity. Over the course of the film, Cahill demonstrates himself capable of calculated brutality and of equally measured generosity. (At one point in the film, he distributes infant care packages to the poor. At another, he nails to a pool table an employee suspected of disloyalty.)

The narrative also insistently articulates instances of the dubious morality of the middle-class world upon which Cahill preys. One early scene, for example, shows Cahill robbing a well-to-do family, including stealing a toy for one of his own children. During the robbery, viewers see a middle-aged man leaving the bed of a woman, stupefied by pills, who appears to be his wife, and going to the room of a young girl, perhaps an au pair, perhaps his daughter.

As with many gangster films, *The General* incorporates the working-class ethos from which Cahill emerges into the identity of its central character. However, it does so in a fashion that eschews the simplistic representation that harsh living conditions inevitably produce a sociopath or psychotic, narrative approaches made familiar by American movies from *White Heat* (1949) to *Scarface* (1932 and 1983). In contrast, Boorman shows a man whom we understand by his environment but who nonetheless shapes the world around him rather than vice versa.

Cahill cultivates his independence and develops an abiding antipathy toward civil authority while growing up in the corporate flats of Hollyfield, a place he always recalls with affection. At the same time, he cannily manipulates to his advantage this image as someone tied to his neighborhood. When, for instance, developers attempt to clear Hollyfield, Cahill refuses removal, staying in a caravan in the middle of the rubble from already demolished flats and claiming to represent the residents who have been displaced. He agrees to leave only after the authorities offer him housing far better than what was afforded to those residents who departed when asked.

That is not to say that he functions as a pure pragmatist. Unlike stereotypical mobsters, Cahill sets standards, albeit idiosyncratic ones, for both his business and his personal life. He disdains the use of drugs and alcohol, and feels contemptuous of men who indulge themselves. At the same time, although he is married to Frances (Maria Doyle Kennedy), he also has children with her sister, Tina (Angeline Ball), in a ménage that all three accept. In the process, Cahill does not scorn morality but, rather, defines its boundaries according to his temperament.

The narrative gives Cahill's opponents no clearer moral sense. Inspector Ned Kenny (Jon Voight) turns his pursuit of Cahill into an obsession, at one point beating Cahill while holding the latter in custody. Other Gardái allow their behavior to degenerate as well. In one scene they kill Cahill's pigeons to provoke a reaction, and in another they laugh at him while he is going into diabetic shock. And after the withdrawal of the police units that had been conducting surveillance on Cahill's house, Gardái cheer when they learn that the IRA has killed him as he sat in his car.

The General stands as a film rooted in impressions of the working-class environment of Dublin, but it remains far too clever to posit a world that simply champions or condemns Martin Cahill. Rather, it continually defers moral judgments of his actions, leaving the viewer to balance conflicting impressions. In one chilling scene, for example, Cahill tries to convince the grandmother of a child sexually abused by her father, Gary (Sean McGinley), a man in Cahill's gang, not to press charges. He cites loyalty to Hollyfield, promises vigilante justice, and then offers the grandmother and granddaughter a new house. Viewers know that Gary has said if he goes to prison for the crime he might inform on the gang.

In a dexterous fashion, Cahill's behavior demonstrates both a fervent tribalism and a cynical individualism that simultaneously satisfy alternate explanations and authorize the filmgoer to come to an accommodation of the conflict. Indeed, throughout the narrative, Boorman plays with antinomies inherent in the working-class milieu he represents to confront viewers with the conundrum of apparently mutually exclusive conditions. The film draws us into the world of Martin Cahill, and we certainly cannot understand him without coming to grips with that world, and then leaves it to us to find a method for discerning the significance of the social forces that shaped his unpredictable behavior.

Three films, all adaptations of Roddy Doyle novels, offer far less violent, though no less culturally driven, examinations of working-class life. Alan Parker's 1991 motion picture, *The Commitments,* traces the rise and fall of a Dublin blues band organized by Jimmy Rabbitte (Robert Arkins) and made up of working-class men and women with meager employment skills and scant professional knowledge of music. What they do have, however, is a very keen sense of class consciousness and communal identity. (When Jimmy advertises for musicians for the band he is forming, he specifies that rednecks and Southsiders need not apply.)

The group initially lacks direction. However, when Joey "the Lips" Fagan (Johnny Murphy), an older musician, joins them and a bus conductor, Deco Cuffe (Andrew Strong), becomes the lead singer, the band takes off. It moves progressively from small gigs to the chance of a record contract. Sexual and professional jealousy erode the band's unity, and eventually it breaks up, leaving the former members to pursue other musical careers with varying degrees of success.

At one level, *The Commitments* does not represent a very daring narrative approach. The trajectory of the band's development never varies, and early on in his metadiscursive self-interviews Jimmy previews its rise and fall. Certainly, the music itself provides a dominant vitality that allows the story line to elide complexities and still engage viewers. Nonetheless, a number of vignettes highlight the working-class world from which the film emerges, and present it with a texture that goes beyond a programmatic narrative: Mr. Rabbitte's (Colm Meaney) expression of his devotion to Elvis Presley, giving the King's picture pride of place on the wall over the pope's, playfully intrudes American culture into an otherwise determinedly Irish working-class home. Bernie's (Bronagh Gallagher) life with her family in an overcrowded corporation flat poignantly enforces her need to transcend the grinding tedium of the social welfare system by participation in the band. And Dean Fay's (Félim Gormley) satisfaction at being called an unemployed musician rather than an unemployed pipe fitter reminds viewers of how complex configurations of working-class identity function in the world of the movie.

At the same time, the film's emphasis on soul music articulates an interesting international amalgamation. Early on Jimmy tells the band: "The Irish are the blacks of Europe. And Dubliners are the blacks of Ireland. And Northside Dubliners are the blacks of Dublin. And so say it once. Say it now. I'm black, and I'm proud." This ostensible blend of American soul and Dublin working-class values creates an environmental duality that viewers must first judge as real or artificial and then come to understand in a fashion that reconciles these impulses. Like the most challenging films in this category, it brings viewers back to the issue of the degree to which environment and temperament shape individual identity in this genre.[4]

Stephen Frears's 1993 film, *The Snapper*, offers a view of working-class life unenhanced by an engaging sound track and spirited musical performances yet nonetheless quite powerful. In a tightly orchestrated tale of working-class domesticity, it examines the impact of out-of-wedlock pregnancy, focusing on the evolving relationship between a father and his daughter. On the surface, it may seem to take a frivolous view of a serious situation. (One need only look at *Hush-a-Bye Baby*, a film examined in Chapter 5, for instances of much grimmer consequences.) However, such a judgment imposes a far too narrow reading of the elements of the narrative.

The film opens with unmarried Sharon Curley (Tina Kellegher) announcing to her family that she is going to have a baby. She refuses to name the man responsible for her condition, and the family, especially her father, Dessie (Colm Meaney), struggles to come to grips with the situation. Though Sharon faces some prejudice where she works and a bit of abuse from some of the neighbors, over the course of the motion picture, with one important exception noted below, all she experiences does not seem to touch her deeply.

Midway through the narrative, the family learns that George Burgess (Pat Laffan), a bumptious man of Dessie's age whose family lives across the street from the Curleys' house, is the father of Sharon's child. As with the announcement of the pregnancy, the news at first proves shocking, but it quickly becomes a source of comic relief. Indeed, reconciliation and accommodation emerge as the dominant themes of the film. Dessie, initially quite upset by the situation, becomes more and more involved as gestation progresses, to the point of reading books on pregnancy and female sexuality. In the end, he drives Sharon to the hospital and waits there through Sharon's labor, showing a much greater involvement in the birth of his grandchild than he had with the births any of his children.

At a fundamental level, *The Snapper* charmingly plays against the grain. There is just enough community criticism of Sharon to make viewers aware of the difficulty of her position without making single parenthood an insurmountable problem. At the same time, the impact of the pregnancy on Sharon is never fully explored. Instead, the narrative perspective rests firmly on Dessie, showing his incremental, self-directed reeducation as he struggles against the assumptions of his working-class Dublin environment. What prevents this metamorphosis from being simply a sentimental resolution of a difficult social problem is its subtle handling of Dessie's transformation and sharp reminder of the circumstances that led to Sharon's condition.

The announcement of Sharon's pregnancy that opens the film, offhand as it may seem, initially draws attention to the significant shift in her life that is about to occur. However, as the narrative develops, the focus of concern oscillates between Sharon's adaptation to the physical changes she is experiencing and her father's gradual emotional transformation. Like the characters in *Pigs* but with less shattering results, Dessie surprisingly shows a high sensitivity to subtle changes in initial conditions, which has a profound effect on the direction of the narrative. As the household adjusts to Sharon's news, tiny alterations in routine exert an exponential impact on her father, and turn him into a man far more aware of and responsive to the intricacies of his daughter's pregnancy than he was of any of his wife's. The contradictions, or at the very least inconsistencies, that viewers must address in Dessie's shift in attitude become more comprehensible through

an awareness of how the reordering of the bathroom schedules, the altera-
tion in the atmosphere at the pub, and the interest that the other children
have in Sharon's condition all combine to modify Dessie's assumptions
about out-of-wedlock pregnancies and men's responsibilities during the
time leading up to birth.

This concept of high initial sensitivity to change reinforces the film's
tendency to offer an upbeat interpretation of events in the lives of the
Curley family, for it allows them to incorporate shifting situations seam-
lessly into the routine of their lives. It also might seem to suggest a form
of closure that would validate a linear view of the film. However, a scene
that takes stark exception to this condition alerts viewers to a depth in
the movie and to interpretive demands not immediately evident. Midway
through the film, after an evening of heavy drinking, Sharon tearfully rec-
ollects the night she got pregnant. The scene unfolds with grim determination and presents Burgess's act as nothing more than the callous rape of a
drunken girl. The narrative makes no effort to resolve the discordant elements in the episode with the rest of the motion picture. Indeed, this stark
testament of the predatory nature of Burgess's behavior overturns any easy
resolution of the narrative's development.

Beyond forcing a reconsideration of what has happened to Sharon, the
incident suggests the need to rethink initial assumptions about *The Snapper*. As painful as it is to watch, the scene offers a stunning counterpoint to
the seemingly breezy narrative tone of so many other parts of the movie.
Whereas the resilience of Sharon and the openness of the rest of the family offer a charming picture of working-class domesticity, recollections of
Burgess's assault on her emphasize the emotional price that Sharon and
to a lesser degree the others have had to pay for whatever tranquillity they
enjoy. Further, Sharon's memories demand that we hold in tension the
enormity of what Burgess has done and the determination of the family
not to allow the event to scar it permanently.

In this fashion, the film defines the impact of community on individuals without laying down prescriptive patterns for interpreting that relationship. It evokes the power of characters, while conforming to the values of
the working-class environment, to transform personal attitudes and beliefs
and to meliorate seemingly intolerable circumstances even as it reminds

viewers of what characters must suppress to achieve this end. It also underscores the limitations of that environment in highlighting both its ability
and its inability to protect and nurture specific individuals. Most significantly, however, it reminds viewers of the necessary contradictions inherent in the nature of any complex life.

In 1996 Frears released *The Van,* the least critically successful of the
three adaptations of Roddy Doyle's fiction. It follows individuals striving
for economic and social change seen in the earlier motion pictures, but it
lacks the imaginative dialogue necessary to carry it along through the all
too predictable plot development. Larry (Colm Meaney) loses his job as
a tradesman, and he and his friend Bimbo (Donal O'Kelly), who has also
been made redundant, fix up an old van to use to sell fast food. It begins as
a success story, showing how initiative triumphs over adversity. Then petty
jealousies and bickering intervene, and the partnership in the van almost
destroys the men's friendship. The actors play the story for great comic
effect, but the script, instead of exploring the world in which these figures
exist, makes men to be children incapable of sustained mature action. Perhaps if the interactions were not so reminiscent of formulaic explorations
of male inadequacies, the narrative would have a greater uniqueness. As it
stands, it is simply *The Odd Couple* set in a chipper rather than a Manhattan
apartment.

Gillies MacKinnon's *Trojan Eddie,* a film made in the same year as
The Van, and one also turning on commerce, demonstrates a much more
thoughtful approach to the link between economics and individuality.
Without trivializing or romanticizing its characters, *Trojan Eddie* highlights
their struggles between inclinations toward independence and the emotional pull of the community. MacKinnon's motion picture embodies a
cultural hybrid of sorts, for it combines elements of the Traveller's rootless
lifestyle with the gritty concerns of a Moore Street trader. In the process,
the attitudes and actions of the Travelling community and the demands of
it arise from efforts to make an accommodation to an urban environment
combine to evoke very specific Irish resonances in the movie.

The title character, Trojan Eddie (Stephen Rea), is a small-time hustler
employed by John Power (Richard Harris), the leader of a group of Travellers who have established a semipermanent settlement on the outskirts of

Dublin. The plot turns on Eddie being caught in the middle of a romantic struggle between John, who wants to take Kathleen (Aislín McGuckin), a much younger woman, as his bride, and Dermot (Stuart Townsend), a young man who also loves her. Although Kathleen agrees to marry John, at the wedding reception she and Dermot run off with a large amount of money that has been collected as wedding gifts. Much of the subsequent action focuses on the delicate negotiations undertaken to get Kathleen to return to John and the contrast between Power's belligerent personality as a criminal boss and his abject craving for his young wife.

The narrative seems to set up a neat polarity in contrasting Eddie's stable relationship with his girlfriend, Betty (Brid Brennan), with the chaotic triad of John, Kathleen, and Dermot, until a parallel domestic situation arises. Eddie's wife, Shirley (Angeline Ball), who has left him with the responsibility of raising their two daughters on his own, briefly returns. She devotes her time to heaping general abuse on her husband, reminding him of his specific inadequacies, and flaunting her aggressive promiscuity. Eddie's response mixes stoicism and passivity until Shirley finally provokes a reaction when she threatens to take the children away from him. Maddened by the thought of losing the girls, the normally passive Eddie beats Shirley, and then throws her out of the house.

The scene embodies the reversals in individual approaches to domestic relations that take place over the narrative. The normally quiescent Eddie has resolved his marital problems through violence. The bellicose John Power, with Eddie's help, has mildly negotiated the return of his wife. The narrative leaves unresolved what these gestures represent in terms of the natures of both characters. It does, however, make clear that understanding both men requires an amalgamation of their new inclinations into a full sense of their natures rather than a substitution of a new attitude to replace the old one.

The film concludes with John and Kathleen reunited and Eddie growing prosperous as an independent trader. Despite this seemingly happy resolution, in the end the parallel stories turn on what it takes to get along and the amount of moral or emotional compromise in which a person can engage. Kathleen is visibly pregnant, but John's unease as they visit a cinema invites the audience to speculate on paternity. Eddie experiences commercial success, but in an ad for his stall that appears before the screening of the film John and Kathleen are attending it is difficult to discern whether he is a paragon of the prosperous businessman or a caricature of that figure.

Throughout the film identity and a sense of self insistently challenge every major character. John Power compulsively recounts stories of his past, seeking to confirm who he is even as he reinvents himself through his marriage to Kathleen. (In a touching narrative undercurrent, at several points an older woman who is a longtime family friend gently hints that John would have been wiser to marry her.) Eddie balances the brash persona of the huckster against the character of the timid, taciturn husband and employee. And Kathleen and Dermot struggle with the realization that the world around them will have as much influence in shaping their lives as will their own natures.

All this backdrop pushes the viewers toward a fuller engagement with the way conflicting cultural values force characters to adopt multiple and at times contradictory personality traits. For the characters in *Trojan Eddie*, the influence of their surroundings—the customs, attitudes, and conditions particular to a working-class life in Ireland—has a profound and unstable effect on their perceptions and their behavior without imposing an inflexible routine on their lives. The culture of the Travelling community prescribes the reaction John is expected to make to Kathleen's infidelity even as the world that he has created through his own initiative pushes him to a far different, and in some ways more humiliating, response. (Early on he recounts to Kathleen his decision to give up the Travelling life while noting nonetheless that his first wife, like Kathleen, was from the Travellers' community.) Eddie finds himself equally constricted by social expectations regarding the way he should behave toward his wife, his family, and his boss, yet no prescribed pattern of behavior proves adequate to his needs.

In the end, cultural values prove to be both essential and insufficient, and the film demands we find ways to resolve this antinomy before we can come to an understanding of any of the characters. With both John and Eddie, the narrative offers individuals who cannot escape their environment yet who seemingly cannot find satisfaction living within it. Dermot and Kathleen offer younger versions of characters confronting the same sort of struggle with no better initial understanding of its limitations. Over the course of the film, even a minor character like Raymie (Sean McGinley), who shows himself willing to betray Eddie whenever it suits his purposes, proves capable of reversal. He gives his life to protect Eddie by needlessly taunting Power's thug, Ginger (Brendan Gleeson), with references to cuckoldry. In all these instances, characters come to some sort of accommodation with their world through the compromises they negotiate that both acknowledge and deflect social forces.

The first years of the twenty-first century produced a series of films focusing on the gritty life of characters struggling, not always successfully, to cling to the ethos of the working class, and they provide a final commentary on how this group reflects the most Irish elements of any narrative category. Lance Daly's 2000 film, *Last Days in Dublin,* proves the least technologically polished, but nonetheless offers an engaging if sometimes discursive narrative. Shot in digital video, it mixes black-and-white and color footage. It opens, after chaotic scenes of the Moore Street Market, with Monster (Gratton Smith) leaving a run-down tenement and the landlord (David Norris) giving him a tongue-lashing that establishes Monster's role as a victim. Monster subsequently roams around Dublin telling anyone who will listen that he is leaving Ireland. Interpolated into the narration are scenes of the main character imagining himself in New York City, Paris, London, and the Sahara Desert. Monster is robbed by two druggies with a syringe. He borrows money from a female loan shark (Nel McCafferty). He is beaten by her thugs, and he spends the night walking around the town. Throughout the film a hobo, Freddy (M. C. Wuzza), dogs Monster's tracks with the same ambition to travel around the world. Monster and Freddy unsuccessfully attempt to cash a lottery ticket, steal liquor, and get drunk. The next day Monster and some old friends go to the track. The film continues with a series of episodic vignettes that cannot always sustain the narrative. In the end it is clear that the ethos of working-class Dublin has stamped Monster's character, and the challenge to understand that world engages viewers rather than the question of whether Monster will succeed in his wish to leave it.

The weaknesses that accrue over the course of the motion picture relate to its execution. Daly has perhaps too precise a sense of the working-class world, for he often leaves significant gaps in his exposition. Though view-ers benefit from the freedom of his narrative, more background would give those audience members unfamiliar with this environment a clearer sense of how to proceed with interpretations. Nonetheless, *Last Days in Dublin* effectively highlights the place of working-class films as the most cultur-ally relevant category of contemporary Irish-themed motion pictures. It remains the task of subsequent movies to offer fully coherent articulations of that condition.

Three years later Daly released *The Halo Effect*. The film has well-known actors—Stephen Rea, Mick Lally, Gerard McSorley, Kerry Condon, and Simon Delany—in the cast, and a budget that allows for much better pro-duction values. Unfortunately, Daly's script lacks the originality and com-plexity that make *Last Days in Dublin* so engaging. Like Daly's first film, *The Halo Effect* centers on a simple problem—Fatso's (played by Rea) gambling addiction. Its setting in a late-night café allows the narrative to introduce a range of eccentric characters, but in the end that backdrop becomes an impediment. The characters rarely rise above types, and fine acting can-not overcome a pedestrian plotline.[5] *The Halo Effect* shows that Daly has mastered the technical complexities of feature-length filmmaking, but the experience of the first film seems to have turned him from presenting a story that draws on strong cultural inflections to an approach that falls back on familiar stereotypes.

Intermission, the John Crowley motion picture released in 2003, shows that one need not face an either-or choice between craftsmanship and cre-ativity. It offers a satisfying approach to a narrative based on vignettes of working-class life, one that provides structure without prescribing mean-ing. The film combines the discursive method of *Pulp Fiction* and the Dogme 95 style of *Last Days in Dublin*. It examines, through a series of interrelated stories, the travails of marginally employed and in some cases criminal Dubliners, and highlights the schemes they concoct to get money and find happiness. Perhaps with a view toward broad commercial appeal, what could have been a very dark account of the lives of self-absorbed bun-glers turns into a skewed romantic comedy that uses slapstick to downplay some of its more serious implications. (Unlike most Irish films, *Intermission* did have a fairly wide U.S. distribution, and three of its featured actors,

Colm Meaney, Colin Farrell, and Killian Murphy, were already familiar to audiences in the States at the time of its release.)

At the same time, its generic affinities remain stable. Although the film does have some middle-class characters—most notably Sam (Michael McElhatton), the philandering bank manager; Noleen (Deirdre O'Kane), his angry wife; and Seamus Ruane (Gerry Moore), the television reporter—these individuals define themselves through the working-class figures with whom they associate. The disgruntled store clerks, John (Cillian Murphy) and Oscar (David Wilmot); Deirdre (Kelly MacDonald), John's ex- and Sam's current girlfriend; Lehiff (Colin Farrell), the thuggish petty criminal; and Jerry Lynch (Colm Meaney), the psychotic police officer all provide a working-class intensity that drives the narrative. Jerry's macho pretentiousness, John's inept courting, Oscar's needy sexual appetites, and Lehiff's harebrained criminal schemes offer comic relief, but it is the nature of the world that these figures inhabit that engages the reader's imaginative response.

In a slightly more contrived fashion because of the coincidences involved, *Intermission* evinces the same sensitivity to initial conditions that one finds in *Pigs* and *The Snapper*. Examples abound, but the most graphic is the rock thrown by a small boy (Taylor Malloy) at a bus early in the film. It results in Sally's (Shirley Henderson) television interview, which makes her aware of her "Ronnie," which leads her to go for a makeover, which produces her encounter with Oscar, which ends with their becoming a couple. It also causes Mick (Brian F. O'Byrne), the bus driver, to be fired, facilitates his participation in the attempted robbery, and concludes with the wreck of his car in the Grand Canal.

Certainly, it would be easy simply to dismiss all these events as contrivance, but to do so would truncate interpretation of the film. Turbulence stands as a more effective image for comprehending the action. Though characters seem to lead haphazard lives shaped by events that often appear capricious, in fact they exist in a tightly structured environment and subscribe to clearly articulated goals that give direction to their behavior. Oscar, John, Deirdre, Sally, Sam, and Noleen all seek to define themselves through relations with others, and no matter how hectic their existence, these romantic needs shape the viewers' sense of them. Jerry and Seamus see notoriety as the key to their identities, and the quirkiness of each becomes clearer with this fact in mind. Even Lehiff, driven by animal appetites and the most unpredictable of all characters (as the opening scene in which he seems to be flirting with a café waitress, Kerry Condon, and then assaults and robs her makes clear), follows a clearly delineated path toward self-gratification.

These characters hold the viewer's interest not because of what they accomplish but because of what they accept. *Intermission* insistently relates their struggles to the world in which they exist. By the end of the film, none has escaped that world, though all have come to some sort of accommodation. As with the conclusion of *Trojan Eddie, Intermission* gives viewers a putative happy ending even as it suggests that individuals may merely have become less restive in their condition.

Perhaps the least-satisfying film in this group of recent motion pictures is Ian Fitzgibbon's 2003 *Spin the Bottle*. The movie offers an extended view of selected characters who rose to prominence in the extremely popular RTÉ comedy series *Paths to Freedom*. Though the motion picture is relentlessly working-class in its ethos, and for that reason a difficult film for non-Irish or even non-Dublin viewers to comprehend, it never transcends the TV sitcom format from which it derives. The central characters, Rat (Michael McElhatton), Tomo (Peter McDonald), and Brainer (Donal O'Kelly), parody a mindless Northside-inflected approach to life, and the plot to raise money for Rat's obese aunt to go to Lourdes falls disappointingly between camp and clever. Though it depends on Irishness for much of its meaning, it also allows its depictions to slip from burlesque to stereotype without the keen sense of irony that redeems this strategy in other motion pictures. For a film apparently steeped in social identity, a surprising lack of cultural awareness permeates its narrative. The rigidity of its characters, fixed in predictable modes of behavior no matter what they experience, inhibits the development of this motion picture. A far more challenging motion picture, made a year later, *Francis*, engages all of the grittiness of *Spin the Bottle* with a much more genuine sense of the parameters of the world that it depicts.

In a departure from the style of his other feature-length films, *The Solution* and *Tin Can Man*, or his short, *Bandage Man*, Ivan Kavanagh's *Francis*

presents a narrative heavily inflected by Irish culture. Like Lenny Abrahamson's *Adam and Paul* (a motion picture that I will take up at the end of the
chapter), it examines the life of a clearly defined if only remotely understood portion of the underclass surrounded by the affluence of upwardly
mobile Dubliners. Instead of heroin addiction, the street person who is the
title character of Kavanagh's film emerges as a riveting figure, despite or
perhaps because of being crippled by shame and lack of hope.

The narrative unfolds in a measured, episodic fashion. It follows a documentary style, featuring interviews with both Francis (Gerry Shanahan)
and Joe (Christopher Kavanagh), another street person. In a very brief
exchange, Francis explains that he began living rough after the death of
his young daughter. Francis feels complicity in her passing because, when
his wife (Helene Meade) told him of the girl's illness, he refused to believe
it serious and would not interrupt his drinking in a pub. Though never
explicitly stated, it seems clear that he drifted into vagrancy as a way of
punishing himself and of avoiding the family setting that would remind
him of his shame.

Later vignettes fill in the details of his daily life and offer some explanation as to why he remains on the streets. They show an attempt at reconciliation with his wife failing presumably because Francis cannot overcome
the humiliation that he continues to feel. They present a man still in the
grip of some self-delusion, initially lying about how he earns a living, telling the interviewer that he never really begs for money when scenes on the
street clearly contradict him, and showing a willingness to degrade himself
in a variety of ways—clumsily performing a shambling dance and eating
rotten food out of bins—simply to continue to survive.

In the closing scenes it becomes clear that Francis has finally con-
quered his sense of ignominy and wishes to return to his wife. However,
he cannot bring himself to go home empty-handed. He sells his shoes to
another vagrant, and buys a bus ticket and an expensive cake. When he is
robbed of both, Francis seems to relapse into despair, and the film ends.

Several features distinguish *Francis* as a model contemporary urban
Irish film. In a fashion evocative of *Adam and Paul* and *Intermission*,
Kavanagh and Colm Downey, who serves as cinematographer, wonder-
fully present grim, recognizable cityscapes of the Dublin under erasure by

Bord Fáilte. Though homelessness has become a generic urban condition, representations of Francis and of others on the street take on a cultural uniqueness colored by the sudden materialism of middle-class Ireland, the erosion of Catholicism as an institution that offered stability in ordinary lives, and the fragmentation of national identity into groups reminiscent of the tribalism of the Middle Ages.

Perhaps most distinctively, Kavanagh's narrative grace signals what a skillful filmmaker can achieve from a minimalist point of view. As with the other top filmmakers in Ireland today, Kavanagh trusts his audience. His exposition outlines conditions for the viewers, and leaves ample latitude for a variety of imaginative engagements with the film. We are not told explicitly how Francis feels or why he behaves as he does. Rather, we see him acting, we are shown the context in which he finds himself, and we are allowed to cooperate with the filmmaker in the creation of meaning. The narrative unfolds without an oppressive sound track, elaborate gestures, or detailed explanations. Its sophistication demands an equally sophisticated response, yet its sharp-edged acknowledgment of the humanity of its title character ensures imaginative accessibility to a wide range of viewers.

Francis succeeds as a film because it rejects any manipulation of its audience and instead relies on straightforward, though not uncomplicated, representations of the human condition. This film is not a motion picture that attempts to persuade viewers of the validity of a particular point of view. Nor does it seek to evoke a specific emotional reaction. Rather, like the fiction of Joyce, the greatest chronicler of Irish urban life, it offers sharply delineated descriptions of Dublin and trusts viewers to make their own interpretations of these images. *Francis* and Lenny Abrahamson's film *Adam and Paul*, examined below, suggest that the urban underclass remains a rich narrative source for Irish-themed films.

A Paradigmatic Reading: *Adam and Paul*

For most of the films considered in this chapter, the dominant influence of the urban working-class settings ensures that a strong Irish identity will inflect the discourses. At first glance, the structure of Lenny Abrahamson's 2004 release, *Adam and Paul*, seems to take on a very different form, focusing on characters too isolated and too self-absorbed to demonstrate any social markers shaping Irishness in an individual. In fact, the starkness and alienation that characterize the lives of the motion picture's central figures have the paradoxical effect of throwing into relief the communal conditions from which these marginalized figures have excluded themselves. The contrast becomes crucial for interpreting the film, for the working-class ethos that emerges in *Adam and Paul* sets down parameters for viewers seeking a clear sense of the conflict and continuity informing contemporary motion pictures in this genre.

From the start, an aura of universality challenges the value of *Adam and Paul* as a paradigmatic Irish-themed working-class film. The story of a day in the life of two junkies trying to gather the resources they need simply to buy some drugs and survive another twenty-four hours would be equally convincing were it set in any urban environment, from New York to Moscow. The features that give the film its specific Irish character and evoke in viewers a sense of the particular hopelessness of a Dublin drug addict emerge from the background: in the near-impenetrable dialect spoken by all of the characters, in the deft emphasis on scenes of urban grit beneath the patina of Celtic Tiger Dublin, and in the clannish patterns of behavior of the figures who populate the narrative. Against this determinedly working-class setting, the story unfolds in a fragmented manner, befitting the disoriented sense of the world held by Adam and Paul. Nonetheless, as the viewer teases the unifying cultural elements—the structure of seemingly dysfunctional families, the rhythm of the working-class day, the tendency of social welfare both to channel and to drain the energies of marginalized figures—out of the narrative, a clearer and more discernibly Irish picture emerges.

Having said the foregoing, I must admit that no matter how one chooses to read its Irishness, the nature of the film challenges conventional modes of analysis. Although Adam and Paul seem doomed from the opening shot, anarchy governs their lives and makes their motivations, beside their fundamental and relentless need for drugs, unclear and their actions often difficult to follow. In this respect, the concept of turbulence, already apparent in a number of other working-class motion pictures, provides for viewers a model for acknowledging the chaos of individual lives

Adam and Paul: Adam (Mark O'Halloran) and Paul (Tom Murphy) mug a young man with Down syndrome. Courtesy of Speers Film/Element Films and photographer Jonathan Hession.

while perceiving how the mores of the working-class world impose a general sense of order.

The film opens at daybreak with Adam (Mark O'Halloran) and Paul (Tom Murphy) awakening on a filthy mattress in a garbage-strewn field. The fact that neither man has any idea how he ended up there simply underscores the sense of randomness dominating their existence. As the day unfolds, they move in a state barely more than catatonic through the city, being acted upon rather than imposing any direction on their day. Like the banks of a river, the urban environment encloses and directs the turmoil of the pair's lives, defining social boundaries rather than delineating individual natures.

To heighten the impression of rampant disorder playing out in tension with the expectations of a regulated system, Abrahamson's motion picture develops episodically with only the cityscape of working-class sections of the town and the progression of time providing unifying transitions from scene to scene. (The technique of featuring the geography of lower-income Dublin neighborhoods stands as characteristic of this genre, and it remains in sharp contrast to the predilection of middle-class films for highlighting tourist landmarks. Both choices underscore the way each type of Irishness functions in either category of film.)

Ineffectiveness functions as the hallmark of the action. Adam and Paul go to a housing project to find the local drug dealer, and they cannot even get him to open the door. They attempt to ride a bus into the city, but must disembark almost immediately when Paul becomes sick to his stomach. They can barely negotiate city thoroughfares, and in fact Paul sustains one of the injuries that will mount throughout the film when a motor scooter clips his leg as he attempts to cross the street. The nihilism that defines Adam and Paul makes viewers that much more aware of the environment that they inhabit, for their stark isolation gains its definition in contrast to the communal rhythms around them.

Understanding the film, however, requires more than simply acknowledging the antinomies of its distinguishing features. The image of turbulence becomes increasingly appropriate as filmgoers see the complete isolation of Adam and Paul. They have cut themselves off from the working-class world of their origin, and therefore lack definition and even identity. In a public park, Adam and Paul meet a series of acquaintances. Georgie (Gary Egan) is playing soccer with his son, and directs the pair to Marian (Deirdre Malloy), Orla (Mary Murray), and Wayne (Paul Roe). These former friends greet the pair with varying degrees of hostility. They remind Adam and Paul that this day is the one-month anniversary of the death of Matthew (presumably from a drug overdose), a young man who had been a close friend of the two. The group berates the pair for missing the memorial mass, said that morning, and warns Adam and Paul to stay away from the party that evening commemorating Matthew's death.

This exchange not only underscores the pair's isolation but also highlights the erosion of their individuality. In a deft touch that recurs throughout the film, the narrative makes it extremely difficult to identify which character is Adam and which one is Paul. They never call one another by name, and others who see them address the pair simultaneously as Adam and Paul. This confusion in turn exposes viewers to the kind of vague, general disorientation evocative of the larger concerns that plague the pair throughout the motion picture.

Adam and Paul: Drinking on St. Stephen's Green. Courtesy of Speers Film/Element Films and photographer Jonathan Hession.

Over the next few hours, in contrast to the ordinary working-class lives unfolding around them, their physical and emotional disintegration increases in an accelerated, entropic fashion. Indeed, any contact they have with the world of quotidian Dublin seems only to hasten their decline. The pair not only prove themselves inept at various forms of larceny but also consistently come off the worse for their efforts. Paul injures his arm attempting a smash-and-grab on a passing car. Adam is caught in a café trying to steal a woman's purse, and runs off hearing the abuse of the café owner. And Paul, like an inept Jean Valjean, is thrown out of a convenience store for attempting to steal a loaf of bread.

After the debacle over the bread, Adam and Paul fall into a bitter argument over identity and a sense of place with a Bulgarian immigrant sitting on a public bench near the river. (The incident is prefigured by Paul's comment in the opening scene and echoed again during their argument with the man that Adam's jacket is from Romania.) An obvious irony infuses the exchange when Adam and Paul, despite their alienation from the world that surrounds them, assert that the man is lucky now to be living in Dublin. However, the narrative gracefully avoids heavy-handedness by playing on the pair's naive insularity. When the Bulgarian speaks of having to leave Sofia, for example, they assume he refers to a pregnant girlfriend and not the capital of his country.

In a desperate search for cash to buy drugs, Adam and Paul visit the apartment of Janine (Louise Lewis), a former junkie who had been the lover of both men. The scene there contrasts concepts of community and isolation, and stands out as both a poignant testimony to the human need for order and an emphatic declaration of the self-absorption of drug addicts. Janine's flat is unlocked and apparently deserted. Despite their past ties to this woman, Adam and Paul immediately set about trying to steal her television set. Before they can, however, they discover a baby in the adjoining bedroom. They become enthralled with it, forgetting everything else in a brief hiatus from their determined solipsism. When Janine returns, her reaction is first guarded and then sympathetic. By the time the pair leaves, she tells the infant to say good-bye to its father, making it clear that neither she nor Adam nor Paul is sure which man it is and reasserting the aura of ambiguity and anarchy.

As the day unfolds, Adam and Paul become progressively desperate for drug money and increasingly inept at securing it. Their attempt to mug a young man suffering from Down syndrome teeters toward the comedic, but in the end its bathos suggests that Paul and Adam are more afflicted than the person they have attempted to rob. They are forced by a man named Clank (Gerry Moore), who bears them a grudge based on an unfounded rumor, to accompany him on a gas station robbery. There they fail as look-outs, and the Gardái arrest Clank. When the two men do stumble upon a stolen television, they prove incapable of disposing of it. However, as they sit on the steps of the housing project that they had visited early in the day, a vigilante mob ransacks the flat of Martin, the drug dealer who had refused to help them. The mob throws packets of heroin from the porch above them, and Adam and Paul happily pocket the contraband. Were their day not so chaotic, these events would strain credulity. However, in a world dominated by misrule and disorder, nothing seems unlikely.

Now fortified with dope, they go to a bar called the Coal Bunker, where friends are gathering to commemorate Matthew. Again they face a chilly welcome, because many in attendance see Adam and Paul as responsible for the addiction that led to Matthew's death. What is most striking about it all, however, is the profound indifference that Adam and Paul display toward this antipathy. They do not simply prefer heroin to anything else; they don't think of anything else but heroin. This point is highlighted by their unresponsiveness to Janine's struggles with the temptation to go back to drugs when she realizes that they are high. In a deft fashion, the narrative humanizes the scene and underscores the identity that Adam and Paul have lost through Janine's poignant ambivalence about addiction and the banal expressions of grief voiced by the others in the bar.

The final scene of the film parallels the opening. It shows Adam and Paul stretched on a sand dune, apparently sleeping off the effects of the heroin. Paul awakens. He attempts to rouse Adam, only to discover that his friend is dead. Paul gets up and leaves. After a few moments, he returns, rustles through Adam's pockets, and takes the remaining heroin.

Although one cannot ignore the universal elements of this tale of addiction, Irishness remains an important interpretive feature. Adam and Paul may effectively efface their identities, but the narrative continually foregrounds the need to contextualize them to form an interpretation. From the bleak council flats of Ballymun to the litter-strewn patch of St. Stephen's Green and the gritty cityscape along the River Liffey quays, the film insistently reminds viewers of the world of working-class Dublin as a means of measuring the alienation that Adam and Paul have embraced.

Although *Adam and Paul* offers a searing portrayal of the degraded lives of the two addicts, it does not turn into a didactic condemnation of substance abuse. Rather, the film simply suggests the pain and turmoil that must characterize the existence of such figures. By integrating into the narrative images that suggest the sort of ordinary lives they might otherwise have led, the movie presents viewers with a keener sense of the pair's chaotic world careening toward disaster. It disrupts any causal efforts at interpretation, and instead, through the anarchy of its discourse, the film invites us to experience without endorsing it the world that Adam and Paul inhabit. From this understanding, viewers are left to consider what alternatives, if any, are open to the pair.

Despite the social instability of the world delineated in *Adam and Paul* and of many of the other working-class films examined in this chapter, these motion pictures offer a cultural constancy not found in other genres. Although many of the movies in this category demand a sense of multiplicity to comprehend fully their narrative options, they all stand apart from other Irish-themed films. They remain rooted in a recognizable Irish environment clearly defined and consistently evoked from film to film. In subsequent chapters, the genres considered face a continuing struggle to find solidity in their categories as changing social forces determinedly undermine the stability of their social markers.

4

Down on the Farm

The Calcification of Irish Rural Drama

Urban middle-class films increasingly offer highly nuanced impressions of contemporary Irishness. In fact, as they endeavor to reflect the cosmopolitan ethos of city life, they often struggle for distinctiveness in the face of a universality that strips such motion pictures of any local identity. Rural films, despite foregrounding a very different ethos, have over the years also encountered strikingly analogous problems in efforts to capture unique aspects of the Irish agrarian milieu. However, whereas films of middle-class city life generally retain a vigorous if universalized narrative direction, motion pictures of the country have increasingly shown signs of fatigue and a loss of direction. This loss may be due in part to the erosion of their environment.[1]

Living in the country once meant experiencing a markedly dissimilar world from the one that people residing in Dublin, Cork, Galway, or Belfast encountered. Now satellite television and the Internet have made the parochial uniqueness of the life outside cities less and less discernible.[2] In consequence, motion pictures examining contemporary rural life strain to find any elements that mark the experience as unique to the countryside or even to Ireland. Although contemporary filmmakers have responded to this problem by seeking greater distinctiveness through retrospective and at times nostalgic narrative arcs, the number of viewers able to empathize with these depictions grows smaller every year.

This condition changes the expectations that filmmakers can presume that viewers bring to rural movies, and it demands significant shifts in interpretive protocols from what obtained a half century ago. As alluded

115

to in the Introduction, one of the prototypical country motion pictures, *The Quiet Man,* lays out a near-perfect pattern for constructing an authentic Irish-themed film. It highlights topics of unique interest to Ireland: immigration and return, land distribution and its subsequent use, the impact of religion on everyday life, sexuality in and outside of marriage, alcoholism as a communal bond, and the conflicted effects of a rigidly enforced yet sharply undermined family structure.

At the same time, the structure of *The Quiet Man* illustrates both the range of imaginative opportunities within the genre and the thematic limitations that filmmakers encounter. It explores the consequences to an individual who enters into a close-knit world ignorant of the communal lines and collective obligations that are rigidly defined though generally not precisely articulated. In the process, Ford's motion picture examines the complex and sometimes harsh social, economic, emotional, and spiritual rhythms of Irish country life, and it accentuates the necessity of an outsider like Sean Thornton coming to some accommodation with these conditions before gaining communal acceptance. Additionally, the film highlights the often contradictory features of gender roles in a rural community, even as it underscores their crucial function in the regulation of society.

Through it all, *The Quiet Man* captures a great deal of the complexity of rural Ireland in the 1930s, and it neatly plays off fact and fiction. It takes up all of the clichés and distortions various individuals and groups have perpetrated about Ireland, and it shows not simply the falseness of those positions but also the dangers of trusting in them. As a counterpoint, *The Quiet Man* outlines a stark, calculating world fully capable of preying upon those individuals whose sentimentality has obscured their sense of their surroundings.

Ford's motion picture offers a searing depiction of the process of amalgamation into communal life, even as it demonstrates how that society can blunt an individual's awareness of the corrosive force of this initiation. As a result, Sean Thornton at the end of the motion picture is no less wounded for his ignorance of his condition. Indeed, his unquestioning acceptance of the man he has become—adopting a nature ultimately little different from the temperament of his overbearing brother-in-law, Red Will Danaher—adds a measure of pathos to his final portrayal. *The Quiet Man* pays its viewers the compliment of assuming they can see this anomaly without it being presented in a heavy-handed, didactic fashion, and the narrative is all the more powerful for its understated critique of the socializing process of a parochial world.

The fact that Ford's film no longer reflects the condition of contemporary rural living does not invalidate the legitimacy of subsequent motion pictures that follow the thematic pattern laid down by *The Quiet Man,* but it does change the viewers' protocols for understanding them. Comparison with a similar condition in American cinema illustrates my point. For decades U.S. filmmakers have animated the westerns that they produced with powerful narratives. At the same time, each successful movie has increased the challenges to subsequent projects to create original narratives while sustaining generic expectations. John Wayne's later films, for example, work well because they self-critique his earlier personae, and those viewers familiar with movies from *Stagecoach* (1939) through *The Searchers* (1956) could react to the poignancy and humor of *True Grit* (1969) or *The Shootist* (1976). Clint Eastwood's *Unforgiven* (1992) and the HBO series *Deadwood* (2003–2006), to cite two other examples, both follow traditional form and also explore profound issues of morality that earlier motion pictures elided. This layered narrative approach defers the closure of simple causality, and it sustains and even relies on a range of alternative viewer responses to enhance its imaginative impact.

Similarly, for Irish-themed rural films, the imperative to find new ways of seeing becomes a cooperative task for directors and viewers. In imaginatively successful motion pictures, filmmakers need to acknowledge the expectations that filmgoers bring to the genre while simultaneously offering more than predictable story lines. In conjunction with this approach, the audience must be aware of the cinematic heritage that informs the genre without seeing that tradition as laying down a prescriptive pattern for interpretation.

Much as the early westerns did for their genre, *The Quiet Man* has provided a wonderful starting point for both filmmakers and critics interested in rural motion pictures. By engaging stereotypical attitudes and subverting them, it forces us to confront the consequences of linear readings. Accepting the superficial representations of characters in the film causes one to produce at the very least a naive interpretation and arguably a deeply flawed analysis that overlook subtle aspects of the environment from which these characters emerge. As an alternative, elaborating on the material presented in the narrative, reconciling rather than banishing ambiguities, underscores the interpretive benefits that derive from acknowledging the subjectivity of viewers' perceptions of Irish identity.

Unfortunately, in a number of instances, subsequent filmmakers failed to embrace the same openness or to engage complexities in a fashion similar to the one employed by Ford. Instead, they offered shallow, prescriptive narratives not open to multiple responses.[3] Within two years of the release of *The Quiet Man*, director Mario Zampi filmed a shameless knockoff, *Happy Ever After* with David Niven and Yvonne DeCarlo in the leading roles and Barry Fitzgerald parodying his portrayal of Michaeleen O'Flynn. (Although the film itself remains less than successful, it reinforces the paradoxical aspect of Irish-themed motion pictures: the propensity of foreign directors to take up these narratives, for better or worse.)

More imaginative, less exploitative efforts evolved, but only slowly. *Ryan's Daughter,* for example, tries to engage these issues, but ultimately melodrama overwhelms all other forces in the film. It was not until the mid- to late 1970s that one could begin to see how skillful filmmakers could exploit the paradigm that *The Quiet Man* had established, in both the issues the film raises and the approach it takes to engaging them.[4]

Directors such as Bob Quinn in his 1978 production *Poitín* could examine the brutality of country residents knowing that Ford had laid the groundwork for many of the viewer assumptions upon which the narrative was based. Ford had dispelled the fatuous supposition of mindless conviviality and had established in its place images of the dominating, predatory impulses of many whose lives revolved around farming communities. As a result, Quinn was free to take these concepts as givens and then to elaborate on the viciousness that such insularity could breed. This interpretation does not lead to a diminution of *Poitín*'s complexity. Rather, it focuses attention on the range of impressions one can derive from such an environment.

For instance, the harsh conclusion of *Poitín,* with the whiskey maker, Michil (Cyril Cusack), engineering the drowning of his erstwhile associates, provides an arresting moment for viewers, but it is one for which Sean Thornton's beating of Red Will Danaher had prepared them. The significance of both scenes lies less in the violence that occurs than in the unvoiced motivations for control and retribution propelling characters in both films. After engaging the complexities of *The Quiet Man,* with its current of emotional upheaval subtly counteracting the ostensible happy ending, moviegoers necessarily feel greater freedom not only in determining how to understand the final scene of *Poitín* but also in accepting and sustaining contradictions as inherent to its narrative.

In a paradoxical fashion, although *Poitín* derives its complexity from its manipulation of relatively simple images, a key element remains the extratextuality on which it relies. Quinn echoes familiar rural Irish scenes from numerous previous films, building on viewers' impressions to provoke reactions not simply to what appears on the screen but to the narrative tradition from which the images emerge. Despite associating individuals with types—the whiskey maker, the bootleggers, the farmer's daughter—examples from *The Quiet Man* of how seemingly narrowly defined individuals in fact sustain a range of diverse attitudes insistently urge viewers to look for complexity and contradiction. As a result, Quinn could strip his narrative of extended exposition and instead offer impressionistic scenes for the viewers to elaborate and interpret. This approach produces a highly evocative film that succeeds because of, not in spite of, its ambiguities.

Quinn was not alone in benefiting from the practice of reiterating images introduced by *The Quiet Man* upon the consciousnesses of filmgoers, but it is also true that his work enhanced the range of expectations that viewers brought to films set in the countryside. With each successive motion picture elaborating the audience's sense of the complexity of rural Ireland and fostering a tolerance for ambiguities, viewers can be expected to approach Joe Comerford's *Traveller,* released in 1981, open to its exploration of individual aspirations in conflict with restrictive communal values and without needing prolonged explanations of the environment in which the struggle takes place.[5] Instead, with a sense of the emotional desolation embedded in rural life, audiences can concentrate on interpreting the bleakness of the prospects of Comerford's itinerant central characters.

The basic narrative details unfold in a fairly straightforward fashion. The film opens with a young man, Michael Connors (Davy Spillane), and a woman, Angela Devine (Judy Donovan), both members of the Traveller community, being forced by their families into a loveless marriage. After a raucous wedding reception, Devine, the bride's father (Johnny Choil Mhadhc), sends Michael and Angela to the North to buy radios to smuggle into the Republic. On their way to the border, they pick up Clicky (Alan Devlin), a hitchhiker and IRA man, whose presence exacerbates the conflicted relations between Michael and Angela.

After the couple succeeds in buying goods to smuggle, the narrative introduces in episodic fashion a number of material and psychological complications. On the return trip, Michael wrecks the van. Subsequently, Angela reveals to Clicky that she had been imprisoned for hitting her father with a bottle when he tried to rape her. Desperate for money, Michael robs a post office. He and Angela go on the run, hiding in Travellers' camps in the West of Ireland. In the interim, Clicky goes back to Devine's caravan and unsuccessfully confronts Angela's father over the attempted rape. Angela, meanwhile, reveals to Michael the details of her father's assault. When Clicky finds them, the three drive to a seaport. Michael returns to the Travellers' camp, shoots Angela's father, and then tries to comfort the wounded man by giving him the money they owe him. Michael then rejoins Clicky and Angela, and as the film closes Clicky announces apocalyptically that they will leave Ireland and return after the Civil War.

As this spare plot summary suggests, *Traveller* delineates physical and emotional environments even bleaker than the ones in *Poitín,* and unfolds its story line in the heavily inflected patois of the Travellers that may seem less intelligible to many viewers than the Irish spoken by Quinn's characters.[6] Comerford's film eschews even the veneer of civility that characters assume in Quinn's motion picture, and it has none of the optimism, however misplaced, of the individuals in Ford's movie. Alienation relates directly to community. Michael and Angela reject the values of the Travellers, but the absence of an alternative system leaves them stripped of identity. In consequence, the narrative presents burned-out individuals stripped of every emotion. Their lack of drive or goals precludes even the possibility of despair. Ennui permeates their existence. Nothing character-izes their natures but the stark awareness of the hostile atmosphere sur-rounding them and a feeling of a tentative control, at best, over the forces continually assaulting them.

Nonetheless, I believe it equally important to note that this bleakness plays out through a tradition, unique to rural motion pictures, that has through repetition foregrounded increasingly nuanced impressions of Irish country life. The marginalization implied in the conclusion of *The Quiet Man* and the isolation revealed at the end of *Poitín* establish defining features for every scene of Comerford's film. At the same time, this aura of alienation effectively engages interpretive attention because viewers remain aware of the romanticized version of country life that it debunks. Responding to the edginess of Quinn and Comerford requires one to recall the world already overtly dismissed in *The Quiet Man.*

Since *The Quiet Man,* the best films of country life overturn objective assumptions and demand subjective responses. Recognizing this condi-tion in turn gives viewers a greater confidence in their abilities to con-struct unique Irish identities and articulate independent analyses. From the example of *The Quiet Man,* one comes to see that gaps and incongrui-ties do not represent breakdowns in the narrative; rather, they are expres-sions of complexities that undermine types. With this tradition in mind, a quarter century after its release, *Traveller* remains a powerful representa-tion of the claustrophobic effects of Irish rural communities on individu-als seeking simply to come to a clear sense of their own natures because it frees viewers to understand those conditions through highly individual responses.

The interpretive options inherent in *December Bride* (1990) underscore the best aspects of this individual approach to imposing meaning on rural Irish-themed films. The sexual and societal mores for which *The Quiet Man* and its successors had prepared viewers allow the director of *December Bride,* Thaddeus O'Sullivan, to engage without preface or introduction their consequences. The starkness of country life highlighted in *Poitín* provides a gloss for the tone of the film. And the clannishness of *Traveller,* often clearly in conflict with individual development, has prepared viewers for the claustrophobic world of O'Sullivan's motion picture. At the same time, evocations of this narrative tradition do not inexorably prescribe a particular interpretive approach. Rather, they highlight the analytic options opened up by the structure of the film.

Like a number of the motion pictures in this category that preceded it, *December Bride* has a deceptively straightforward plot.[7] It is set in a rural Presbyterian community in the North at the turn of the last century, and it introduces the Echlins, a father and his two grown sons, as a prosperous farming household. When their boat capsizes on a lough and the overturned craft appears unable to support the weight of all who are clinging to its sides, Andrew Echlin (Geoffrey Golden), the patriarch, releases his grip and allows the water to take him to save the lives of his sons, Hamilton (Donal McCann) and Frank (Ciaran Hinds), and of one of the family's servants, Sarah (Saskia Reeves).

After Echlin's funeral, the pattern of life on the farm alters. Martha (Brenda Bruce), Sarah's mother, becomes disturbed because everyone else at the farm has stopped attending Sunday church services. She leaves the farm, and Sarah begins an affair first with Frank and then with Hamilton. Sarah becomes pregnant, but the narrative never identifies which brother is the father.

After some initial friction between Hamilton and Frank based on sexual tension, the three settle into life as a reconfigured family, but nonetheless they remain aware of the community's hostility, embodied by the local minister, Sorleyson (Patrick Malahide), over their unconventional relationship. Hamilton would be happy to remove the source of controversy by marrying Sarah, but she is unwilling to relinquish her independence. At the same time, despite her fierce desire for recognition and respect for her individuality, Sarah shows appalling prejudices toward Catholics who move into Martha's cottage after the old woman dies. Ultimately, Frank becomes restive in the ménage, and tries to rejoin the community. However, when he attempts to court a young woman at an Orange Order picnic, her family gives him a crippling beating.

Thereafter, Frank, Hamilton, and Sarah fall into a quotidian routine, including another pregnancy, until the older child, Martha (Dervla Kirwan), wants to marry. She persuades Sarah to formalize her relationship so that the wedding can take place in church. Sarah reconciles herself to it

December Bride: A determined Sarah (Saskia Reeves) confronts the rural Protestant world. Courtesy of Donna Walsh and Little Bird Productions.

by seeing her marriage to Hamilton as a sacrifice much like the one made by Andrew Echlin at the film's beginning.

December Bride establishes itself as a striking achievement for a number of reasons. It stands as a rare film in its sustained and evenhanded portrayal of the Protestant community. It shows a deft ability to play off sweeping cinematic beauty against claustrophobic, provincial attitudes. And, rather than falling into the easy division of black-and-white dichotomies, it explores the complexities that accrue when dogmatic religious attitudes abut the pragmatic values of individuals. Donal McCann's Hamilton presents a wonderfully balanced portrayal of a patriarchal figure whose beliefs are informed by kindness and understanding. Saskia Reeves's Sarah, on the other hand, offers a view of a courageous, strong-willed woman whose anti-Catholicism plays nicely off her own resentment of biased community values. Finally, Ciaran Hinds's Frank foregrounds a figure with simple needs and little interest in introspection. Together, they unfold a complex and engaging narrative that takes up the issues outlined in *The Quiet Man* and extrapolates from that film's perspective to examine what happens when one refuses integration into the community.[8]

More important, *December Bride* does not seek to impose a meaning on its narrative, but rather it trusts viewers to come to their own understanding of the events it depicts. O'Sullivan's film highlights parochialism and its stifling consequences. It does not, however, offer those individuals who resist this condition a privileged position in the narrative. Rather, it engages viewers to articulate their own sense of the environment, Irishness in a very specialized form, and then apply that assessment to an understanding of the film.

For better or for worse, the imperative for active responses to motion pictures in this category has grown greater in recent years. In the decades that have passed since the release of *The Quiet Man,* and particularly since the Irish economic boom of the 1990s, rural films have become increasingly divorced from everyday experiences. As with movies that examine middle-class life, a shifting sense of group identity has produced a marked change in audience reactions. By the 1990s affinities with the rural lifestyle had all but disappeared from the lives of most Irish, and with European Union funds supplementing farm incomes and access, through satellites and the Internet, to worlds well beyond the confines of the community, even those Irish living in the country were themselves significantly distanced from the rural milieu by and large represented in this genre.

Over the past few years, a further difficulty has emerged, paradoxically growing out of the genre's success, to impede its imaginative development. With highly skilled directors such as Bob Quinn, Joe Comerford, and Thaddeus O'Sullivan building on John Ford's achievements, the pattern for representations in rural films has become fixed, and filmmakers have needed to employ greater and greater innovations within a fairly narrowly defined structure to produce imaginatively engaging work.

Unfortunately, with the filmmakers already noted having explored central issues, their successors proved generally content to reexamine the same topics without offering new perspectives. In short order a predictable pattern emerged:

- Motion pictures that take up rural issues cannot find narrative leverage in contemporary life.
- As a consequence, they content themselves with retrospective issues, relevant decades ago but now no longer germane.
- They deal with generational conflict over diverse perspectives that have ceased to matter.
- They take up the pull of urban living and the threat of modernization to the rhythm of traditional life, issues that have already been done to death, albeit to the dissatisfaction of many.
- They often inculcate, overtly or covertly, nostalgia and sentimentality into their narratives.

A brief examination of some representative films underscores the degree to which works in this category have become programmatic, and it reflects the greater pressure on viewers to recuperate meaning from a narrative form that has lost vigor and complexity.

The same year that Thaddeus O'Sullivan directed *December Bride*, Jim Sheridan made *The Field*. O'Sullivan's examination of the Protestant community and his exploration of hierarchical family structures and sexual mores produced an inventive story line. Sheridan's screenplay highlights the particularly Irish challenges of rural life during the period between World Wars I and II even as it suggests the growing difficulty of producing innovative work on the subject.

The film is based on a play by the same name written by John B. Keane and first performed in 1965. Keane set his story in a rural village called Carrickthomond in the 1960s, though Sheridan has moved the time period back by three decades.[9] The central character, Bull McCabe (Richard Harris), emerges as a small farmer obsessed with land. He bullies his son Tadgh (Sean Bean) and lives in chilly silence with his wife, Maggie (Brenda Fricker), who blames Bull for the suicide of their older son, Sheamie, years ago. Tadgh clandestinely harasses the widow (Frances Tomelty) who owns the field that Bull's family has rented for several generations and Bull hopes to buy. When the widow puts the field up for sale, McCabe intimidates all in the village so that no one plans to bid on it save an American, Peter (Tom Berenger), who wants to turn the land into an industrial site. Before the auction of the land, Bull engineers a fight between Tadgh and Peter down at the river. When Tadgh loses, Bull intervenes and, perhaps inadvertently, kills the American. Peter is reported missing, and the authorities suspect foul play, but the villagers provide an alibi for McCabe. The local priest (Sean McGinley), out of frustration at the communal collusion, locks the parishioners out of church for shielding a murderer. More pragmatically, the widow brings in a crane to drag the water in search of the American's body. Meanwhile, Tadgh has become infatuated with a Traveller girl (Jenny Conroy). He runs away with her, abandoning his family and the land, at the moment the police find the American's body.

This combination of events seems to unhinge Bull's mind. He drives his cattle to the edge of a cliff, and when Tadgh tries to intervene the animals knock him over the precipice to his death. The film ends with Bull, in Cuchulain-like fashion, madly fighting the waves of the sea.

In terms of production values, one cannot fault *The Field*. Time and again, Sheridan demonstrates his abilities as a highly skilled director. The cinematography creates quite beautiful effects, and the cast list boasts top-notch actors who give first-rate performances.

The story deals with issues of ownership and generational ambition unique to the Irish countryside. A key communal issue, the image of rural Ireland on the verge of industrialization, gets less attention than it merits, though Sheridan does avoid casting the issue in terms of polarities. Although one should not fault the film for the emphasis it chooses to follow, it does reveal the challenges already facing films in this genre. Like many American westerns, a formulaic tendency periodically surfaces in the narrative, and the danger of programmatic representation, one that will manifest itself far more forcefully in films made near the end of the decade, is already becoming evident.

The film's narrative unfolds in a causal, linear fashion. Bull McCabe's obsessive attachment to the land invites one to see this approach as corrosive. It leads directly to the deaths of his two sons and of the American. It alienates McCabe from his wife. And it leaves him in an unbalanced state.

It invites associations with a Lear-like tragedy without producing the powerful Shakespearean soliloquies that illuminate characters' natures.

These conditions do not preclude the kind of interpretation that favors multiplicity, but they do place greater demands on any analytic effort to contextualize contemporary responses. Depending on how one judges the impact of materialism on Irish society, particularly the consumerism of the Celtic Tiger, McCabe's dominant attitude and his progressive mania may appear to be an inevitable, even logical, response to an entropic environment. McCabe's fight with the sea, mimicking ancient tradition, can accommodate both heroic and pathetic dimensions. Indeed, McCabe stands simultaneously occupying a series of conflicted roles: relentlessly controlling his tiny portion of the world with an obsessive inflexibility and inextricably caught in a pattern of behavior to which he adheres with a religious-like fervor, though without any real understanding of its ontology. If Sheridan has not explored complexity as fully as one might wish, he certainly brings a measure of sophistication to familiar issues.

Two years later, in 1992, Gillies MacKinnon made *The Playboys,* and it marks the beginning of a series of motion pictures progressively less and less interested in exploring the Irish nature of rural life. The film is set in an Irish village in 1957. Tara Maguire (Robin Wright) is an unwed mother who will not identify her child's father. She is pursued by the local Garda, Hegarty (Albert Finney), an older man who did in fact impregnate her. Tara resists Hegarty, and instead becomes enamored of Tom (Aidan Quinn), an actor in a traveling theater group, whom she meets when the entertainers come to town. The story turns on Tom's courtship of Tara and Hegarty's growing jealousy. Out of frustration, the alcoholic Hegarty, who has been a teetotaler for some time, turns to drink again, and his behavior becomes increasingly erratic. First, he arrests Tom on flimsy charges of involvement with the IRA, and then, after Tara forces Tom's release and the two become lovers, he provokes a fight with Tom. After the fight, Hegarty is disgraced and departs. Tara and the baby join Tom and the players, and they all leave town together. In a precious nod to feminine independence, Tara drives the motorcycle, while Tom with a broken arm rides in the sidecar.

Though typographically Irish, *The Playboys* relies on a nondescript plot developed in a predictable and unimaginative fashion that underscores the difficulties of finding innovative approaches to films set in this genre. Although Tara experiences some social disapproval, she and her sister, Brigid (Niamh Cusack), manage surprisingly well in such a supposedly close-minded community. The IRA subplot and Tara's efforts at smuggling goods across the border stretch credulity, but more to the point they act as shortcuts to narrative development. Just as the final tragedy was inevitable in *The Field*, the happy ending of *The Playboys* is never in doubt. That conclusion in itself would not be insupportable if the narrative ever troubled to go beyond its clichéd representations of the characters and the social life.

The Playboys does, however, allow viewers the possibility of making nonlinear connections, though these links highlight the minimal range of alternative readings struggling against a highly prescriptive narrative. Specifically, it provides a metatextual basis for examining the perpetuation of clichéd Irishness. Several of the principals, including Robin Wright and Albert Finney, are not Irish, whereas Aidan Quinn spent time in both Ireland and America while he was growing up. Others, such as Milo O'Shea, Alan Devlin, and Niamh Cusack, have well-deserved reputations as indigenous actors. The international cast implicitly invites viewers to examine the tension between script and players—a contrast highlighted when the theatrical group led by O'Shea does an impromptu burlesque of *Gone with the Wind* as a means of counteracting the impact of the rebroadcast of the 1939 film on a television recently smuggled across the border—to determine to what degree the makeup of the film critiques its own flawed representations. However, as subsequent examples illustrate, this sort of metacritique becomes itself repetitive in the face of little imaginative variation.

Ironically, the problem of interpretive circumscription comes to the foreground at the same time as the growing technical achievements of Irish-themed films. Unfortunately, slick production values cannot redeem superficial efforts to explore the issue of cultural identity. Rather, they become self-parodic, like Bord Fáilte promotions that create an Ireland of clichés and anachronisms. I have presented detailed summaries of these motion pictures not to belabor their shortcomings but to illustrate how far they depart from the standards set by films of the previous decades.

Cathal Black's *Korea*, released in 1995, stands as a good example. It is a beautifully photographed motion picture set in 1952 in a village in County

Cavan, with a plot turning on a variation of *Romeo and Juliet*. Unfortunately, like *The Field*, the narrative of *Korea* shows little inclination to explore the psychological complexity of the conflicted identities that animate Shakespeare's characters, much less to engage the cultural features that inform the conflict.

Una Moran's (Fiona Molony) older brother, Luke, has been killed fighting with the U.S. Army in Korea. The film opens with a scene showing his body being returned to the village for burial. Eamon Doyle (Andrew Scott) and Una are in love, but a number of factors stand in the way of their relationship. Eamon's father, John (Donal Donnelly), still feels enmity for Ben Moran (Vass Anderson) because they were on opposing sides during the Civil War. The Morans' affluence contrasts with the Doyles' poverty. Exacerbating the situation, eeling, the Doyles' occupation, is disappearing, and Moran is working to develop the lake for tourism. Eamon Doyle's father wants his son to emigrate to the United States to get him away from Una, but Eamon resists. He fears he will be drafted into the army and will end up like Una's brother. Ultimately, Eamon confronts his father, and the father accepts Una.

As with a number of other films about country life already mentioned, one can find little cinematically to criticize about *Korea*. From Black's sure-handed directing to the confident performances of actors such as Donnelly, the motion picture exudes a polished professionalism. At the same time, it barely acknowledges the imaginative potential of Irish-themed rural films. Rather, it signals the diminishing cultural relevance of the genre. Like the movies already mentioned, *Korea* falls back on the familiar story of class and political differences seeking accommodation in the midst of social changes in country life, and it makes no effort to explore the complexities of any side of the issue. The plot of *Korea* would already have been dated a generation before the film was made, and the repetitiveness of its thematic development underscores my point about the narrative limitations that have arrested the evolution of this form of Irish motion picture.

In 1998 Pat O'Connor directed *Dancing at Lughnasa*, a film version of the Brian Friel play about events that take place one summer in rural Donegal in the lives of five sisters (Meryl Streep, Catherine McCormack, Kathy Burke, Sophie Thompson, and Brid Brennan) and their missionary brother (Michael Gambon) recently returned from twenty-five years in Uganda. It is told from the point of view of the now adult but then young illegitimate son of one of the women, Michael. (The narration is voiced by Gerald McSorley, and the young Michael is played by Darrell Johnston.) Gerry Evans (Rhys Ifans), the father of Michael, arrives on his way to Spain to fight in the Civil War, and the visit stirs up the passions of his mother. It is a bit sentimental, but ends with a flash-forward to show how hard the lives of the women were and how idyllic that one summer was in contrast.

Perhaps because it was based on Friel's play, the film goes further than other recent rural dramas in exploring the complexities of country life. It takes up the claustrophobic world, the social and sexual constrictions, and the pain and dangers of emigration. It too derives its power from retrospection, and, like the western, it must negotiate the risk of being seen as mythologizing a period that never really existed.

On its own, the narrative shows the promise of a complex rendering of seemingly mundane conditions, and certainly it remains open to multilayered interpretations. Its drawback comes from the type of story the film tells. *Dancing at Lughnasa* repeats the tale of rural frustration and conflicted values found in any number of its predecessors. It succumbs to linearity, offering a good account from a single perspective but doing little to introduce complexities into a plot already quite familiar to filmgoers.

Despite the criticisms I have offered, the retrospective motion pictures released in the early 1990s, though not nearly as imaginatively ambitious as the Irish-themed rural films of the 1970s and 1980s, retained a measure of cultural specificity. By the middle of the decade, several filmmakers turned to projects that addressed more recent developments in country life. Although one might argue that the films themselves stand as true to type, they also signal a generalizing trend in the category that makes their Irish associations increasingly less relevant.[10]

Kevin Liddy's *Country*, made in 2000 and set in rural Ireland in the 1960s, suggests themes that could remain valid in a contemporary setting, but it never develops ideas beyond all too familiar types. Jack (Dean Pritchard) is a young boy living on a farm with his widowed father and older brother, Conor (Gary Lydon), who has a drinking problem. The father, Frank (Des Cave), is a reformed alcoholic. Conor is involved with a local girl, Sarah (Marcella Plunkett), and her uncle is jealous. Frank's sister-in-law, Miriam (Lisa Harrow), comes to put in order the home of her brother, who has died but who was a great friend to Jack. She stays in her brother-in-law's home, and changes the tone of the household, even to the point of prodding Conor to action by advising Sarah to leave for the city. This advice upsets Conor who feels he cannot leave Jack and accompany Sarah.

Before any change takes place, a series of events break up the communal affinities that have formed over the course of the narrative. Sarah's uncle rapes her, and her family takes her to England. Miriam has developed an affection for Frank, until Conor claims that while drunk Frank knocked his wife down the stairs. Frank asserts it was an accident and that it made him stop drinking, but he admits that it did kill his wife. Miriam is appalled, and decides to leave. The uncle, shortly after raping Sarah, tells Conor that she was involved with Travellers, and Conor agrees to go on a vigilante raid to the camp. There he runs into Jack, who has a Traveller friend. Men from the town burn the camp, but one of the Travellers kills the uncle. The next day Conor leaves for England. The Traveller camp is in ruins, and Jack and Frank are left alone.

Country highlights the difficulties that face filmmakers currently working in this genre, but it offers no satisfactory solutions because it takes familiar themes—alcoholism, sexual repression, rural isolation, and bigotry—and deals with them in a programmatic fashion. The motion picture unfolds during the Lemass period of economic expansion, yet it projects an ahistorical view that relies on a rigid rather than a fluid sense of social conditions. Without the psychological complexity of *The Quiet Man* or the searing social critique of *Poitín*, Liddy's film never rises above the level of melodrama.

Films with contemporary rural settings have an even greater difficulty going beyond the predictable or the prescriptive, and they reiterate the impression that the rural film genre has become a stagnant area of Irish filmmaking. Peter Yates's *Run of the Country*, released in 1995, is set in the present, but it offers no insights to the similar problems of courtship that it outlines. In a border village eighteen-year-old Danny (Matt Keeslar) and his Garda father (Albert Finney), a widower, argue over the boy's future. He leaves home to live with a friend, Prunty (Anthony Brophy). Though a Catholic, he meets and becomes attached to Annagh Lee (Victoria Smurfit), a well-to-do Protestant girl who lives just north of the border. When she becomes pregnant, Danny struggles unsuccessfully to find money for an abortion. After she miscarries, Annagh's relatives tar and feather Danny, and she is sent away. He is reconciled with his father, and decides to go to college in Dublin.

Although the narrative reflects themes so familiar as to become tedious, elements in the motion picture hint at what could distinguish it. The testosterone-fueled braggadocio that characterizes many of Danny and Prunty's experiences, such as the frenetic trips to a local disco in an overcrowded delivery van, implies a desperateness overlaying recollections of life in the Midlands. Indeed, these scenes suggest a topic that would revive contemporary rural films: the uneasy transition from the isolation of country life to the sophistication of urban living. The ambivalence of existing between two worlds indicates that explorations of rural Irish identity can still produce a unique representation that goes beyond the familiar types featured in *The Run of the Country*.

Eugene Brady makes an effort to play off even larger stereotypes in his 1997 film, *The Nephew*, set in a small fishing village. After the death of his mother, Chad Egan-Washington (Hill Harper), the title character, journeys to the village to find his uncle Tony (Donal McCann). Tony had no contact with his sister, Karen, Chad's mother, since she emigrated to New York years before, and had never seen her child. Chad's father, conveniently for the story line also dead, was African American. In a predictable fashion, the narrative deals with how Chad comes to terms with life in the village and with the way that the village comes to terms with him. Pierce Brosnan, looking as if he wandered into the wrong movie, plays a former lover of Karen's whose daughter is now attracted to Chad.[11]

The Nephew stands as another missed opportunity to explore transition in country life. Given the recent appearance of political and economic refugees in Ireland, the film may seem to be raising an important issue. However, the plotline delves no deeper than offering the hypothesis that prejudice is bad and tolerance is good. It may be impossible to know whether the motion picture was inspired by simpleminded or cynical motivations.

In either case, it comes nowhere near meeting the standards set by the best films in the genre. As with several previous movies, the premise never goes beyond superficialities, and the highly predictable story line is barely salvaged by good performances.

Johnny Gogan's *Mapmaker* (2001) encapsulates all of the difficulties relating to identity that arise when a filmmaker attempts to make a motion picture set in contemporary rural Ireland. Though ostensibly concerned with articulating a sense of self and of place, in the manner of Brian Friel's *Translations,* it never achieves a perspective that seriously addresses either issue. Indeed, outside of the almost peremptory inclusion of the IRA, the Irish nature of the film receives little emphasis. Nonetheless, it offers an important opportunity for understanding contemporary rural Irish motion pictures, for it shows the effacement of a country ethos.

As with the other films I have criticized, *The Mapmaker* has a fine cast and is technically well made, though I think it would have benefited greatly from a much stronger script. What strikes me most about *The Mapmaker* is its manifest discomfort, an attitude shared by a number of contemporary movies in this genre, with the subject of a rural Irish film. Though announcing itself—through its location, discourse, and characterizations—to be an Irish-themed film, *The Mapmaker* shows a reluctance to take up any issues that would define it as such. Instead, it injects a universalizing tone, offering a narrative viable in any number of settings, which diminishes rather than expands its imaginative scope.

The problem that has arisen for commentators on films set in the country stands as analogous to the issue that dogs contemporary middle-class motion pictures. The internationalizing impulse in Irish society may not have erased all cultural and social differences between urban and rural dwellers. However, the gap is not nearly so wide or so distinct as it had previously been. With the intrusion of popular culture everywhere in Ireland, the loss of a distinctive rural identity becomes a more valid narrative topic for a motion picture seeking to be Irish than an exploration of country life from outmoded perspectives. However, contemporary filmmakers seem uninterested in teasing out the cultural significance of this conflation. As a result, recent rural films, consciously or not, have defined themselves either through retrospections or anachronisms.

The consequence inherent in such approaches too often involves the creation of a false sense of Irishness that can lead to distorted readings based on faulty cultural premises. I do not mean to say that any contemporary film set in the Irish countryside is inherently flawed. However, I do feel that an effective approach to understanding films in this category based on assumptions about cultural markers of Irishness is becoming increasingly difficult to achieve. Even motion pictures exploring earlier periods where cultural distinctiveness would presumably remain a valid feature have an international quality that challenges the efficacy of interpretations based on features of a national ethos. One finds a good example of this condition in a film released in 2001, *How Harry Became a Tree*.

I have made the analogy, at several points in this chapter, between films of Irish country life and American westerns. My argument has been that both categories have evolved as highly prescriptive forms that demand a great deal of creativity to avoid seeming thematically derivative. Unfortunately, in the survey of rural Irish films that I have undertaken, I have found that, since the groundbreaking work of *The Quiet Man* and the stunning motion pictures of the mid-1970s, few filmmakers have shown the dexterity necessary to represent the complex features of country life in an imaginative fashion, and in consequence, in motion pictures such as *How Harry Became a Tree*, an overarching interpretive strategy for examining the cultural features of the genre tends to emphasize deficiency rather than accomplishment.

I realize, of course, that the point I seek to make about rural films engaging Irish identity at times can seem to contradict directly the evidence of artistic merit in particular projects. It is not my intention to dismiss well-made motion pictures on dogmatic, chauvinistic grounds. However, as I have noted earlier in this study, when filmmakers overtly employ social markers of Irishness in their narrative and invite viewers to make these elements part of the analytic process, I do feel it is important to develop a clear sense of how seemingly definitive cultural features function or fail to do so within specific works.

Because interpretation depends so heavily on association, I am concerned with how the assumption of Irishness in certain rural films can distort understanding across the genre. In derivative motion pictures that repeat clichéd views of country life, the failure to explore elements of a genuine Irish identity stands as fairly obvious. However, a more insidious problem arises from dealing with technically and artistically polished works that nonetheless provoke distorted readings because of an assumed Irish identity that in fact does not exist within the narratives.

Of all the recent Irish-themed rural films, Goran Paskaljevic's 2001 movie *How Harry Became a Tree* seems the most open to complex interpretation, but in fact its imaginative structure makes the validity of a culturally based analysis highly problematic. The artistic and technical achievements of *How Harry Became a Tree,* featuring stellar acting highlighted by evocative cinematography, stand as undeniable. Thematically, it takes up a promising topic, for exploring the tensions of suppression and frustration remains a valid concern for rural films. However, in this instance, the narrative's decision to represent the universality of that condition diminishes the Irishness of the motion picture and distorts interpretive assumptions based on its presumed cultural context.

How Harry Became a Tree is set in Skillet in 1924. Harry (Colm Meaney) is a farmer with a shy, timid son, Gus (Cillian Murphy). Harry has a muted, though deeply antagonistic, relationship with a local businessman, George O'Flaherty (Adrian Dunbar). Harry's son feels an attraction for a girl, Eileen (Kerry Condon), whom O'Flaherty has brought to town as a house servant, and Harry grudgingly reaches an agreement to give O'Flaherty half his cabbage harvest for arranging a match between Eileen and his son. However, because Harry resents the bargain, he sabotages the crop, absorbing his own loss as a consequence of spiting O'Flaherty. The two young people are married nonetheless, but they do not consummate their union. George O'Flaherty steps in, and has intercourse with the girl. Harry finds out, and is enraged. He is determined to expose O'Flaherty to the town, but he cannot get his daughter-in-law to corroborate his accusations. Harry becomes obsessed with disgracing O'Flaherty. After Harry catches O'Flaherty and Eileen again engaging in sexual intercourse, he hatches a plan to have his son kill O'Flaherty. The reluctant Gus shoots O'Flaherty's dog instead, and then the son and daughter-in-law leave. O'Flaherty comes with men to take the slates off Harry's roof in compensation for the killing of the dog. Harry, in frustration, literally turns into a tree, and another servant with whom O'Flaherty had an affair shoots him.

As outlined above, *How Harry Became a Tree* may seem to have impeccable social and cultural credentials. Certainly, the complexity of the characterizations suggests that the film projects a range of perspectives that one would find in an Irish identity. However, an internationalism pervades its structure, and calls the nature of its references to a specific national character into question.

How Harry Became a Tree is based on a Chinese story adapted to an Irish setting. In consequence, the central issues it engages enforce a tone of universality that belies any national association. And in fact in dialogue, action, and setting, the film works self-consciously to suppress evidence of any identifying cultural markers.[12]

Indeed, *How Harry Became a Tree* derives its narrative power from its unwillingness to limit its imaginative development to localized representations. The tension of the film turns on a familiar struggle between peasant and petit bourgeois perspectives. The visceral antipathy that Harry feels for George comes from a class resentment that one could find in any agricultural community. The ineffectuality of Harry's efforts to best George grows out of advantages that the latter enjoys through economic differences rather than because of any inherent ethnic features. Finally, the magic-realism ending makes no connection to Irish folklore or mythology but rather illustrates in its graphic simplicity the common depth of frustration that class and economic inequities provoke in any society.

Even the most fundamental markers of place, distinguishing typography, remain absent from this film. Unlike other internationalized motion pictures that attempt to assert a measure of Irishness through distinctive scenery, *How Harry Became a Tree* strives instead, through its nonspecific representations of country locations, to suppress any particular impression of an Irish landscape. This movie is set in Ireland and was filmed there as well, but it self-consciously emphasizes nondescript geographic features.

Specific observations on the absence of an Irish identity in *How Harry Became a Tree* stand as emblematic of the issue explored throughout this chapter. The film's relentless drive toward universality underscores the tendencies contributing to the decline of the Irish rural motion picture, even as it illustrates the imaginative quality of the work itself. In a very direct way, *How Harry Became a Tree* announces the demise of the Irish rural film in a fashion analogous to *The Quiet Man* proclaiming its viability a half century earlier.

John Ford's work highlights key features of how motion pictures in this category can present a powerful, though not necessarily positive, representation of the uniqueness of life in the Irish countryside: the strong sense of communal values, suspicion of outside influences, intense social pressure to conform, and the alienation of any individual who seeks an independent existence. Subsequent rural films have endeavored to vivify narratives taking up those topics, but in an increasing number of instances they have highlighted an antithetical condition. As the fundamental themes noted above are reintroduced in movie after movie with little or no variation, the repetition has a cumulative effect of enforcing on the viewer a sense of stagnation.

Films made by Ford, Quinn, Comerford, and O'Sullivan have gone beyond demonstrating individual achievement. They have laid down the pattern for motion pictures in this genre for generating insightful explorations of culturally specific studies of country life. For whatever reasons, subsequent filmmakers have produced movies that neither lived up to these standards nor provided alternative approaches. Instead, for most contemporary films in this category, Irishness serves merely as a convenient label without delineating distinctive features for imaginative engagement.

The change in narrative emphasis in many recent Irish-themed rural films places new interpretive demands on moviegoers in a manner already familiar to viewers of other genres. Hollywood motion pictures such as *Blood Simple, The Last Picture Show,* and *Brokeback Mountain* are all set in the same geographic locations as *Stagecoach, High Noon,* and *Unforgiven,* but no thoughtful critic would bring the same analytic expectations to the first group as to the second. Audiences of Irish rural films need to assert the same awareness of the changing atmosphere and to read contemporary works as growing out of rather than replicating their predecessors. At the same time, for this category to retain any claim to representing aspects of Irish identity, filmmakers need to demonstrate greater curiosity in exploring the new ambivalences that characterize country life. Though such changes would bring a welcome vitality to this area of filmmaking, at present reading motion pictures in this category from a cultural perspective distorts rather than clarifies their meanings.

A Paradigmatic Reading: *Garage*

That is not to say that one can no longer make an Irish-themed rural film, but it does suggest the need for a different approach. Lenny Abrahamson's motion picture *Garage,* a wonderful rural complement to Ivan Kavanagh's urban chronicle discussed in the previous chapter, meets that need. Just as *Francis* offers a defiantly different world from what is presented in *When Brendan Met Trudy, Wild about Harry,* or *About Adam, Garage* resists the formulaic view of rural Ireland—as seen in retrospective films such as *Korea* or *Country* or contemporary versions such as *The Mapmaker.* Nor does it create an Ireland that does not seem to exist anywhere, as in *Small Engine Repair,* a film with all the improbability of *Eat the Peach* but with none of the latter's whimsy. (I fully realize and acknowledge the incongruity of a foreigner commenting on inauthenticity in an Irish film. I will say, however, that in traveling around Ireland and in watching representations of Ireland on film, I have never seen such a proliferation of weapons—not being used by paramilitaries, that is—country and western music, and pickup trucks. All that seems lacking is Burt Reynolds and a muscle car.)

The films that I have just mentioned in the preceding paragraph weigh themselves down with complicated plots and detailed characterization. Lenny Abrahamson, like Ivan Kavanagh, trusts his views. He presents a spare, but not flimsy, story line that invites the imaginative engagement of his viewers.

Josie, the central character of the film—played brilliantly by Pat Shortt, whose command of subtle variations of gesture and expression evokes the powerful response one experiences in seeing the best silent film actors—is a character who inhabits the margins. He lives in a Midlands small town at the limits of the economic boom. He works at a gas station on the edge of town at a job that consists of little more than occupying time and space. And his social contacts, though numerous, remain consistently peripheral.

Garage: Josie (Pat Shortt) being taken in for questioning. Courtesy of Speers Film/Element Films and photographer Jonathan Hession.

Like Abrahamson's urban film *Adam and Paul,* the narrative of *Garage*
uses discrete accounts to develop the story line. (Also like *Adam and Paul,*
the powerful script for *Garage* was written by Mark O'Halloran.) Music
functions only incidentally during the opening and closing credits and in
a brief montage near the end of the film. Language has a laconic feel to it,
conveying a sense of the claustrophobia felt by speakers who have known
each other so long that conversation has lost its ability to engage, much
less surprise or delight. And movement reflects the rhythms of exhaustion,
with characters refusing to undertake any but the most fundamental gestures and acts.

Through it all, Abrahamson constructs a powerfully defined yet teas-
ingly subjective Irish context for his narrative. The film conveys isolation
without presuming angst. It catches a sense of entrapment without imposing overt panic or despair on its characters. And, perhaps in its most Irish
gesture, it outlines the complex rituals of tribalism that define behavior
while withholding social, spiritual, and emotional support. In ways in
which other rural motion pictures have only gestured, *Garage* is a prison
film, without the conventional frenzy of movies in that genre.

With infinite patience, Abrahamson constructs Josie's identity, and the
character of the world he inhabits, through a series of carefully delineated

Garage: Sully (Andrew Bennett) and Josie (Pat Shortt) in a moment of reflection. Courtesy of Speers Film/Element Films and photographer Jonathan Hession.

but self-consciously nonprescriptive episodes. One first sees instances representing Josie's routine of work at the gas station, his interaction with customers and with others in the town, and his bachelor life in a small room off the station. The scenes convey a sense of careful choreography, with every movement and gesture planned, but not a feeling that the director seeks to use the action to impose a single interpretation on viewers.

Narrative complications arise when the gas station's owner, Mr. Gallagher (John Keogh), brings a teenage boy, David (Conor Ryan), to help Josie while the station remains open longer, and it is suggested to allow the owner more time with David's mother, Vivian (Anne Byrne). In short order, Josie's indignation at the intrusion of another gives way to affection. At the same time, David's resentment at being put to work in the gas station turns to a kind of tolerance. If the film did nothing more that explore the consequences of the juxtaposition of the sullen teenager and the patient adult, it would be hard-pressed to rise above cliché. However, the narrative brilliantly transforms conventional expectations of the situation to bring out subtle elements in the natures of both characters.

The interaction between Josie and David quickly underscores the limits of Josie's social skills and hints at a mild retardation as well. Josie does not have the ability to make fine or complex distinctions, and so he treats David in much the same way that he does the adults with whom he interacts every day. This approach includes initiating the practice of ending the day with several cans of beer as they survey the unvarying landscape at the edge of town, and expands to supplying beer for David and his friends. Without articulating the problem, Abrahamson's narrative underscores just how limited Josie is and how tolerant the townspeople are, despite occasional bullying by men such as Breffni (Don Wycherley), of Josie's shortcomings.

Representations of David prove to be equally understated and similarly powerful. Actor Conor Ryan presents David with all the stiffness, hesitation, and insecurities that beset everyone who has had to endure being a teenager. However, he goes well beyond the expected type in representing the suffocating despair that an ordinary young person feels in a town with little distraction besides the stupefaction of drink. Again, the skill of the narrative comes from a trust in its viewers. David is not a brilliant artist or intellectual trapped among philistines in the country. He is an ordinary young man, yet one still capable of engaging our interest.

A tenderness toward the main characters infuses the film, and so the reversals that form its climax and denouement come with painful rapidity. When a trucker gives Josie a pornographic video, Josie in a combination of camaraderie and social inappropriateness shows it to David. The shocked young boy tells a friend, who tells his mother, who tells the Gardái. From David's initial reaction, Josie has had some sense of the inappropriateness of what he has done, but when he is brought in for questioning and his room is searched, he is devastated. Again, Abrahamson and O'Halloran show their ingenuity by resisting expectations. The Garda (Denis Conway) who questions Josie is a middle-aged man whom some viewers might expect to erupt in moral indignation. Instead, an understated gentleness infuses the interrogation. In the end, the Garda, Michael, advises rather than admonishes Josie, but even that counsel proves to be too much for the man to take.

The penultimate scene shows Josie at the edge of a river, putting rocks in his pockets and preparing to take his life. By this point viewers have a graphic representation of the fragility of Josie's psyche and of his tenuous emotional connection to the community. With this image in mind, the exchanges that have occurred throughout the film take on a much more complex meaning. The usual representations of narrow-minded country folk or of simpleminded rubes fall away, and viewers are confronted with evidence of a sophisticated and sensitive community that, for a time at least, can shelter without smothering someone like Josie but unfortunately can only defer tragedy.

5

Suffer the Little Children

Reconstructions of the Family

Up to this point in my study, I have focused on demographic features to demarcate various cultural dispositions in Irish-themed films. My premise has been that social evolution manifests its effects on different classes in different ways. As a result, interpretations of films examining particular social groups require sensitivity to the reconfigured communal markers that delineate each. At the same time, regardless of generational shifts, when using class and location as delineators, one encounters a measure of internal consistency. Despite ambiguities along the margins, the social position that most people occupy remains clear and distinct. Likewise, residency remains unambiguous: one lives in the metropolitan area or in the country. This categorical stability has allowed me to introduce methods of examining the subjective experiences of individuals within these groups in a fairly controlled atmosphere.

Other elements informing identity work in a more mercurial, more amalgamated fashion, but nonetheless command equal attention. Social institutions—family, church, and state, the "nets" that Stephen Dedalus sought to fly over in James Joyce's *Portrait of the Artist as a Young Man*—have had and continue to exert a profound impact on the formation of an Irish character. Although in explorations of identity filmmakers have consistently chosen to emphasize the effects of one of these entities over the influences of the others, these categories often seem to intermingle in a way that class and location do not. This tendency highlights the plurality of features shaping a national character and reflects the contingencies of ordinary Irish life. The most satisfying films on these subjects challenge

143

viewers to show an awareness of the uniqueness of each institution while considering the impact of interactions between them.

To this end, it is important to acknowledge from the start that representations of these groupings in motion pictures have a permeability that depictions focusing on any of the three previous categories lacked. At the same time, although Irish identity can be shaped by any combination of the forces of the family, the church, and the state, more often than not a cinematographic examination of the impact of one far overshadows the others. For example, *Some Mother's Son,* because of its emphasis on the Hunger Strikers, foregrounds its credentials as a political film, though the changes to two specific families remain a significant feature of the narrative. *Hush-a-Bye Baby,* on the other hand, despite the impact of British troop occupation on daily life in the Bogside, highlights the familial problems for a child who becomes pregnant.

In the next three chapters I will examine the dynamics of groups of films that define their Irishness through representations that emphasize each of three institutions—in essence, seeing identity created primarily by the family, by the church, or by the state. In particular, I will stress the inclination, already noted in some contemporary films in other categories, to deconstruct these institutions and move toward an erasure of a specific Irish identity. With this thought in mind, I will explore the interpretive demands raised by each, beginning with motion pictures relating to children and families.

Despite the recent well-documented changes in economic and social conditions, the common cultural heritage surrounding everyone born in Ireland combined with the tightly delineated structure of the nuclear family, the pervasive influence of the Catholic Church, and the relative uniformity of the Irish educational system would seem to create an atmosphere of broadly similar experiences for anyone growing up in the country. However, as with so many other conditions examined in this study, diverse demographic changes have powerfully inflected the Irish awareness of childhood. As the features of traditional Irishness become less evident in the lives of many living in both urban and rural areas, the elements of a national character that come to bear upon maturation remain more evident in the marginalized communities. As a result, despite the seeming universality of broad experiences encountered in the process of moving from infancy to adulthood, a related kind of subjectivity governs individual understanding.[1]

Predictably, artistic representations of the events and attitudes shaping an individual's maturation vary greatly. The best-known account of an Irish childhood—albeit a fictional one, though derived from personal experience—remains James Joyce's *Portrait of the Artist as a Young Man*. It offers the clearest sense of how dominant Irish institutions—the family, the church, and the state—confront individuality and endeavor to foster conformity. The challenges to his independence and identity that Stephen Dedalus faces stand as clear-cut, and, though his responses may differ sharply from the reactions of his classmates, the narrative underscores the uniformity of their experiences.

Of course, Joyce depicts conditions more than a century old unfolding in a world that no longer exists. Nonetheless, cinematic examinations of the family continue to address the same issues that engaged Stephen Dedalus. In contemporary life, however, rebellion proves more difficult to trace because of the mutability of the institutions with which the individual must contest.

Diarmaid Ferriter's examination of Irish memoirs offers a recent example of studies highlighting the variety of experiences, impressions, and interpretations that children encounter.[2] Like so many other elements that delineate Irish life, accounts of childhood, even for those children not as precocious as Joyce's main character, stand as very much individually constructed concepts, emerging from a common cultural environment but informed by specificity. The Irish may well feel that they share general reference points and consequently similar experiences. However, the evidence suggests that the diverse forces and varied responses to them within families produce highly subjective notions of the individuals and the world they encounter in the process of growing to adulthood.

That point does not mean that certain common elements do not shape experiences across Irish society; rather, a tension exists between the received opinions on a common environment and the individual's subjective reaction to it. The Irish family, as it has been delineated for generations, either in its presence or absence, remains at the center of any story of childhood. However, like so many other Irish social constructions, since 1922 the family's status and structure have undergone tremendous social pressures. In oscillating valences, the family directs itself inward in interactions with individual members and outward as it copes with the world surrounding it. In this manner, the family functions as both an independent social institution, acting as a shaping force upon its constituents, and an entity defined through its relations with other elements of the establishment such as the church and the state.

This condition has led some to easy generalizations about all three, but, as Clair Wills has perceptively argued, efforts to understand these interactions by applying simplistic dichotomies between family and church, family and state, and even delineations among family members themselves quite often miss the subtle aspects of all of these institutions but most particularly of the family. Like Tolstoy's view of the beleaguered family, "each . . . unhappy in its own way," the individual Irish family, though formed from identifiable social forces, retains a uniqueness that must be acknowledged to exploit its rich imaginative material.[3]

Nonetheless, filmmakers in Ireland proved slow to tap this resource. Perhaps because of the instability of so many other social, political, and economic forces, stories of interactions of the family and its shaping impact on identity have played little part in the development of Irish-themed films until the past few decades. Earlier motion pictures, such as *The Quiet Man* or *Home Is the Hero,* may unfold their narratives around domestic settings, but they generally focus on adult characters whose behavior and sense of self evolve under the influence of broad community values rather than through the more directed attitudes of the family.[4]

Joe Comerford's 1977 motion picture, *Down the Corner,* reversed this approach and set the standard for examining the nature of the Irish family. It highlights economic upheaval, the struggle between patriarchy and matriarchy, and generational alienation. Its gritty documentary style and straightforward narrative present snapshots of the lives of five working-class children between the ages of twelve and fourteen from a housing estate in Ballyfermot, on the west side of Dublin. The narrative follows an episodic format, offering loosely connected scenes of the boys interacting at home, in school, and on the street. With a deft interplay of energy and stasis, the camera highlights the isolation that these boys feel from the world that surrounds them even as it shows the insistent influence of that environment.[5] There is an almost feral quality defining the boys, and it is hardly surprising that their adventures end in a hospital where one of them, who has been injured stealing apples from an orchard, has been taken. As a counterpoint to the boys' frenetic activity, the film plays on the economic stagnation of the area, and it conveys an undertone of hopelessness in its references to the adult world, summed up in a man made redundant who turns to drink and the grandmother of one of the boys who remembers a gruesome murder during the Easter Rising.

Chaos dominates the environment, but it does not preclude understanding the way milieu shapes the lives of a group of children as often as not acted upon by the world around them as acting on it. In delineating this ethos through a series of indeterminate exchanges with family members, schoolteachers, and the local authorities, Comerford neither idealizes nor demonizes the young boys. Rather, without prelude or exposition, the narrative unfolds in a disruptive, episodic fashion that mimics the disorder of the children's lives and the lives of the adults around them. The Irishness of the film comes across through selective references to economic blight, alcoholic despair, and a tortured nationalism, but, as with the natures of the children that it influences, it remains an evolving condition. From these fragments Comerford invites viewers to construct a sense of identity, leaving it to the individual filmgoer to access each character and to come to an opinion of how the environment shapes each.

Jim Sheridan's 1989 film, *My Left Foot*, presents a sharper and ostensibly more judgmental focus on family life, but one that still resists prescriptive interpretation. The narrative introduces and then blurs stock images of the brutal Irish father, the nurturing Irish mother, and the plucky Irish child who seemingly can overcome all obstacles. In this fashion it performs a both-and gesture of conferring legitimacy and insinuating doubt on readings that follow the exclusionary patterns of linearity. It is the narrative's implicit demand for a "compensation for disunity," Kenneth Burkes's phrase referenced in the Introduction, that gives the film its imaginative power.

In *My Left Foot*, Sheridan presents the story of the wheelchair-bound Christy Brown (Daniel Day-Lewis), from birth to his success as an artist and autobiographer, told in flashbacks while Christy waits to speak at a fund-raising gala at a big house. In covering Christy's childhood, the film emphasizes the affection of his mother (Brenda Fricker) and the rough treatment of his father (Ray McAnally). It shows Christy accepted by his family but seen as a freak by others in the community because of his cerebral palsy. Nonetheless, from the start *My Left Foot* works to disrupt conventional impressions as Christy struggles relentlessly to mark off a place for himself in the family and the neighborhood in which he exists.

Early on, the film shows Christy, whose illness has severely affected his ability to speak, making some progress at communication on his own, but the big steps come when, as a young man, he is given therapy by Dr. Eileen Cole (Fiona Shaw), who also encourages his artistic talent. Perhaps predictably, Christy falls in love with her, but the violence of his response when she does not reciprocate breaks conventional melodramatic patterns and reminds viewers of the anarchic environment from which he has emerged. At the same time, the motion picture celebrates his success as a painter and as a writer. The film ends with him leaving the gala with the nurse, Mary Carr (Ruth McCabe), who has minded him and heard his story, and a postscript informs viewers that they later married.

Although the plotline, even with the complexities already noted, seemingly unfolds in a straightforward fashion, *My Left Foot* avoids a simplistic presentation of Christy by introducing his development in contrast with ambivalent portrayals of the father. In an understated fashion, Mr. Brown assumes not merely the role of adversary to Christy. His life presages the variety of conflicted situations that Christy will face, and Mr. Brown's behavior does much to explain both the strengths and the flaws in Christy's character. Mr. Brown shows a stubborn pride that gets him fired from a job site for insubordination and has him brawling in a pub over perceived slights. Despite the squalor and chaos in which the family lives, he has a high-handed, puritanical reaction to his eldest daughter's out-of-wedlock pregnancy, worrying what the neighbors will think. At the same time, he does not cease to make sexual demands upon his wife, despite the poverty, overcrowding, and abuse that his existing children must endure. And, in perhaps the greatest irony of the motion picture, for all his bluster, he has such a fragile sense of his own worth that his wife must urge her sons not to surpass their father's masonry efforts as they labor to complete an addition to the house for Christy.

All these events initially seem to unfold quite apart from the maturation of his son. Christy's stubborn determination to develop a means of self-expression, his petulant resistance to efforts at rehabilitation, and his fierce jealousy over Dr. Cole's engagement to the art gallery owner, Peter (Adrian Dunbar), who gives Christy his first exhibition may seem simply events serving as ways of defining his identity, and they certainly do so. However, in light of Mr. Brown's behavior, echoes of the father's nature and of the chaotic world from which he emerges are unmistakable in Christy.

Developing implication of this juxtaposition leaves viewers with their own interpretive challenge, based on their sense of the Irish family. Do Mr. Brown and Christy condemn themselves by repeating cycles of violence and frustration? Do they reflect the inevitability of certain patterns of behavior given the nature of slum life in Dublin? Or do they require the filmgoer to redefine their roles in order to come to some sense of them? No matter how one responds to these questions, the crucial factor lies in the viewer's construction of the Irish family. Time and again, the most satisfying films in this genre are the ones that invite these imaginative completions.

A specific aspect of family life, out-of-wedlock pregnancy, plays a prominent role in several films that trace the coming-of-age experience. Like Christy Brown's cerebral palsy, teenage pregnancy disrupts the normal family routine, and reactions to it provide diverse interpretive possibilities for the development of a child's nature.[6] Most prominently, it illustrates the tension growing out of conflicting attitudes expressed in Catholic dogma: the sanctity of human life and the restriction of sexual intimacy to marriage. When represented in a stereotypical, hackneyed fashion, this subject can produce deadly dull movies. However, in the hands of a capable filmmaker, this topic can elaborate on inherent complexities and contradictions in Irish life and engage the viewer with a broad range of interpretive possibilities.

Margo Harkin's 1989 film *Hush-a-Bye Baby*, set in Derry in 1984, lays bare the antinomies that this condition can produce without pretending to offer clear solutions to the consequent disruptions of family structure. Goretti (Emer McCourt) is a fifteen-year-old Catholic living in the Bogside.

Hush-a-bye Baby: Goretti (Emer McCourt) and Ciaran (Michael Liebman) at the internment center. Courtesy of Margo Harkin.

(Her forename is taken from Saint Maria Goretti, a young Italian girl who died at the age of eleven from stab wounds received while resisting the sexual assault of her twenty-year-old neighbor.) At an Irish class, she meets Ciaran (Michael Liebman), whom she had earlier seen at school and at social clubs. They begin a relationship that escalates to intimacy before it is disrupted when Ciaran is "lifted" by the British army. Shortly afterward, Goretti discovers that she has become pregnant by Ciaran. Because she is profoundly ashamed and confused by what has transpired, she writes to Ciaran in Irish to tell him of her condition. Unfortunately, since prisoners are not allowed to receive letters written in Irish, he does not learn of Goretti's pregnancy until much later and so does not respond to the letter that the authorities never delivered.

Goretti feels increasingly isolated as she tries to interpret her status as a child, an expectant mother, and a Catholic—represented as profoundly contradictory conditions. On a trip to the Gaeltacht, where Irish is the predominant language, she hears a radio debate about abortion, and her sense of guilt and frustration only increases. The film concludes with a disturbing scene depicting Goretti, at home in the Bogside, either giving

Hush-a-bye Baby: Goretti (Emer McCourt), Sinéad (Sinéad O'Connor), and Majella (Julie Marie Reynolds) in the gym. Courtesy of Margo Harkin.

birth or having a miscarriage, with the ambiguity of the ending underscoring Goretti's divided sense of self.

As with *My Left Foot,* how one responds to *Hush-a-Bye Baby* depends on how one constructs Goretti's Derry environment, but a sense of its specificity remains crucial to any interpretation. *Hush-a-Bye Baby* demands that viewers clarify the status of childhood in the film, particularly as it is inflected by cultural conditions. The sectarian struggles going on around her have an impact on her environment, and religious beliefs assert themselves forcefully as well. They contribute to the way Goretti and her family see the world. The dominant interpretive question, however, remains how all these factors inform Goretti's sense of self, and their representations leave the viewer obligated to form a specific interpretation of their impact on her childhood.

In scene after scene the narrative insistently reminds us that Goretti is still a child. In one instance, for example, Goretti and her friends stand on a bridge over a walkway, yelling catcalls at young men, and then hiding before being observed. Throughout the narrative *Hush-a-Bye Baby* offers a clear delineation of the elements that surround both Goretti's childhood and her friends'. At the same time, because each character asserts a highly individualistic nature—Sinéad (Sinéad O'Connor) daydreams of being a nun, whereas Fidelma (Julie McDonald) cultivates a reputation as a wild girl—the film leaves to viewers the obligation of forming those features into coherent impressions. In this fashion, *Hush-a-Bye Baby* wonderfully emphasizes the individuality that emerges from common cultural experiences.

Motion pictures, like the ones noted above, that explore the complexities of Irish family life provide rewarding engagement for viewers. They offer a sense of the multiplicity informing familial relations, and invite filmgoers to balance individual experiences and societal expectations to form full responses. Unfortunately, as is the case with motion pictures relating to the middle class and to rural life, most movies made the 1990s dealing with children and families in Ireland reflect a failure of cultural imagination. Approaching them with a sense of the potential of multiplicity in representations of the environment can be frustrating, for so many fall back on reductive approaches. In the long run, however, by keeping the pluralism of an Irish childhood in mind, viewers can at the very least come to a clearer sense of the state of Irish-themed films about families.

As Irishness itself becomes more problematic, movies in this category, like the recent rural films examined in the previous chapter, take on an exhausted quality. Whether they offer retrospective explorations of how families used to live or trace their contemporary mores, these motion pictures seem to have little to say and only glancing contact with cultural determinants. Only when filmmakers turn to marginalized groups do their projects convey a sense of cultural specificity.

John Roberts's 1994 *War of the Buttons,* for example, does little more than remake the 1962 French film, *La guerre des boutons.* The film is set in rural Cork in the 1970s, though like its French predecessor, it has a universality that minimizes its Irish identity. It chronicles the activities of warring gangs of boys from adjacent villages. Buttons and shoelaces become the trophies taken from members of the opposing gangs during fights. The action follows the two leaders, Geronimo (John Coffey) and Fergus (Gregg Fitzgerald), and details their struggles for supremacy. At the end, they become friends, and are both sent to reform school. As with *How Harry Became a Tree,* one finds Irishness as an attribute overlaid on the film, and as such it can never dispel the impression of being contrived.

Pat O'Connor's technically skillful but imaginatively stilted 1995 film, *Circle of Friends,* follows the same pattern. It bears the strong stamp of its origin as an HBO production. With its melodramatic moments and stock characters, it proves only marginally effective at integrating an Irish ethos into the narrative. Further, it exemplifies the flaws that accrue when a film relies on retrospection rather than introspection to explore Irish identity. A nonindigenous cast plays all the major characters, who veer toward stereotypes in a narrative that is both unimaginative and predictable.

A fundamental narrative laziness mars the motion picture. The theme of sexual repression in Ireland in the 1950s has simply been done to death, and *Circle of Friends* offers no new insights into the subject. Instead, the film takes the simplistic approach that most viewers would accept as self-evident: a healthy attitude toward physical intimacy is good and one based on exploitation is bad. Unfortunately, the narrative never attempts to examine why characters hold to or reject various sexual or social attitudes. Rather, *Circle of Friends* adopts the cynical view that the best approach to an Irish-themed film is to make it reductive to the point of cliché. Though ostensively benign, its narrative arc in fact hints at a movement to efface definitive features of family that will become stronger in subsequent motion pictures.

Geraldine Creed's 1996 motion picture, *The Sun, the Moon, and the Stars,* demonstrates what can become of a motion picture seemingly highly sensitive to specific cultural conditions when it presents a reductive response to them. The narrative is set in motion by the friction between Mo (Gina Moxley) and Tom (Vinny Murphy), a husband and wife now separated and bickering over caring for their children, Shelley (Elaine Cassidy) and Dee (Aisling Corcoran). The chaotic lives of single parents are manifest in contrasting scenes in which the girls confront Tom's new girlfriend and Mo is denied a promotion at the bank where she works because of the perceived demands of her family. Shelley, Mo, and Dee respond by going off on their summer holiday. At the seaside, the girls encounter an eccentric-looking American woman (Angie Dickinson), whom Shelley decides is a sea witch. In the meantime, Mo becomes involved with Pat (Jason Donovan), a peripatetic Australian. As Mo unsuspectingly eats hallucinogenic mushrooms and Shelly takes up tarot, the message seems to be that a lack of inhibitions is the best reaction to a claustrophobic society. An improbable reconciliation of the girls and their father ends the film.

Lance Pettitt has given qualified praise to the film, calling its happy ending plausible and noting its concern for "difficulties faced by some women in Irish society."[7] Without denying the generosity of Pettitt's assessment, I think it fair to say that whatever its social aims, good intentions cannot redeem *The Sun, the Moon, and the Stars*—which seems to have very little faith in viewers' capacity to make imaginative responses—from being anything more than pedestrian representations of recycled ideas. The character of Noleen in *Intermission* offers a much richer, far more complex examination of the challenges faced by a middle-aged woman abandoned by her husband. The same flatness inhibits the representations of the children, where eccentricity is introduced as a substitute for complexity. Indeed, when contrasted with motion pictures such as *My Left Foot* or *Hush-a-Bye Baby*, the lost opportunities for a more imaginative examination become evident.

Angelica Huston's 1999 production of *Agnes Browne,* a movie based on the Brendan O'Carroll novel *The Mammy,* proves to be even more disappointing. The film, set in the 1960s, traces the life of Agnes Browne, played by Huston, a Moore Street trader left on her own with seven children after the sudden death of her husband. The narrative contents itself with presenting the main character as a watered-down version of the "whore with a heart of gold" stereotype—in this case, a plucky, though not promiscuous, heroine with a foul mouth and a sense of humor—a sure indication that cliché has triumphed over creativity. The attention Pierre (Arno Chevrier), a French baker improbably opening a patisserie in Browne's working-class Northside Dublin neighborhood, pays to court to Agnes thus supplies a detour into romantic comedy, and the narrative draws a cloying amount of cuteness from Agnes's obsession with Tom Jones, who makes a cameo appearance. All these factors, however, underscore what the film sacrifices rather than what it achieves.

Sheridan's *My Left Foot* has shown how a skilled director can use the Dublin slums to create an imaginatively engaging examination of family life. Unfortunately, in *Agnes Browne* neither O'Carroll nor Huston seemed willing to take the material far enough beyond safe laughs to create that sort of experience. In the end, the viewer's attitudes about the Irish family do not matter, for he or she is never given sufficient opportunity to examine them through what transpires on-screen.

The heavy-handed narrative style of a film such as *Agnes Browne,* however, exerts a minimal impact on the cinema in Ireland. Motion pictures such as Alan Parker's well-received 1999 motion picture, *Angela's Ashes,* on the other hand, work in a much more insidious fashion. The film is a beautifully photographed and well-constructed adaptation of Frank McCourt's best-selling memoir of an impoverished Irish Catholic childhood in 1930s Limerick. It follows McCourt's book closely, and in consequence it has many of the same strengths and weaknesses.

McCourt's memoir remains engaging because of his ability to play off the misery of the deadening poverty and hopelessness of his family with incidents of macabre humor. Unfortunately, the account of young Frank's movement toward adulthood and emigration heavy-handedly mixes equal parts nostalgia and self-pity. When the screenplay overlays these elements with the unrelieved gloom of McCourt's childhood surroundings, one finds little leeway for interpretation. Although the film's narrative holds the viewers' attention because of the skill of the original storytelling, it does little beyond making the obvious point that childhood suffering is bad.

Worse, *Angela's Ashes* offers an intense view of the shortcomings associated with Irishness without any effort to examine the forces motivating them. It plays on the idea that seemingly frank descriptions of horrid circumstances provide certification of authenticity: the more bleak and hopeless the conditions, the more genuine they must be. In fact, *Angela's Ashes* reinforces stereotypical anti-Irish biases: drunkenness, sentimentality, and fecklessness. It is a caricatured version of *A Portrait of the Artist as a Young Man* with a working-class accent but without the sense of complexity in the environment or the redeeming possibility of creative talent developing the narrative beyond the tale of a straightforward melodrama.

Bruce Beresford's unabashedly sentimental *Evelyn,* released in 2002, offers even less imaginative engagement. After Desmond Doyle (Pierce Brosnan) loses his job, his wife, Charlotte (Mairead Devlin), abandons the family. Because of an antiquated Irish custody law, civil authorities do not allow Doyle to keep custody of his three young children, Evelyn (Sophie Vavasseur), Maurice (Hugh McDonagh), and Dermot (Niall Beagan). Instead, they are taken away and put into orphanages. With the help of friends, Desmond takes on the Irish Supreme Court, as well as the Catholic Church. Ultimately, he is reunited with his children.

This film is a good example of how watching a straightforward drama with a plot for which most viewers will feel sympathy can turn into an experience akin to having one's teeth drilled without Novocain. The moral issues present themselves in black-and-white contrast. The bureaucracy remains predictably insensitive. And justice triumphs in the end with the rehabilitation of the Brosnan character and the reunification of the family. Such a simplistic narrative line leaves little for the moviegoer to engage. What could have developed as a sophisticated examination of the influence of Irish culture and social conditions on parenting, lawmaking, and religious practices—a study that could have examined what elements in each are necessary and what flaws are tolerable—never rises above a simplistic view. As a consequence, regressive Irish laws serve simply as an excuse for producing a predictable Dickensian melodrama.[8]

Certainly, the type of social advocacy one sees in *Evelyn* and similar films foregrounds uniquely Irish conditions. However, as Irish society changes and as the Irish legal system moves toward conformity with other European Union countries, the disparities that produced these glaring injustices have begun to disappear. More to the point, and this issue is why I have discussed them in some detail, children's advocacy films, like rural dramas, have become fixed in the past. Reductive motion pictures like the ones I have just referenced pander to a false sense of recently acquired communal justice, then versus now, that in fact undermines any serious cultural criticism. Unlike so many of the movies made in the 1970s and 1980s, these feature-length films fail to explore the imaginative range of a particular genre. Instead, they undermine the concept of Irish-themed films on the family by a relentless invocation of universal banalities.

Though not completely satisfying, Neil Jordan's *Miracle*, released in 1991, provides a brief disruption of this tendency toward the lowest common narrative denominator. It shows what a director with a solid respect for the complexity of issues relating to sex and sexuality in an Irish setting can accomplish. And it offers insights on how exceptional teenagers deal with these concerns by featuring subtle elements that make their experiences unique.

Two fifteen year olds living in Bray, Jimmy (Niall Byrne) and Rose (Lorraine Pilkington), are bright and precocious and, predictably, bored. They spend their summer inventing stories about people whom they see around the town. Rose has a crush on Jimmy, and she tries to make him jealous by announcing her intention to seduce a young boy working at a circus that has come to town. Jimmy, meanwhile, becomes infatuated with an older woman, Renée Baker (Beverly D'Angelo), who comes down to the beach to swim. Jimmy has a troubled relationship with his musician father, Sam (Donal McCann), which becomes intensified by sexual rivalry when Jimmy learns that Sam has had some previous connection with Renée. As Jimmy pursues Renée, she alternately leads him on and repulses him.

The dramatic emphasis of the film shifts markedly when viewers hear Sam and Renée arguing about why Sam has not told Jimmy that she is his mother. Although Renée clearly resents Sam's silence, she takes no steps to enlighten Jimmy. Throughout the film the narrative has represented family relations as strained but important. (At times there is a desperation for connection, as Rose risks being hit by a train in an effort to attract the attention of her father, who is preoccupied with his golf swing.) This construction of a family changes with the introduction of an ambiguous scene that hints at intercourse between Renée and Jimmy after Jimmy has learned that she is his mother. The next day Jimmy appears completely unaffected by the events of the preceding night. He finds that Rose has seduced the circus boy, stolen his keys, and let loose the circus animals in Bray. The film ends with Jimmy and Rose back on the promenade in Bray, once again making up stories about the people whom they see.

Cleverness is the strength and weakness of the film. It captures nicely the claustrophobia and imaginative frustrations of inventive teenagers in an Irish context circumscribed by convention and repression. It also neatly highlights the effect of their sheltered environment that allows them to combine sexual naïveté with recklessness. At the same time, the narrative works so hard to show their cleverness that it truncates the opportunities to explore their relationship with each other and with their families. The circularity of the ending provides an artificial assurance that, despite the emotional travails of the two young people chronicled in the film, order and normalcy of a sort have been restored by simply refusing to acknowledge the enormity of what has transpired. Like the sentimental conclusion of *Circle of Friends,* for thoughtful viewers the coy ending of *The Miracle* suggests more what the film failed to achieve than what it has done.

Six years later, Jordan's 1997 production of Patrick McCabe's novel *The Butcher Boy* offers a much more forceful assessment of the impact of environment on an individual's identity, standing out as a stunning exception to this inclination to rely on retrospection as a substitute for imagination. In this film Jordan offers a powerful examination of the extreme pressures of Irish childhood and the ultimate failure of the family, particularly in the pre–Vatican II world, to act as a shield from the grinding insistence of a society demanding discipline and conformity. In the early 1960s Francie Brady (Eamonn Owens) lives in a rural town with his alcoholic father (Stephen Rea) and psychotic mother (Aisling O'Sullivan). He is great friends with Joe Purcell (Alan Boyle) and antagonistic to the well-off Nugent family. When Francie is sent to reform school after vandalizing the Nugent home, Joe forms a friendship with Phillip Nugent (Andrew Fullerton).

Joe's ties to Phillip and the deaths of his mother and then his father set Francie off on a delusional path of destructiveness, informed by images of the Blessed Virgin Mary and scenes of nuclear holocaust. He has tormented the Nugents throughout the film, but with this dissolution of the conditions that had given his life some stability, Francie's actions become increasingly vicious. Eventually, he kills Mrs. Nugent (Fiona Shaw), dismembers her, and hides the body parts all over town. The authorities eventually apprehend Francie, and send him to an asylum, where he remains until he is a man well into his thirties.

Although a surrealistic tone dominates the film, its narrative marvelously concentrates the viewer's attention on the fundamental features of Francie's life. The parochialism of a small town, with all its complex rituals and attitudes, dominates the motion picture, and Francie's struggles with his own religious belief add a poignancy rarely captured by filmmakers attempting to reflect the church's influence on Irish life. All of it creates an imaginatively satisfying experience because, like the book on which it is based, in *The Butcher Boy* Jordan takes narrative risks, cultivates ambiguities, and trusts viewers to respond.

Further, *The Butcher Boy* wonderfully combines the sophistication of modern cinematographic techniques with a sure sense of a uniquely Irish identity. It evokes the past without dragging in nostalgia. It portrays poverty without relying on clichéd images. And, most important, in terms of this study at least, it plays on viewer expectations of cultural institutions— the family, Catholicism, small-town life—without forcing a prescribed response.

Francie's mania offers an intense version of the nonlinear discernment that characterizes all human perception. Indeed, as one traces the associations between experience and reaction in a broad, nonexclusionary manner, the motivations for Francie's actions become clearer and one's judgment of them becomes less prescriptive. Francie has organized his life around a series of elements that have taken on iconic stature—his home, his friendship with Joe, and his dialogues with the Blessed Virgin—that allow him great freedom within his environment while anchoring him as well. He desperately endeavors to sustain them. The film starkly represents both the poignancy and the ineffectuality of his efforts when, after his father's death, he dons an apron and cleans the house in determined—and some might say transgressive—attempts to sustain the normalcy of family life. The violence of Francie's response to the people around him who threaten the maintenance, however artificial, of these institutions underscores the most powerful statement of the narrative. Francie's world remains stable until the hold of these anchors is broken, and their dissolution is inevitable because they no longer exert a shaping influence.

In this regard, *The Butcher Boy* offers a grim prediction of the trajectory for representations of the family. In a film set a half century ago, the defining features of an Irish childhood are already slipping away from Francie Brady. In accounts that grow out of contemporary settings, these markers have lost what little efficacy they had earlier displayed.[9]

To some degree, motion pictures of the past decade and a half that have turned their attention to examining contemporary childhood experiences have broken from this pattern by downplaying didacticism and returning to the sort of representation seen in *Down the Corner*. The most intensely personal movies in this broad category dispassionately examine social structures emerging within groups of children, often forming alternative communities in reaction and resistance to adult domination. This subgroup offers unique interpretive opportunities, for it highlights specific features of Irish society, often underscoring the antipathy of these elements to the needs of children. These efforts have not proved to be universally satisfying. However, even in flawed attempts, when filmmakers take the trouble to explore the complexity of the situation, the results can powerfully engage viewers' imaginations.

Focusing on marginalized communities increases the likelihood of artistically complex explorations of family identity in contemporary Ireland. Mike Newell's *Into the West,* released in 1992, offers a story about children growing up in and around a Traveller community.[10] In the opening scene, a white horse appears by the sea where Grandpa Ward (David Kelly) is sitting, and follows him to an encampment near Ballymun corporation housing on Dublin's Northside where his grandsons Tito (Rúaidhrí Conroy) and Ossie (Ciarán Fitzgerald) live with Papa Riley (Gabriel Byrne). Riley's wife died giving birth to Ossie, and Riley subsequently rejected the Travellers' way of life to reside in the city. Counterpointing their urbanization, Ward tells his grandsons the myths of Ireland, and then leaves with the boys the horse that has been following him. After some misadventure by the boys with adapting the horse to life in public housing, the police come and take the animal away, selling it to a businessman. Tito and Ossie discover the horse's whereabouts when they see it in a television news story about racing. In short order, the boys steal the horse and head west with it. Eventually, they come to the sea, and when the horse plunges in with Ossie on its back, the young boy sees his dead mother under the waves. The horse disappears. After rescuing Ossie, Papa Riley and the boys burn the caravan where Mary, the mother, died, and the boys see their horse in the flames.

Although its narrative provides insightful moments into the lives of Traveller children, *Into the West* fails to coalesce into a unified presentation. It cannot decide whether to become a myth, a cautionary tale, or a simple melodrama. Identities never develop to the potential initially suggested. The corrupt Garda, played by Brendan Gleeson, and the sleazy businessman (Dave Duffy) are wooden characters. The performances of these talented actors, as well as by Colm Meaney and Johnny Murphy, struggle against inadequate characterizations. Comic scenes often have a recycled feel to them, such as the horse in the elevator, copied from *The Commitments,* and cute overwhelms creative, leaving the viewer as passive apprehender.

Nonetheless, the narrative at times has a complexity that fosters a range of responses and encourages pluralistic understanding. Sporadic moments show the desperateness of the lives the children lead, as when Tito struggles to read the most rudimentary of sentences, and they provoke viewers to go beyond the romanticism of the plot to consider the legitimacy of the Travellers' stubborn adherence to a nomadic lifestyle in light of the demands that contemporary society places on the children. In consequence, despite its creative shortcomings, *Into the West* requires consideration from anyone exploring the range of Irishness that films can convey.

Perry Ogden's 2005 film, *Pavee Lackeen: The Traveller Girl,* further explores the world of marginalized children and shows the rich results one can still achieve in narrowly delineated approaches to the subject. In circumscribed fashion, it deftly comments on the complexities of Irish family life. The movie focuses on the stress endured by a mother and her children—Winnie (Winnie Maughan), Mum (Rose Maughan), Rosie (Rosie Maughan), and Leroy (Paddy Maughan)—living in caravans on a busy road in Ringsend. The plot deals with relatively straightforward problems. Winnie is suspended for fighting in school because the girls there had insulted her. Local authorities pressure the family to move their caravans up the road, and they are struggling to find a permanent home. Winnie and Rosie are coping with maturing physically while remaining outside the normal world of teenage Irish girls. The frustrations that accrue to the characters highlight the difficulties that arise when attempting to resolve any of these issues.

Despite the hardship it chronicles, *Pavee Lackeen* makes a concerted effort to avoid didacticism or even linear exposition while engaging significant aspects of family life in contemporary Ireland. Instead, with chilling detachment it underscores a randomness that comes close to chaos in the lives of Winnie and her family by simply presenting viewers with a

Pavee Lackeen: Winnie (Winnie Maughan) and her mother (Rose Maughan). Courtesy of Perry Ogden.

series of episodic events, often no more connected to one another than the everyday occurrences of anyone's life. Winnie and her family occupy a liminal position in Irish society and show little interest in engaging the mainstream culture. Whatever background one gleans comes from impressions drawn out of the behavior and actions of the characters.

The narrative unfolds in a minimalist fashion, highlighting the clash between the principles of the majority and the ethics of the minority. The central feature of the movie demands that viewers impose a kind of order by coming to a sense of a communal value system imperfectly applied and often at odds with one's own expectations. In this fashion, viewers replicate the experiences of Winnie and her siblings, struggling to find a unified sense of self amid conflicting and often disappearing cultural markers.

Pavee Lackeen poses sharp questions about identity for indigenous and nonindigenous viewers alike. It sketches a world divorced from the rituals and conventions of ordinary Irish society yet formed from the same social environment. In light of the rapidly changing conditions of childhood represented throughout Irish-themed motion pictures, the process of understanding *Pavee Lackeen* consists more of engaging the ambivalences in any Irish family situation than in defining the otherness of the Traveller community.

Although the dysfunctional nature of Winnie's family is evident, it retains a maddening passiveness that slows the narrative development. A much more hectic film, *Disco Pigs*, offers a richer opportunity for extended analysis. With characters more violent and more deeply disturbed than any save Francie Brady but without the surrealistic narrative embellishments of *The Butcher Boy*, this film challenges viewers to find an approach that can encompass its complexity while resolving the antinomies in its representations of childhood.

A Paradigmatic Reading: *Disco Pigs*

Because of the economic and social changes outlined in Chapter 1, it is a rare film that can convey a sense of the unique attributes of contemporary Irish families with the unadulterated power and authenticity that one finds in Kirsten Sheridan's *Disco Pigs*, released in 2001. Indeed, its stark, nihilistic approach, an extension of the narrative style of *Down the Corner*, enables *Disco Pigs* to foreground the ineffectual efforts of modern Irish cinematic families trying to delineate the experiences of childhood. The film follows the lives of two feral children, tracing events from their births to their untimely deaths. In the process it questions the efficacy of an institution long seen as the defining feature of Irish identity, and by extension it suggests to viewers that the best approach to motion pictures in this category inverts conventional, linear interpretive expectations.

Disco Pigs focuses on the troubled childhood of two Cork children—Sinead/Runt (Elaine Cassidy) and Darin/Pig (Cillian Murphy)—who are born on the same day, have lived in houses beside one another for seventeen years, and from a very early age have made their families and indeed the world in which they find themselves redundant by becoming deeply and completely intertwined with one another's lives. What at first seems charming mimicry evolves into an effacement of individuality, a merging of personalities, a solipsistic dismissal of the relevance of all elements outside themselves. As symbolized by the nicknames that they, and no one else, use to identify one another, the two reject the power of the family or of society to shape them as individuals, and instead appropriate the task for themselves by redefining the boundaries of their identities.

As they near their seventeenth birthdays, the dynamics of their relationship subtly change. Runt remains committed to Pig, but she has also begun to realize the limitations of their relationship, striving ever so slightly to develop elements of an identity independent of his. Pig, if anything, has grown more reliant on Runt and more determined to circumscribe their world. Despite Runt's gesture toward transformation, each remains keenly attuned to the other. Nonetheless, the restiveness that Runt has begun to evince threatens Pig's security by questioning his sense of who he is.

When Pig responds with behavior that becomes increasingly controlling, unstable, and violent, Runt's parents, in a tacit admission of their failure to form her identity, put their daughter into residential care to break the hold on her of the relationship with Pig. There Runt makes friends with a young woman who seems every bit as disturbed as Pig, suggesting that moving Runt from marginalization to integration stands as a far more difficult task than her parents had anticipated. Nonetheless, her gesture toward someone else redefines the dynamics of identity in her relationship with Pig, and delineates a subtle interpretive challenge for viewers.

In fact, Runt's nature has taken a more radical turn than Pig's, as she moves, even tentatively, toward becoming Sinead. Pig continues to define himself in relation to her, as half of a single entity. Runt seems now to be drifting toward a wider definition of identity though one that still asserts itself through negation. Her association with marginalized figures beyond Pig does not so much embrace a new nature as expand her opposition to conventional characterization. Whereas Pig demands claustrophobic entanglement, Runt moves toward a complex self-sufficiency. She stands open to engagement with selected elements of the world around her, but they simply reinforce her sense of self. In essence, she has expanded her solipsism by finding reflections of herself beyond engagement with Pig. At the same time, Runt shows no inclination to integrate with society. (The narrative presages this inclination earlier in the film when Runt is inadvertently locked in the trunk of a car and rides around in it for several days. When Pig releases her, she emerges with a beatific smile, apparently none the worse for her solitary experience.)

Predictably, separation only accelerates Pig's commitment to violence and madness, and precipitates his frantic search for Runt. After finding Runt and taking her out of the home, the pair return to Cork. They spend the night clubbing, and Pig's brutal possessiveness becomes all too clear. In a jealous rage, Pig beats to death a young man who has, in Pig's view, shown Runt too much attention. The violence seems to shock both of them, and they go to a deserted beach that they had frequented earlier in the film. After having intercourse, Runt suffocates Pig, probably to save him from the trauma of separation that incarceration in prison would bring, and then walks into the ocean, seemingly intent on suicide. Even their deaths highlight the divergence in their natures. Pig dies literally smothered by Runt, a condition to which he has always aspired. Runt moves solitarily to her death, stepping into the sea and thus erasing all evidence of her presence.

Despite the power of its narrative, or perhaps because of it, *Disco Pigs* is a difficult film to watch and an even more difficult film to understand. Pig's penchant for explosive violence gives an edginess to every scene in which he appears. Runt's oscillation between a gleeful participation in Pig's brutalizing others and a clear expression of interest in finding a life independent of their relationship continually disrupts a viewer's interpretation of her character. Although the delineation of their natures becomes evident over the course of the narrative, coming to an understanding of the forces motivating them proves to be extremely challenging.

A full engagement of Pig's and Runt's natures depends, to a great extent, on one's ability to reconcile the apparent arbitrariness that motivates their actions. However, accepting a measure of randomness within a unified narrative does not mean reading without a purpose. Runt and Pig careen around their world, seemingly oblivious to all restraints, yet their behavior has a coherence when one accepts the idea that absence has created a presence. The ineffectuality of the family has created a strongly articulated dependence on one another. Although the individual actions of these characters hold a great deal of the viewer's attention, their behavior

Disco Pigs: Runt (Elaine Cassidy) and Pig (Cillian Murphy) in a rare moment of tranquillity. Courtesy of Ed Guiney.

offers an implicit critique of the institution of the family that demands imaginative engagement as well.

Getting a clearer sense that boundaries exist in Runt and Pig's world gives the viewer a solid point of reference for understanding their natures, and the real crisis develops only when, because of Runt's incipient independence, Pig senses the erosion of those boundaries. In this regard, one can anchor the subjectivity of Irishness of which I wrote in the Introduction on an assumption that its aspects highlight the identities of the central characters, even if only through the negative effect of showing the resistance that the solipsistic natures of Runt and Pig have to any cultural forces. Further, this awareness of overall order surrounding a chaotic existence allows viewers to let the milieu that shaped Pig and Runt emerge subtly and indirectly—in references to their schooling, in comments on living in Cork, and in the tempo of their daily lives. The Irishness of their environment inflects rather than informs the lives of Pig and Runt.

Viewers of *Disco Pigs* sense Irishness most strikingly through its nonappearance, but this void is not a replication of the generalizing social impulses of lesser films. The cultural opaqueness of Runt and Pig underscores their self-conscious inhibition of identity. They literally exist only for themselves, and filmgoers are much more aware of the Irish world that surrounds them than they are, though even for filmgoers the features of this environment remain sketchy. In consequence, interpretations need to hold both worlds in tension to come to a clear sense of the options for understanding the pair. The film does not offer clear guidance as to whether the relationship of Runt and Pig presages the complete disintegration of the family or simply reflects their own sociopathic deviation; rather, it leaves to viewers the task of resolving or sustaining the conundrum.

Disco Pigs represents a sophisticated effort at portraying the fractured quality of contemporary life for children in Ireland. However, the dominant factor in motion pictures in this genre remains retrospection. This gesture involves much more than a narrator simply looking backward on his or her youth. It entails contrasting examinations of family structures in previous generations and acknowledging those times as eras in which the uniqueness of childhood was sharply defined. Like films set in the country, few contemporary motion pictures concern themselves with childhood, suggesting that the singularity of the Irish experience is quite literally becoming a thing of the past.

All this clarification leads to my point that, as with any narrowly defined genre, even with the benefit of a highly subjective perspective, reliance on a limited number of issues can lead to stagnation. In the preceding chapter, I examined the repetitiveness of the struggle for definition in rural Ireland. And, as noted in the past few pages, without a highly imaginative approach, generational conflict rapidly takes on features indistinguishable from one country to another. In the next chapter, I will take up motion pictures dealing with Catholic education and with the impact of Catholicism on emotional, spiritual, and even physical maturation in Ireland. I will trace the range of cinematic approaches to religion, not only in films examining how it shapes the lives of children but in those movies that explore how it informs the social consciousness of Irish adults.

6

In the Name of the Father

Images of Religious Beliefs

As Tom Inglis, in a very useful survey of the topic, has noted, for centuries religion has dominated life in Ireland, and, despite some recent diminution of its role, it still exerts a strong, if often inflected, influence in the shaping of Irish culture.[1] Filmmakers have shown little interest in this evolving, nuanced attitude, tending instead to offer a more polarized view of religion, often bringing their own grievances to the screen. In consequence, rather than reading diverse communal perceptions directly into motion pictures in this category, understanding religion in Irish-themed films demands an awareness of the dichotomies that obtain between the sociological evidence of its continuing though evolving impact and the dramatizations of specific experiences unique to Irish life.

From the Reformation onward, religious beliefs, and even more significantly sectarian affiliations, have played a prominent role in defining the scope of political, economic, and social life on the island. Whereas Protestantism, specifically the Church of Ireland, initially exerted overriding control, from the Devotional Revolution of the nineteenth century through the constitutional privileging of the twentieth century, Catholicism has displaced it as a prevailing cultural force. A number of factors marked this rise in prominence, including the church's expanded role in education and, with churchmen in Rome acting as mediators between Ireland and England, its function in the efforts to secure nonviolent political change.[2]

With the establishment of the Irish Free State, the prestige of the Catholic Church in the mind of ordinary citizens increased.[3] As Ireland's separation from colonial rule became more pronounced, a concomitant rise of a distinctly Catholic (though not necessarily catholic) personality within the bulk of the citizens, similar to the loyalty to a Protestant identity held by the Anglo-Irish before the Treaty of 1922, became increasingly evident. The Catholic Church continued its commitment to social services and to education. Additionally, the Irish constitution afforded a privileged position to the church and its teachings, and the de Valera administration offered it unabashed preferment.[4]

Despite the economic, social, and cultural changes of the past few decades, even today in Ireland, more than in any other western European country, attitudes toward religion remain an important aspect of national identity. However, as I will note below, contemporary filmmakers have become more inclined to explore instances of its absence from Irish life. Consequently, understanding the way religion defines identity in Irish-themed films often becomes a matter of balancing the idiosyncratic, and at times ossified, response of the filmmaker against the complicated ethos of religion that continues to evolve in the country. Such films emphasize individuality to a greater extent than do movies in any other category, and viewers must proceed toward understanding with a sense of the imperatives that such distinctiveness exerts.

Inglis has identified the communal feeling that arises from a religion's cultural presence as *habitus*—a collective religious consciousness.[5] It applies equally to diverse denominations across the country, and it distinguishes itself from the more precisely defined theology of these faiths. *Habitus* represents a state of mind identified with the culture of a particular religious group, and it serves as a useful designation for the attitudes about Catholicism and Protestantism that one finds in Irish-themed films.

A striking parallel exists between the idea of *habitus* and the concept of Irish identity relevant to this study. Subjective and objective perceptions inform both. Individuals broadly apply their idiosyncratic impressions of each condition across the cultural landscape, and a continual process of negotiation, self-conscious and otherwise, goes on in public discussions of these terms. Perhaps more than any other genre examined in this study, religious motion pictures clearly lay out the tension between subjective perceptions and assumptions of universality, and they demand a nonexclusionary assent to both for a full understanding.

Like any social condition, of course, *habitus* finds itself subjected to dynamic evolution. Over the last decades of the twentieth century, Protestantism, at least in the republic, has struggled to avoid becoming an anachronism, whereas perceptions of Catholicism have ranged from staunch traditionalism to indifference to a profound resentment. A growing secularization, reflected according to Inglis in a drop in Sunday mass attendance from 91 percent in 1974 to just over 60 percent in the late 1990s, has demonstrated an appreciable lessening of the influence of the church.[6] Likewise, the series of clergy scandals—sexual, financial, and otherwise—have further eroded the authority of the Catholic hierarchy. In consequence, determining how religion conveys identity in Irish-themed films calls for care and insight, and, as with other institutions, it provokes highly individualized responses from viewer to viewer.

Getting a sense of how films reflect Irishness through representations of religion and religious attitudes becomes even more difficult than it is in other aspects of Irish society because of the paucity of motion pictures on the subject. Perhaps because of religion's pervasiveness across the cultural landscape—RTÉ One still interrupts programming to signal the time for praying the Angelus, a Catholic devotion traditionally recited at 6:00 A.M., noon, and 6:00 P.M.—the topic receives less detailed scrutiny and occupies a more or less permanent position in the background. Even this subject matter can be problematic, for often what should be the most Irish of elements is portrayed in clichéd fashion.[7]

Current events have doubtless contributed to the tendency to draw on stereotypes. Some of the most prominent contemporary films dealing with the church in Ireland focus on what has sadly become a timely topic: abuse in religious-run institutions. The spate of scandals in the 1990s has certainly fueled interest. Unfortunately, many of these efforts never get beyond the self-evident proposition that sexual or any other abuse of children is a bad thing and the distorted implication that the clergy in the Roman Catholic Church in Ireland are hypocrites, weaklings, perverts, sadists, cretins, or some dreadful combination of these traits. Although the sentiments of moral outrage expressed in such motion pictures stand as commendable ethical positions, they provide very few imaginative alternatives to interpretation. This approach to the topic stands as particularly disappointing since a full decade earlier Cathal Black showed that it was possible to present a powerful assessment of the abuse of power while exploring the complex dynamics of the situation.

At a scant thirty-five minutes' running time, Black's 1981 motion picture, *Our Boys,* qualifies as a short rather than as a feature film. Further, its narrative structure often blurs the distinction between documentary and fictional material. However, like *Down the Corner,* Joe Comerford's contemporaneous motion picture, *Our Boys* sets creative standards by which subsequent films on the topic must be judged. In particular, Black uses brevity and eclecticism to present a powerful episodic assessment of an intolerable situation without falling into the reductionism that has marred other efforts to deal with this topic.

Our Boys looks at the Christian Brothers' approach to education, and announces an oscillating point of view with an ironic title that can apply as much to the men who administer the institutions under scrutiny as to their students. Nonetheless, despite acknowledging a measure of ambiguity, it never flinches from highlighting the determinative features of the painful story it seeks to tell. In the end, the narrative places evidence of intolerable abuse within a context that frustrates easy explanations of the situation.

The format of the film deftly introduces a sense of ambiguity. It mixes documentary footage of a Saint Patrick's Day parade, the 1932 Eucharistic Congress in Dublin, and other national events with fictional exchanges among the Christian Brothers, scenes with the brothers and the boys interacting at the school, and reactions of the parents. The integration of actual and dramatized events effectively highlights the multiple levels of analysis that the motion picture demands, and it precludes narrow, exclusionary interpretations.

At the same time, the social concern of *Our Boys* remains unambiguous. It offers unmistakable criticism of the way that the Christian Brothers run the school, foregrounding the climate of brutality informing the teachers' relations with the boys. Black emphatically avoids any appearance of trying to excuse the behavior of these men, and he deftly conveys the frustration and anger felt by a number of students and their parents over the boys' treatment. At the same time, Black shows an interest in presenting

Our Boys: Mick Lally as a Christian Brother. Courtesy of Cathal Black.

the uniqueness of the environment of Irish education that would foster the complex effects of abusive behavior.

Toward this end, Black works to capture the humanity of all the participants. Interviews with former boys give a horrific sense of the conditions that they endured, and make very clear the trauma with which they still live. Black deftly leaves the viewer to determine how such circumstances could come about, and in the process the film silently calls for judgment of the society that simply allowed this sort of behavior to continue with no concern for what was going on. Exchanges with the brothers are conflicted and pathetic. These men now seem confused and at times ashamed of the way they treated their charges. Most strikingly, they also project a sincere concern for their responsibilities to form or reform the children in their care. Despite their appalling treatment of the boys, many of the brothers come across not as monsters but as limited individuals given tasks beyond their ability to perform. Compounding this impression is the fact that these men have clearly led a sheltered existence. After receiving the news that their school is being closed down by the government, many of the brothers are simply at a loss at what to do.

Unfortunately, not many cinematic examinations of Irish Catholic institutions prove as willing to scrutinize organizational complexities. Though a number of directors show great skill in their representations of the diverse and even contradictory forces shaping individual religious identities, their depictions of aspects of the church's establishment continually run the risk of slipping into stereotypes. Colin Gregg's 1986 motion picture, *Lamb,* based on the Bernard MacLaverty novel, presents a sensitive individual study of a young Christian Brother's efforts to meliorate the life of a troubled boy. At the same time, the intransigence and insensitivity of the brother's religious superiors become simple, and even simpleminded, plot devices for moving the story forward.

The narrative follows a straightforward path. Owen Kane (Hugh O'Connor) is put in a Catholic orphanage because his epileptic fits have disrupted the relations of his mother (Frances Tomelty) with a series of men. Although the head of the orphanage, Brother Benedict (Ian Bannen), openly expresses his disgust toward the mother's behavior, he nonetheless makes no exceptions for Owen, subjecting the boy to the brutal treatment that all of the orphans presumably receive. At the same time, the boy gains the protection of Brother Michael Lamb (Liam Neeson), who is vehemently opposed to Brother Benedict's harsh approach to the management of children at the orphanage.

When Michael's father dies, Brother Benedict pressures Michael to donate to the order the money that he will receive as an inheritance. Instead, Michael and Owen use it to run off to London. They stay there for some time, eventually finding a room in a squat, but the pedophilia of one man there puts Owen in danger and compels them to leave. While they are on the run, Owen finishes the last of his epilepsy medicine, and the situation seems quite hopeless. In a gesture conveying both defeat and melioration, Michael brings Owen back to Ireland. After spending a day at the seashore doing things that Owen has always wanted to do, Michael drowns the boy and unsuccessfully attempts to take his own life. The film ends with Michael in despair on the beach.

Although a melodramatic tone dominates the broad narrative lines, an openness to the complexity of characters' emotions, insights, and desires allows one to see beyond its predictable plot development. Although the movie makes a straightforward representation of institutional brutality and insensitivity, the interactions between Owen and Michael show how difficult it can be to deal with recalcitrant children with special needs. It also demonstrates how corrosive the system can be on practitioners with sensitive natures, highlighting the irreparable damage that someone with good intentions can sustain. The botched escape attempt and the sordid and desperate life that Michael and Owen lead on the run only heighten the ambiguity of the ending. The film leaves the viewer to decide whether the pair would have been better off had they remained in the orphanage and to wonder where personal responsibility ends and communal concern emerges.

To be fair to Gregg, and to MacLaverty who adapted his novel for the screenplay, one needs to remember that the thrust of the film, although solidly set in the context of Irish religious institutions, is not a detailed examination of the orphanage system. Rather, it seeks to explore concepts of belief, goodness, and justice in the relationship between Owen and Lamb. At the same time, it does not engage in great detail the environment that shaped their natures.

This is not to say that *Lamb* ignores the world surrounding its central characters. In fact, it does hint at a complexity inherent in the system, as manifested by Brother Benedict, about which viewers can only speculate. When Brother Benedict speaks of Owen's mother, he exudes a barely concealed contempt for her selfishness. When Lamb protests the punishment of Owen for an offense that the boy could not have committed, Brother Benedict shows a sophisticated if cold sense of group psychology. Indeed, Brother Benedict arguably stands as a more interesting figure than does Lamb, for Benedict manifests himself as both a product of the religious institution in which he finds himself and a shrewd critic of the world that it encompasses. In this context one can see the narrative asking whether Brother Benedict embodies a model for an evolving religious perspective whereas Lamb stands as an idealistic anachronism.

Audiences will wrestle with the scenes cited above and with their own attitudes toward the Catholic Church in forming their interpretations of the film, but this conflict represents only the background to the narrative that unfolds. In fact, *Lamb* focuses its attention on the efforts of Michael and Owen to come to understand one another rather than on attempts at the grinding down of the human spirit made by institutions within the church. At the same time, viewers who wish to come to a fully satisfying analysis need follow an approach that acknowledges how subjective attitudes about Irish Catholicism inform both the construction and the interpretation of the film.

Further, *Lamb* signals a new approach to Catholicism as an institution. The sensitivity of Brother Benedict to the complexity of situations stands in stark contrast to the organizational ineffectuality at addressing these conditions. *Lamb* suggests, without elaboration, what will become a more insistent perspective in subsequent films: perceiving Catholicism as a threat to Irish identity.

Because the Catholic Church in Ireland can provoke extremely strong responses, viewers must keep in mind how easily narratives can slip into polemics even when attempting to resist that impulse. Peter Mullan's 2002 film, *The Magdalene Sisters,* unfortunately, makes no effort to eschew didacticism or to extend to the audience the opportunity to make an interpretation of the events it depicts. Rather, the film purely and simply undertakes an unapologetic assault on the administration by religious orders of homes for unwed mothers in Ireland.[8]

This is not to deny the importance of the subject or the validity of some of the film's criticisms. In recent years the abuses that have occurred within Magdalene homes have been well documented. However, with Mullan's outrage exerting such a strong influence on his project, the credibility of his assertions would have been greater had he presented a documentary rather than a fictional account or had he, like Cathal Black, demonstrated a capacity to see complexity in the natures of all of the participants in his narrative.

For those readers who link art and didacticism, this objection may seem unfair, though even the didactic approach demands a balanced perspective. More tellingly, for those who feel that an aesthetic work is not complete without the opportunity for the viewer to interact imaginatively, films such as this one seem little more than secular sermons. Further, Mullan does not take the trouble to elaborate on more than the basic elements inform-ing the issue. No one of sound mind would endorse the brutal behavior inflicted upon young girls by the nuns in the film. At the same time, when the narrative makes no effort to explore the attitudes that underlie the callousness of the religious, the insensitivity of families, and the general public apathy toward such institutions, one must question whether *The Magdalene Sisters* achieves much beyond the filmmaker's chance to settle old scores, real or imagined.[9]

The motion picture opens with three scenes explaining why the girls who are the film's protagonists have been placed in an asylum. Margaret (Anne-Marie Duff) is raped by her cousin Kevin, and her outraged father sends her off to the home. Bernadette (Nora-Jane Noone) is already con-fined to an orphanage, and, when she begins to show a mild interest in boys, the horrified nuns put her in the Magdalene facility. Rose (Dorothy Duffy) has given birth to an illegitimate child. Her parents force her to give up the baby, and pack her off to the institution. In each instance place-ment seems more like incarceration, and time in the home stands as a form of punishment for actual or anticipated sins.

Their introduction to the head of the home, Sister Bridget (Geraldine McEwan), emphasizes the cold insensitivity of the nuns and their concern with money. (Mullan's repeated shots of Sister Bridget's hands counting money or of her face gazing with pleasure at the safe in her office quickly become tedious.) Women of all ages are in the home, and a sense of their hopelessness fills the film. The narrative unfolds episodically, showing how the spirits of the girls are broken by physical abuse, how they are humili-ated (as in the nude shower scene when two nuns amuse themselves by ridiculing the bodies of a line of girls asking "who has the biggest bum," "who is the hairiest," "who has the smallest breasts," and other demeaning questions), and how the inmates lead austere lives in comparison with the physical comforts enjoyed by the nuns, particularly at mealtimes.

There is a chilling scene when a father (played with a bit too much gusto by the film's director) brings back his daughter, Una, who had fled the home. He literally drags the helpless and terrified young woman into the dormitory as Sister Bridget and the girls look on. He has beaten his child, and now declares he has no daughter. With barely controlled rage, he casts accusatory glances around the room, and calls the other young women "bitches." (It seems out of character for Sister Bridget to tolerate such coarse language, but perhaps it accentuates the sense of her as a bully, unwilling to confront any but those individuals over whom she has power.) When Una later joins the religious order, the narrative misses an important opportunity by failing to explore her motivations. However, this lack of curiosity regarding the inner lives of characters typifies the perspective of a film more interested in moralizing than in artistic expression.

This is not to say that *The Magdalene Sisters* lacks narrative force. Strong performances by all of the principals draw as much out of their characters as possible. Bernadette, for example, boldly uses her sexuality in an unsuccessful effort to get the laundry boy to help her escape. At the same time, while she hates the world of the home, she has conflicted feelings about the women with whom she lives. She steals Crispina's Saint Christopher medal, and later vacillates over whether to return it. She ridicules an old inmate who is on the point of death, yet she kisses the forehead of the woman's corpse. Time after time Nora-Jane Noone, the actor portraying Bernadette, through expression, gesture, and intonation, masterfully conveys the girl's abiding fear of growing accustomed to her life in the home.

Anne-Marie Duff gives an equally powerful, though more understated, performance as Margaret. Of the three, she shows the greatest sympathy for others and the greatest sense of the injustice of her situation. In a rare display of unbridled emotion, she tears apart the dormitory to find Crispina's medal, and is flabbergasted when no one seems as shocked as she is by Bernadette's larceny. After she sees Crispina giving oral sex to Father Fitzroy (Daniel Costello), she punishes the priest by putting nettles in his undergarments and enjoys his public humiliation when the itching from the nettles becomes intolerable and he tears off his clothing. Nonetheless, when she has the chance to flee out the back-garden gate, Margaret cannot summon the courage to accept a ride into town from a passing motorist.

Perhaps the most stunning performance, given the simplicity of her character's nature, is Eileen Walsh's portrayal of Crispina. She is a young unwed mother who has never been allowed to have contact with her child. She has been sexually exploited by Father Fitzroy, and generally patronized by everyone around her. Nonetheless, she displays a powerful and touching simplicity of spirit. When, for example, Margaret finds the stolen Saint Christopher medal in Bernadette's things, Crispina does not care that Bernadette stole it, but expresses how happy she feels now that the medal has been restored to her.

Though all of these women endure, none escapes the effect of the asylum. Crispina eventually goes mad, and dies in a mental hospital. Margaret is finally taken out of the institution by her brother, though her resentment of him mirrors the bitterness that has infected her. Rose and Bernadette blackmail Sister Bridget into allowing them to escape, yet they cannot mask their unease even when they are free of the home's control. The epilogue suggests that none of them ever recovers from the experience. However, despite the pain that any sensitive viewer will feel over the girls' sufferings, the film asks little of us but passive condemnation of all we observe.

More to the point, Mullan wastes the stellar performances of his cast to present a narrowly focused and simplistic attack on the Magdalene institutions. As Leanne McCormick has noted in a detailed examination of both the film and of actual Magdalene asylums, the narrative of *The Magdalene Sisters* goes beyond objective reporting or even advocacy to present a reductive account of life in these homes. McCormick is certainly not an apologist for these institutions. However, her article does seek to offer a dispassionate and balanced assessment of the conditions of the facilities and of the administration by the staff in contrast to Mullan's emotionally manipulative presentation of his material.[10]

As the work of Tom Inglis has demonstrated, Irish views on religion have become increasingly fragmented and therefore increasingly difficult to represent on film. Nonetheless, it remains puzzling, with religion, and specifically Catholicism, standing as such an integral element in Irish culture, that more sophisticated examinations of its manifestations and practices have not appeared. Instead, a number of filmmakers have simply truncated imaginative development by employing simplistic archetypal figures to create narrative tension. Aislin Walsh's 2003 film, *Song for a Raggy Boy*, based on Patrick Galvin's factual story, takes this all too familiar approach. It focuses on the lives of boys incarcerated in a Young Offenders' Institution run by a religious order in Cork in the 1930s. The boys face a life of intolerable cruelty, initiated by their losing their identity upon arrival, being thereafter referred to by the numbers assigned to them.

The head of the school, caught between a struggle with his conscience and the orders of his superior, the bishop, is eager for changes in the institution's regime and hires its first lay employee, an English teacher played by Aidan Quinn, who has just returned from fighting on the communist side in the Spanish civil war. From there the story becomes predictable. Quinn's character treats the boys as human beings, and defends them from the sadistic actions of the brothers. A power struggle ensues, which in turn leads to a tragic outcome. Without calling into question the sincerity of this type of motion picture or the justification of its anger over the brutality of such an institution, the fact remains that motion pictures such as *The Raggy Boy* or *The Magdalene Sisters* allow didacticism to overwhelm creativity and in the process erase the role of the viewer.

When filmmakers shift the topic from consideration of the church's institutions to its impact on society—the *habitus* characterizing ordinary life—the emphasis moves to individuals, and the opportunity for a rich representation of the complexity of this condition increases. Arguably, almost any Irish-themed film will reflect this *habitus,* but for this element to affect interpretation it needs direct and extended representation in the narrative. For dramatic purposes, this depiction often focuses on the clash between individuality and community mores, with the emphasis on the intolerance of the group rarely challenging viewers to offer anything more than a programmatic response. However, even with that narrow approach, skillful filmmakers have shown the ability to offer great latitude for viewer interpretation.

The insularity of rural communities, particularly in the period before the push for industrialization in the 1960s, provides a very stable environment for detailed examinations of religious attitudes, and a canny filmmaker can draw on this condition to explore the features and contradictions of the institution. Thaddeus O'Sullivan's *December Bride* scrutinizes that sort of world. Although I have already discussed this motion picture in some detail in Chapter 4, its unique perspective on dissenting Irish Protestants makes it worth revisiting.

December Bride: Andrew (Geoffrey Golden) and Sarah (Saskia Reeves) discuss life on the farm. Courtesy of Donna Walsh and Little Bird Productions.

Though a synopsis of the story gives the appearance of the religious attitudes it explores being presented in a cut-and-dried fashion, O'Sullivan and his actors do a marvelous job of bringing ambiguity into the mix. Andrew Echlin offers a model for the ideal man in this situation—wise, tolerant, self-sacrificing—yet with his early demise, the others can only struggle to approximate his nature. Hamilton and Frank seem less introspective and more inclined to take life as they encounter it, yet they retain a self-confidence that enables them, for the most part, to exist outside their Presbyterian community. Martha has a fierce stubbornness that shows an admirable independence, but her narrow-minded prejudices toward Catholics demonstrate a self-righteousness equal to that of the community she disdains.

Even the supporting characters project a range that disrupts quick and simplistic interpretation. The Reverend Edwin Sorleyson seems at first simply an archetypal prig with no tolerance for alternative views of the world, yet in the scene when he urges Hamilton to marry Martha (and has a lamb urinate on him for his troubles), signs of vulnerability and manifestations of humanity invite the viewer to explore the conflicts within his character. Later, a scene with Martha heightens this representation. In the midst of his remonstrations, Sorleyson becomes aware of Martha's attractiveness and has an epiphany regarding his own sexual appetites that terrifies him. The narrative goes on to show Sorleyson fleeing the community rather than confront the temptation again. In both instances the film portrays the minister neither as sympathetic nor as odious. Rather, it leaves to the audience the task of sorting out his nature, particularly as informed by his religious beliefs.

Therein lies the overall strength of *December Bride,* set in striking contrast to a movie such as *The Magdalene Sisters.* O'Sullivan's motion picture clearly outlines the rigid religious attitudes of the community in contrast with the no less determined if sharply contrasting views of the people living on the Echlin farm. However, it does not take a polemic position regarding either. Though highlighting the flaws of both groups, *December Bride* refuses to deal in the Manichaean perspectives of more simplistic renditions. Instead, it requires the viewers to come to their own sense of the place of established religion in Ireland and to grapple with the implication that it has lost its force in shaping identity and has become instead a superficial cultural marker. (Whether this loss is in fact actually the case in Irish life is not within the scope of the study to debate. What I am asserting is that filmmakers seem increasingly less inclined to see religion as a distinguishing element of Irish identity.)

Whereas *December Bride* shows the wealth of material available to a director who embraces complexity, Sydney Macartny's 2001 motion picture, *A Love Divided,* offers yet another instance in which even excellent acting cannot salvage a narrative demonstrably less inclined to resist the pull of didacticism and stereotyping. Protestant Sheila (Orla Brady) and Catholic Sean Cloney (Liam Cunningham) wed in the '50s in what was then euphemistically called a mixed marriage. As was commonly the case, Sheila promises to raise any children as Catholics. When it comes time for the elder of her two girls to begin her education, Sheila resists the pressure of the local priest, Father Stafford (Tony Doyle), to send her to the Catholic school. Perhaps unsurprisingly, her husband sides with the priest, and in response Sheila flees to Scotland with the children. In retaliation, Father Stafford organizes a boycott of Protestant businesses that gradually escalates to violence. Ultimately, Sheila returns, and she and her husband demand an end to the boycott. The local Catholic bishop intervenes, and Father Stafford must end the boycott and apologize to Sheila for his behavior.

Although the film is based on a true story, that fact in itself cannot justify the simpleminded anti-Catholic bias that blunts the effectiveness of the narrative. Characterizations are black-and-white—violent Catholics and peaceful Protestants—ignoring facts that complicated the moral delineation of the actual case, such as a young Ian Paisley traveling to the South to foment Protestant reaction during the conflict. Though one can readily find examples of religious intolerance in the Catholic Church in Ireland, a slanted account of a situation like this one reduces characters to caricatures, and treats a complex subject with disdain. This type of film misses a wonderful opportunity, as Thaddeus O'Sullivan's *December Bride* shows, to elaborate on the complex demands made by religious belief on both sides and to trust viewers to come to a satisfying interpretation of the action.

Suri Krishnamma's *Man of No Importance,* released in 1994, falls midway between the achievement of *December Bride* and the failure of *A Love Divided.* Like the other motion pictures, it examines a religious ethos of the past. Set in 1963 Dublin, the film follows the life of Alfie Byrne (Albert Finney), a bus conductor who wishes to stage a production of Oscar Wilde's *Salome* in a local church hall using passengers who regularly ride on his bus as the actors. Carney (Michael Gambon), the butcher, does not like being cast as Herod, and he tells Alfie's sister, Lily (Brenda Fricker), that the play is blasphemous.

Whereas Alfie's effort to bring a production of *Salome* to the stage remains the central event moving the narrative forward, the film derives its emotional power from several other complementary narratives. The interplay between Alfie and Adele Rice (Tara Fitzgerald), a pregnant single girl whom Alfie wishes to play Salome, highlights a tolerance counterpointing the bigoted self-righteousness of the overtly religious Carney and Lily. It shows a tender, generous side of Alfie, and gently introduces the concept of his emotional rather than simply highlighting his physical needs. This issue dovetails with the motion picture's examination of Alfie's homosexuality and its implications in Ireland in the early 1960s. He has a crush on Robbie Fay (Rufus Sewell) who drives the bus on which Alfie is a conductor and who is also scheduled to play John the Baptist in Alfie's production. However, the film never makes clear the degree to which Robbie understands and indulges Alfie's feelings.

A Man of No Importance does, however, deftly capture the ambiguity of Alfie's dilemma—a highly principled man whose personal ethics directly confronts public morality—and thoughtfully presents his inability to come to a clear-cut resolution of the issues raised by the narrative. He tries and fails to find a way to help Adele, and, when he realizes that Robbie has a girlfriend, he goes to a gay bar, is beaten up by thugs, and is turned over to his sister by less than sympathetic police officers. At the emotional low point of the film, with his play canceled and feeling shamed by the revelation of his homosexuality, Alfie tries unsuccessfully to drown himself. In a somewhat mechanistic fashion, situations resolve themselves: Adele leaves for England, Carney and Lily cease to be important, and Robbie, who had seemed hostile, is reconciled with Alfie.

The film certainly has its problems, not the least of which is a penchant for showing how clever it is. Its title reworks the name of one of Wilde's plays—*A Woman of No Importance.* Central characters have names out of Wilde's life—Alfie (Lord Alfred Douglas, Wilde's lover); Robbie (Robert Ross, who first seduced Wilde); Bosie (Douglas's nickname); Carson, Alfie's supervisor (Sir Edward Carson, the man who prosecuted Wilde for immoral behavior); and Lily (Lily Langtry, a woman that the young Wilde claimed to adore). The name of Carney, the butcher, a homophone for the Latin word for meat, stands as perhaps the weakest attempt at cleverness. (This cuteness often threatens to turn the narrative into a farce, as when Alfie attempts suicide. He jumps into a canal that is only knee-deep in water, and he has to ask a passing woman to help him out.) Finally, the narrative takes too many lines from Wilde's works, making much of the dialogue seem like an inside joke.

At the same time, the film offers an interesting view of the *habitus* of Dublin in the early 1960s. The narrative does a wonderful job evoking both claustrophobia and naïveté in the responses that Carney and Lily make to Alfie's sexuality. Unfortunately, it never attempts to develop them beyond roles as narrow-minded bigots or to offer some sense of how they came to be that way. Catholicism clearly stands as insufficient for Alfie, Adele, and others, but the reason is never considered.

Sensuality proves an easier topic to develop than morality. In one instance the narrative introduces the phrase "a cuddle," and endows it with a wonderful vagueness. Alfie's close friend, Christy Ward (David Kelly), a widower, uses the term to describe what he most misses about married life, and Alfie, when he finally decides to flaunt his sexual orientation, repeats the phrase in the form of a request to a man at a gay bar. The narrative never makes it clear whether either man means the word to be taken at face-value or uses it as a euphemism for more intimate contact, and such moments of uncertainty underscore the strength of the film.

Most important, although *A Man of No Importance* cannot avoid the simplistic approach to homosexuality that was part of Irish life, and indeed life in many countries, in 1963, the narrative has taken care to make the attitudes of a number of characters ambiguous and possibly ambivalent as well. Alfie may pine for sexual release, or he may simply wish for a kind of emotional intimacy. Robbie's kindness may come from an awareness of Alfie's feelings or simply reflect a good-natured individual with an inability to imagine a homosexual lifestyle. Lily and Carney may each be intolerant bigots, or they may simply be individuals with a simplistic, fearful approach to religion and very limited experience with the world. All in all, *A Man of No Importance* makes good use of a very specific ethos at a very specific time without imposing a narrow or prescriptive response on its viewers.

Perhaps ironically, given the direction of their narratives, the most sympathetic and probing representations of the Irish clergy appear in two complementary films directed by Bob Quinn, *Budawanny* and *The Bishop's Story*. They deal with the loneliness of clerical life while overturning the stereotypical view that associates narrow-mindedness with country folk. In the end, the central character, who appears in both motion pictures, loses his faith, but his attitude represents neither a sweeping condemnation of the Catholic Church nor a reflection of the intolerance of his parishioners. Rather, one sees in the films the incredible emotional demands laid on the clergy, and finds the opportunity to assess that situation without following a prescriptive pattern. (I will offer an extended examination of these motion pictures at the end of this chapter.)

As the concept of *habitus* suggests, as long as religion, for better or for worse, occupies a central position in the ethos of Irish life, traces of it will appear throughout Irish-themed films. A great many key scenes in otherwise nonreligious films have turned on the actions of priests and the beliefs of the Irish people. Perhaps surprising to some are the number of instances in which these scenes depict benevolent or otherwise admirable behavior, and it is useful to point them out if only to dispel simplistic assumptions about an inherent hostility to religion among filmmakers and to clarify the evolution of cinematic attitudes relating to the significance of religion in Irish life. The diminution of such references in recent films, particularly in those movies depicting contemporary life, underscores my assertion of the assumption by filmmakers of the disappearance of religion as a signifying aspect of Irish identity.

One sees very positive references to religion throughout the decades. In the early Kalem Company production *Rory O'More,* the local priest, at the cost of his own life, helps Rory escape hanging. Less perilously, in *The Quiet Man,* Father Lonergin joins the rest of his parishioners in pretending to be a Protestant so that the local Anglican cleric will not be reassigned. In *The Field,* the parish priest (Sean McGinley) is so shocked by the village's complicity in Bull McCabe's murder of the American that he locks the parishioners out of the church. In *Some Mother's Son,* Father Daly (Gerald McSorley), more courageously and certainly taking a more palpable risk, denounces the IRA for politicizing the funerals of Maze Prison Hunger Strikers. Although these examples do not highlight layered representations of complex characters, they remind viewers that the clergy can be represented by a range of attitudes and that attentiveness to them provides insights into the diverse views of the community of the film.

Recently, a number of filmmakers have turned their attention to the flaws that distinguish the Catholic ethos. In *Hush-a-Bye Baby,* the church's views on abortion seem hopelessly intolerant, and certainly add to Goretti's fear and guilt. In *The Butcher Boy,* Brendan Gleeson's portrayal of a good-natured if bumbling priest, Father Bubbles, stands in contrast to

Rory O'More: A British army patrol in pursuit of Rory (Jack J. Clark). Courtesy of the Irish Film Institute.

Milo O'Shea's rendering of the pederast, Father Sullivan. When one adds Sinéad O'Connor's role as the Blessed Virgin Mary in Francie Brady's hallucinations, the variety of representations appears to make religious beliefs anything from ridiculous to dangerous. The gullible curate in *Waking Ned Devine* who takes theology lessons from the child Maurice and is complicit with the rest of the village in swindling the state lotto board comes quite close to seeming like a refugee from the *Father Ted* television series, unselfconsciously underscoring a sense of his own irrelevance.

When considered together, these scenes involving priests and religious illustrate not just the mutability of *habitus* but its increasingly ephemeral quality. It is not simply a matter of giving the clergy varied roles in different motion pictures. These portrayals underscore a movement toward the cinematic marginalization of religion in Ireland. The humanity of these characters highlights the range of personalities who make up the church, and in the best representations it also reminds one of the subjective responses

Hush-a-bye Baby: Goretti (Emer McCourt) and Ciaran
(Michael Liebman) stopped by a British army patrol.
Courtesy of Margo Harkin.

that we each make to Catholicism and its representatives. Increasingly,
however, one sees either in its presence or in its absence assertive views on
the diminishing effect of religion in shaping Irish identity.

A Paradigmatic Reading: *Budawanny* and *The Bishop's Story*

Two connected films directed by Bob Quinn, *Budawanny* and *The Bishop's
Story,* offer a good opportunity for understanding the evolving sense of
the significance of *habitus* and for clarifying a filmmaker's comprehension of both the subjectivity and the general applicability of the force of

contemporary Catholicism on Irish identity. Each motion picture tells the same story with only the frame around the tale shifting. Each depends on a reconciliation of the attitudes toward Catholicism held by the community in the film and by the viewer to shape meaning. And each seems to present the same basic issues without offering a clear-cut resolution. In these motion pictures viewers can see the features of paradigmatic Irish religious narratives, and from that perspective can come to understand the best interpretive approach to the genre.

Indeed, a deceptive redundancy characterizes each narrative, and it provokes the question of why Quinn felt the need to produce such similar motion pictures. Linear reasoning does not offer much help in resolving the issue. However, with an awareness of the inherent subjectivity of interpretations of religious life and of its mutable effect on individuals, one gets a greater sense of the freedom the viewer has in comprehending the events recounted in the films.

Quinn made the first motion picture, *Budawanny*, in 1987. It opens with a bishop (Peadar Lamb) reacting to a copy of a novel that he has recently received, written by one of his priests, Father Thomas Conor (Donal McCann). The book is titled *Budawanny: A Bishop's Tale*. It presents a fictionalized account of Father Conor's experiences as a priest on an island off the Irish coast, and material on the dust jacket indicates that it has already been made into a motion picture.[11]

The film then shifts attention to the central events of the narrative. A young woman, Marian (Maggie Fegan), jumps off the boat on which she is traveling to the island where Father Conor is the parish priest. Before the boat's embarkation, she had inquired whether Father Conor was on the island, and, after her rescue, as a matter of course she is brought to the priest's house to recover. Gradually, Marian regains her strength, and takes on the role of housekeeper. During this period of convalescence it becomes evident that she and Father Conor have had a previous relationship of some sort. Elaborating on this point, Father Conor keeps remembering a time when he and the girl were at a park in London, though the narrative does not make clear their degree of intimacy.

As with Quinn's earlier film *Poitín*, the director uses cinematography deftly to present a number of key issues without taking a polemic position or even pushing viewers toward a particular interpretation. The scenes on the island are in black-and-white and sepia, and they highlight with lingering care its stark landscape. Quinn skillfully contrasts these shots with interpolations in color of the bishop at his residence, surrounded by material comfort, contemplating Father Conor's novel and composing a letter to the priest that offers a response to the latter's struggle with his faith. As in Quinn's previous motion pictures, the director's sure sense of viewer expectations gives him the ability to take an understated approach to evolving complex responses.

Relations with Marian and Father Conor resolve themselves after a fashion when, during a thunderstorm, the girl becomes frightened and runs to the priest's bed. They commit themselves to a physically intimate relationship (which, judging from remarks made by Father Conor the next morning, was apparently the first time he had engaged in sexual intercourse). When Marian becomes pregnant, Father Conor tells the congregation at mass about her condition, and freely acknowledges his responsibility. Generally, the people seem simply to accept matters. However, the sacristan (Tomás Ó Flaithearta), who knew of the affair before anyone else in the village, struggles over how to respond. Feeling no such ambivalent compunctions, the pub keeper (Seán Ó Coisdealbha) reports Father Conor to the bishop, who summons the priest to the bishop's palace for consultation. During Father Conor's absence, Marian leaves the island, and the sacristan hangs himself. As the film ends, the scene reverts to the film's opening. The bishop tears up the letter he has been writing to Father Conor, giving the audience no clear sense of its content, and tells his assistant merely to acknowledge the receipt of Father Conor's book.

The Bishop's Story, which appeared in 1994, reconfigures the original version by changing the framing narrative. This film begins in a monastery with Father Conor, now a bishop and recently returned from the foreign missions, openly admitting to losing his faith. He talks with another priest (Ray McBride) whom church authorities have sent there because of alcoholism and pederasty. Bishop Conor begins to tell the other priest of his experiences on the island, and interpolations punctuating that account make clear to the audience that Bishop Conor now seems to advocate many of the same ideas espoused by the bishop from the previous film.[12]

The dialogue in both of Quinn's motion pictures remains laconic (with intertitles punctuating the scenes on the island), and an aura of tragic inevitability pervades both narratives. The terse interchanges between characters forestall resolution on the film's central issues, and indeed suggest that the exclusionary approach of cause-and-effect logic would produce a reductive perspective. Alternately, the continuing communal significance of religion in Ireland and the individual need to come to some sort of accommodation to it stand as constant imperatives. By reconciling the idea of *habitus* and the concept of subjectivity, one can arrive at a sense of the dynamic tensions that affect not only the priest, Maggie, and the bishop but also the sacristan, the publican, and others in the village.

Further, the parallel between the attitudes of Father Conor and the beliefs of the previous bishop combined with Bishop Conor's admission of a loss of faith call the efficacy of the church as a religious institution into question without going so far as to brand it obsolete. Indeed, the status of religion remains unclear throughout these films, and viewers must decide for themselves whether *Budawanny* and *The Bishop's Story* reflect accounts of the fragility of individual faith or depict an institution undergoing a profound change from religious foundation to cultural artifact. A nonlinear approach allows viewers to sustain both possibilities, leaving the issue of religion's effect on Irish identity open to multiple interpretative possibilities.

More than anything else, the dual narratives encourage us not to assume that an inherent meaning resides in the actions of any of the characters. Father Conor and the bishop, for example, at first appear to be polar opposites, a condition seemingly requiring that a judgment of the nature of one produces the opposite assessment of the other. However, by the end of the first film the bishop has intimated his own loss of faith while at the end of the second Father Conor has adopted the language of the man against whom he seemed to rebel. It does not do simply to say that Father Conor reflects an inevitable movement from resistance to resignation, for the narratives give too much complexity to him and to the bishop to support the idea that intellectual exhaustion stands as the eventual consequence of any rigorous engagement with belief. Nor does it suffice to absolve both as men simply doing their best, for neither shows a willingness to accept such an accommodation. Rather, the skill of Quinn's direction and the mercurial character of *habitus* make it far more logical to accept one's ability to impose an admittedly transient, though no less valid for it, meaning on the actions of these and the other characters as well as on the two narratives every time one sees these motion pictures.

The bishop, Father Conor, Marian, and the others have their characters delineated according to the perspective that the individual viewer brings to the film. The intervention of the observer changes the dynamics of the story, and this presence creates a unique form of interpretation with each viewing. Characters come to life through us, and consequently the unique perspective that each of us brings to the film informs the identities of the individuals encountered in it.

With this notion in mind, as in other imaginatively satisfying films, Burke's "tolerance for disunities" creates a richer sense of the narrative, and it also highlights the shifting ability of religion to imprint Irish identity on a motion picture. Although the puritanical streak in Irish Catholicism may well be evident in *Budawanny* and *The Bishop's Story,* so also are the impulses toward charity and forgiveness that pervade these motion pictures, seemingly at odds with the authoritarian representations of the church. The sacristan's struggle with his convictions and the reliance of the villagers on prayer while searching for a young retarded girl who has become lost underscore the concerns of the narrative as going well beyond simply a tale of a priest's loss of faith. They stand as testimonials to the varieties of belief that grow out of the Irish religious tradition, and they invite viewers to come to their own conclusions about their efficacy. A rush to impose exclusionary meaning on any of these aspects of the narratives simply moves toward a reductive view that gives short shrift to the achievement of the narratives and to the implicit interpretive compact that Quinn makes with his viewers.

Recent directors have not shown Quinn's sophisticated awareness of the relation of religion to the Irish sense of self. Nonetheless, religion remains one of the most mercurial markers of Irish identity employed by contemporary filmmakers. As seen in a number of examples adduced in this chapter, for some religion in general and Catholicism in particular have assumed an anachronistic function in Irish life, evocative of habits of the past but no longer a significant feature in a modern consciousness. For others, religion retains a strong, if at times corrosive, hold on the Irish and on their sense of self. For viewers, these diverse attitudes heighten the subjectivity of each cinematic encounter with religion. As will be seen in the next chapter, when Irish-themed films of the late twentieth century combine both religion and politics, the former seems to lose all its theological significance and metamorphosizes into a strictly social marker.

7

The Struggle for Independence
in Irish Political Films

Of all of the social forces shaping individual identity—family, religion, class, place of residence—the casual observer might see the political milieu as the one most easily defined, most predictably characterized, and most indicative of a specific group. In addition to bearing the distinctive stamp of the local community, political ideas and relationships are freely and broadly disseminated so that a wide spectrum of society has access to the ostensible central concerns of specific parties and factions. Despite the complex human relations that inform political associations, such organizations insistently reiterate their views in speeches and position papers, and the accounts of their successes and failures quickly become matters of public record. Political movements articulate core beliefs in speeches and editorials that attract loyal adherents. They measure their accomplishments by the concrete results at the polls and in legislative bodies. And they shape and in turn are shaped by the world in which they exist. Former Speaker of the United States House of Representatives Thomas "Tip" O'Neill once famously said that "all politics are local." With Speaker O'Neill's admonition in mind, one might readily assume that motion pictures dealing with political events in Ireland should provide the clearest indication of the nature of Irishness of any of the institutions examined in this study.[1]

As with other Irish institutions, however, the human element tempers the perception of conditions, and political opinions express themselves as subjectively and idiosyncratically as the manifestations of any other points of view. In fact, in any careful examination the all too apparent disparities between public pronouncements and personal agendas quickly come

193

to the foreground, and they preclude the possibility of an objective sense of the Irish nature emerging from cinematic examination of the political establishment. Even if one were to take the highly dubious position of assuming that the general behavior of political parties (like Fianna Fáil or Fine Gael) or political beliefs (like Unionism or Republicanism) conformed to the unambiguous delineations found in party platforms or election materials, in fact individuals' conceptions of political attitudes, political influence, and political awareness create a number of extraordinarily different impressions of the political institutions of Ireland.[2] Beyond the attitudes that one brings to the political arena, the events that define political movements—success or failure in armed struggles, victory or defeat in elections, the rise or fall of popular ideologies—certainly remain open to a variety of interpretations dependent on the perceptions of the individual who endeavors to explain them.

Ireland's long experience as an occupied country further complicates efforts to understand this condition. From the waves of invasions that began in the pre-Christian era until the English surrender of Dublin Castle on January 16, 1922, periodic bloody confrontations between native and colonizing forces have characterized the country's development. (And, of course, the partition of the North ensured that sectarian violence would continue until the Good Friday Accord of April 10, 1998.)

Filmmakers, both indigenous and foreign, have found these clashes fascinating, and have used many of them as the basis of feature-length motion pictures. In such films, one finds a close association of national identity and physical force accompanied by the suggestion, increasingly evident though not directly articulated in recent films, that without the catalyst of colonialism or neocolonialism to provoke violence, nationalism and a sense of self through nationalism rapidly disappear.[3] Not surprisingly, these projects evoke emotional, ideological, and cultural responses that often feature visceral and polarized perspectives. Consequently, because of the inherently subjective quality of the topic, Irish-themed political motion pictures, if anything, demand much greater viewer involvement and cry out for more pluralism in one's readings than do films in many of the other genres.

As I will demonstrate later in the chapter, contemporary historical events have provided ample opportunities for rich, digressive narratives of the conflict in the North, but the evocativeness of motion pictures examining contemporary issues has had a retrospective effect as well. (They also raise the question, referenced in the extended interpretation of *Michael Collins* at the end of the chapter, of whether an Irish political identity can exist outside examinations of the violent clashes between those individuals willing to use physical force to forward an ideology.) Focusing attention on the ambiguous moral, cultural, and social positions of individuals and groups involved in the current political struggle has raised the interpretive possibility that representations of earlier political conflicts, long considered clear-cut, in fact turn on antinomian propositions. By the same token, graphic portrayals of the violence characterizing the Troubles of the 1970s, '80s, and '90s, have eroded the political credentials of many of the participants, often obscuring ideological beliefs and evoking parallels between these figures and common criminals, Irish or otherwise. In consequence, the most seemingly straightforward of films can require the greatest imaginative engagement, demanding that viewers avoid the sentimental or emotional manipulation often imbedded, intentionally or not, in accounts of great historical struggles.

That is not to suggest that political films generally take the form of national propaganda. The best foreign and indigenous filmmakers have demonstrated a sophisticated awareness of the potential for imaginative range inherent in politically themed films. From the first productions, the most enduring works in this group never equated ideology with a simplistic worldview, and critics who assume that complexity appeared only with the technical evolution of the Irish film industry miss the point of some of the earliest productions. Indeed, the issues shaping the construction of politically themed films, no matter when they appeared, have consistently pointed up the need for nonexclusionary interpretations.

One of the first, for example, *Rory O'More,* a film made in 1911 by the American-based Kalem Company and set during the turbulence of 1798–1803, does a fine job exploring the gradations of conflict within a politicized society. Black William (Robert G. Vignola), an informer, has told British soldiers of the whereabouts of the title character, an Irish rebel with a price on his head. While making his escape by swimming across a lake, Rory (Jack J. Clark) stops to save a drowning soldier. This act of compassion results in Rory's capture, but the British officer (J. P. McGowan) in charge of the forces who have been pursuing Rory wishes to let him go as a recompense for his kindness. However, Black William, greedy for his reward, demands that Rory be taken in for execution. In the climactic scene, the parish priest, Father O'Brien (Arthur Donaldson), helps Rory escape from the scaffold, but is shot in the process. During the turmoil, Rory makes his way to a waiting boat where, joined by his beloved, Kathleen (Gene Gauntier), he sails away to America.

This seemingly straightforward narrative in fact raises several interpretive problems that will recur time and again in subsequent political films, beginning with the story subtly obscuring what code of conduct governs combatants. If, as suggested by Rory's behavior toward the drowning solider, ethical standards remain the same for military men as for noncombatants, then the validity of violence as an alternative form of action comes into question. How can one save a man whom one might have killed in other circumstances without negating the code that seemingly governs one's behavior? On the other hand, if we condemn the death of the priest, shot while freeing Rory, as a brutal manifestation of force over reason, we need as well consider the legitimacy of the acts of the rebels who also employ violence in an effort to enforce their beliefs.

Additionally, the film concludes in an ambiguous fashion as Rory and Kathleen leave Ireland. Since the mendacious traitor, Black William, profited and the heroic priest, Father O'Brien, suffered, one might legitimately wonder if flight remains the logical response to political violence. Of course, if that conclusion is right, the seeming happy ending of the film becomes bittersweet at best, and the legitimacy of physical force comes into question. In fact, one does not come to a clearer understanding of *Rory O'More* by resolving these antinomies but rather by seeing them working in tension as a means of enhancing the viewer's sense of the inherently conflicted nature of political action.

Ambiguity certainly did not dominate all politically oriented motion pictures released during this period. American companies also made *Robert Emmet* (1911) and *Ireland a Nation* (1914). Both chronicled the efforts of Robert Emmet, and seemed to draw clear distinctions between right and wrong, noble and ignoble, as if the accounts they presented were not open

to interpretation. Irish filmmakers offered a more oblique but no less assertive political perspectives in producing *Knocknagow* (1918), dealing with
land trouble and emigration during the famine period; *In the Days of St. Patrick* (1920), celebrating the change Christianity brought to the island; and
Willy Reilly and His Colleen Bawn (1920), detailing the difficulties that could
arise over a proposed upper-class Catholic and Protestant marriage in the
eighteenth century. In every case, filmmakers tended to elide ambiguities
and ambivalences, and downplay the possibility of alternative readings.
Nonetheless, as with *Rory O'More,* the complexities inherent in the political
contexts of these films allow sophisticated viewers to resist the closure of
dominant interpretations in favor of sustaining diverse responses.

In the decade immediately following the end of the Civil War, the narrative focus of Irish-themed political films shifted to contemporary events.
In 1926 an indigenous production company made *Irish Destiny.* Set between
mid-1920, at the height of the War of Independence, and the Truce of 1921,
the film traces the love affair of Denis O'Hara (Paddy Dunne Cullinan)
and his fiancée, Moira Barry (Frances MacNamara), as they cope with
the political forces reshaping the world around them. After the Black and
Tans terrorize the village of Clonmore, Denis joins the IRA. He is shot
and captured during a Black and Tan raid on Vaughan's Hotel in Dublin.
(Vaughan's is the name of the hotel that was actually used by Michael Collins and his men as a base of operations during the War of Independence.)
British authorities incarcerate Denis at the Curragh Camp, but, with the
film incorporating a dramatic historical event from the War of Independence into its narrative, viewers see images of him escaping with a large
group of prisoners of war. In a burst of melodramatic action, Denis returns
to Clonmore in time to rescue Moira, who has been kidnapped by the
poitín maker, Gilbert Beecher (Brian Magowan). *Irish Destiny* then shifts
from personal back to national issues, ending with the announcement of
the Anglo-Irish truce.

Through a striking cinematic amalgamation of actual and fictional
events, George Dewhurst, the director of *Irish Destiny,* raises formal interpretive issues (unlike the emphasis on thematic concerns dominating most
of the other films in this genre) by punctuating the narrative action with
incidents from the war with the British shown through actual newsreel

Irish Destiny: A tender moment between Moira (Frances MacNamara) and Denis (Paddy Dunne Cullinan). Courtesy of the Irish Film Institute.

clips. These footage include training exercises of Black and Tan auxiliaries, the burning of Cork City on December 11, 1920, the attack on the Dublin Customs House on May 25, 1921, and the aforementioned mass escape from the Curragh Camp on September 9, 1921. Intentionally or not, these interpolations provide an important measure of interpretive flexibility in an otherwise programmatic film. Resolving the significance of this juxtaposition of the real and the fictional stands as just one of the analytic challenges facing viewers, but it very neatly illustrates the larger problem of perspective that jeopardizes the integrity of any historically based political film.

Though no one disputes these events from the War of Independence, their contextualization within the fictional accounts of *Irish Destiny* raises questions regarding examinations of the political issues that surround them. Indubitably, the newsreel footage shapes the viewer's impressions of the rest of the film, but its impact stands open to interpretation. For linear criticism, legitimacy becomes a prime concern: are the film's aesthetic moments compromised by this incorporation of journalistic accounts, or do the events from the newsreel clips lose their authenticity in the context of a fictive presentation?

Resolving these issues by picking one alternative or the other truncates a good deal of imaginative engagement. Instead, just as the motion picture self-consciously crosses genres, a reading of the film that sustains the validity of both the fictive and the factual images creates a commentary on both. It simultaneously draws attention to narrative impulses toward propaganda and romanticism, and in doing so it forestalls the closure that privileging either would impose. Instead, the film's form invites one to remain open to the multiplicity of the vexed relationship of violence, history, and art that comes out of accounts of the War of Independence.

Most films in this category, however, follow less ambitious formal approaches, highlighting content instead. Two motion pictures released in 1935 wonderfully illustrate the power of this perspective, underscoring the variable articulations of the place of violence in Irish political films. John Ford's film *The Informer* explores the clash of individual and political loyalties and the personal consequences of public actions. During the War of Independence, Gypo Nolan (Victor McLaglen), tempted by a twenty-pound reward, betrays one of his IRA friends, Frankie McPhillip (Wallace Ford), to the Black and Tans. He wants to use the money to leave Ireland with his prostitute girlfriend, Katie Madden (Margot Grahame). The British kill Frankie during an attempt to arrest him, and Gypo wanders around Dublin plagued by guilt until IRA men apprehend him. After a summary trial, the IRA condemns Gypo to death. He escapes, but his pursuers shoot him while he is confessing his betrayal to Frankie's mother (Una O'Connor) and begging her for forgiveness.

Guests of the Nation, produced and directed by Irish playwright Denis Johnston, records the personal effect of a retaliatory killing justified by political necessity. A pair of British soldiers are being held by the IRA under threat of death if two IRA men in British custody are executed. Over the course of their imprisonment, the soldiers become friendly with their captors. When the British put the IRA men to death, the soldiers are taken out to be shot. One stoically dons a blindfold, while the other pleads for mercy. Both lose their lives. After killing the men, their former captors return to the cottage where the prisoners had been detained and sit in silent dejection.

In these films the consequences of violence stand out quite clearly, but in each the motivations and the justifications remain troubling and problematic. This ambiguity in turn undermines the integrity of nationalism as a defining factor in identity. *The Informer* presents the ideological integrity of both the IRA and the British troops as a given, yet individual behavior invites careful scrutiny. Gypo Nolan has acted in a way that led to the loss of his friend's life, and as a result Gypo experiences a paralyzing if poorly articulated guilt. In contrast, the British who kill Frankie and the IRA men who eventually take Gypo's life evince no remorse or regret over their behavior. They seem to feel bound to a code of conduct, never openly articulated in the film, which absolves them of responsibility for their actions in a way that Gypo can neither understand nor accept. Interpretations of the motion picture need not make the choice on whether to validate either Gypo or the other violent men. Quite the contrary, the most effective responses hold their behavior in tension as a means of capturing the conflicted values of the world they inhabit.

In *Guests of the Nation,* the violence produces even more chilling responses as it takes on a formidable, if disembodied, role in the action. Once events set in motion the possibility of the captured IRA men and the British soldiers losing their lives, the seeming inability of any individual to forestall these consequences raises the issue of a perverse repudiation of responsibility and hence the suggestion that even those men who take lives become victims in a larger sense. Passing exclusionary judgment on any of these characters imposes a false resolution through the presumption of moral closure. The narrative sustains a sense of ambivalence surrounding its violence, and leaves viewers to reconcile the diverse forces it outlines.

Not surprisingly, personal and public attitudes foreground even greater ambiguities. In *The Informer* and *Guests of the Nation* one finds the guilt that these men bear tied directly to the violence they perpetuate. At the same time, the way that a viewer judges the consequences of their actions remains very much a matter of the cultural and historical perspectives that one brings to the events depicted in these films. The use of violence and the failure of certain individuals to respond to the moral implications of that course of action challenge the viewer's understanding of the relation between culpability and cultural identity in each film, yet resolving the conflict misses the point of both.

Ambiguities surrounding assignment of guilt make powerful state-ments about the dehumanizing effect of violence, and they function inte-grally within the narratives. Judging one as appropriate and the other as inappropriate because of a linear historical perspective threatens to trivi-alize the moral dilemma being dramatized. These films take the colonial experience seriously, and pay it the compliment of representing its com-plexity fully. In the process, they underscore the way ideological violence enforces identity without clearly delineating it.

In contrast to *Irish Destiny*, where assessment turns on the way one per-ceives the formal structure of the Irish images in the film, these motion pictures offer sophisticated contextual problems. They confront viewers with ideologies, political allegiances, and moral values that seem mutu-ally exclusive. At the same time, sustaining the multiplicity informing view-ers' responses becomes an imperative for comprehension. Any number of defensible ethical positions could serve as guidelines for interpretation. The historical context of these films remains a crucial element to under-standing them. However, adopting a single position based on the commit-ment to one set of beliefs over another truncates the aesthetic experience and trivializes the conflict. These political conditions challenge the partic-ipants because seemingly obvious answers do not exist. Replicating this sit-uation in a film's narrative enhances rather than obscures understanding.

Coincidental to the release of these complex films, a handful of sim-plistic political motion pictures appeared, and they are worth noting both because they underscore the profoundness of the other films and because they presage an approach, much more evident in the past few decades, of filmmakers effacing the ideologically complex and diverse features of political films in favor of reductive, universalizing narratives. *The Key,* made in 1934, is an American motion picture that uses the War of Independence as a backdrop for a love triangle. The movie represents the IRA as little more than a gangster organization and a foil for William Powell's devil-may-care behavior as a Canadian officer, Captain Bill Tennant, serving in the British army. Another American-made motion picture, *Beloved Enemy* (1936), offers a highly fictionalized version of the life of Michael Collins. Like *The Key,* it centers on the love story of Helen Drummond (Merle Oberon), daughter of the British envoy to Ireland, and Dennis Riordan (Brian Aherne), leader of the rebels, with the War of Independence as little more than a backdrop. Both movies offer sanitized views of British behavior, and take up admonishing attitudes toward Irish truculence.

In slight contrast, the Irish-made film *The Dawn,* released in 1936, does evince some awareness of the political events of the period, but it presents them primarily as a catalyst for a broad examination of fundamental human impulses. Rather than engage the complexities of the War of Independence, the film turns on the personal drama of loyalty and the price a decent human being must pay to serve his country. Brian Malone (Brian O'Sullivan) is the grandson of a man who was unfairly labeled an informer. Brian feels wounded by the accusations made against his grandfather, and when he is expelled from the IRA he joins the Royal Irish Constabulary. His alliance with imperialism proves short-lived, however. After Malone sees the Black and Tans execute an IRA man, he joints an assault against them. During the fighting, Malone's brother Billy (Donal O'Cahill), who had seemed to be an English sympathizer, is killed, and Malone learns that Billy has served as an IRA intelligence office. The narrative depicts the Black and Tans and the Royal Irish Constabulary as little more than collections of brutes, and portrays the IRA as behaving without fail as noble patriots.

With clear assertions of the shaping influence of historical conditions, *The Informer* and *Guests of the Nation* seek to engage the often conflicted psychological impact of political violence on the individuals involved, forcing viewers to reexamine assumptions about justifiable responses to imperialism. The other motion pictures noted above are weighted down with either didacticism or melodrama. *The Key* and *Beloved Enemy* trivialize and denigrate the War of Independence, whereas *Irish Destiny* and *The Dawn* idealize it. However, taken together they provide several insights into the way politics is represented during one period of Irish-themed films.

With the violence of the War of Independence and the Civil War still very much a part of the national consciousness, the majority of filmmakers and viewers in the 1930s seemed more drawn to narratives of the conflict made less painful by romanticizing or valorizing it. Although the aesthetic worth of such works seems highly questionable, it is useful to note them, for they mark an inevitable stage in the development of political films. These approaches provide a secure way of seeing recent history, asserting purposefulness to the suffering at the expense of reducing the events to Manichaean moralistic tales.

As will be evident when films about the recent Troubles in the North are discussed, a similar strategy still obtains. Though representations of the contemporary conflict have a good deal more grittiness, the same tone of moral absolutism informs many of the less imaginative narratives, even as it works often unintentionally to undermine political identities. Right and wrong and good and evil seem clearly delineated, but the beliefs upon which actions are presumably founded remain as ambiguous in current politically drawn motion pictures as in many of the films of the 1930s.

In the interim, filmmaking turned its attention to assessments, generally apolitical, of the psyche of an individual caught up in the struggle. In 1947 the motion picture *Odd Man Out,* directed by Carol Reed, appeared, with an approach that tended to efface the significance of specific beliefs and focus instead on the struggle between the individual and the organization. Set in post–World War II Belfast, its narrative follows Johnny McQueen (James Mason), an IRA man on the run, as he attempts to break free of the cycle of violence in which he has immersed himself. The British soldiers and police in this case function as little more than the near-anonymous authority with which Johnny must contend. The film devotes its attention to the diminished range of alternatives open to a man of committed political ideals who finds that there is a limit to what he will do to

implement them. The conflict comes from the by now familiar realization
that extricating oneself from such a situation proves to be far more difficult than becoming involved in it had been.

Odd Man Out evinces a tone similar to what one finds in *The Informer*
and *Guests of the Nation*. They all examine the consequences of political violence on individuals. Its effects eclipse the upshot of ordinary domestic or
local mayhem that one finds in many Irish films, and it springs from causes
that go well beyond individual psychoses or can be explained by gross generalizations about the nature of a particular group. Nonetheless, as Irish
film critic John Hill has noted, making specific reference to *Odd Man Out*,
efforts ostensibly aimed at studying the impact of politically inspired violence on individuals have often led to generalizations, producing gross distortions of character traits inherent in the nature of the Irish people while
giving little or no attention to the social forces that led to such behavior.
In this critique, Hill highlights the need for complexity in films seeking
to present accurate portrayals of the Irish condition. "What British films
about Ireland maintain is not simply the traditional inclination to portray
the Irish as violent but also the inability to provide a rational explanation
for the occurrence of violence. Two main attitudes towards violence pre-
dominate. In the first case, violence is attributed to fate or destiny; in the
second, to the deficiencies of the Irish character. Both attitudes share an
avoidance of social and political questions. It is only metaphysics or race,
not history and politics, which offer an explanation of Irish violence."[4]

Hill has clearly pinpointed the weaknesses of many nonindigenous
motion pictures. Admittedly, by arguing that British and American films
dealing with political violence in Ireland "are by their nature inimical to
social and political explanations of *any* human actions," Hill shows himself
prone to the sort of sweeping generalization that he effectively condemns.
Nonetheless, he accurately underscores a universalizing impulse by no
means exclusive to Reed's film when he points out that a movie like *Odd
Man Out* "evacuates socio-historical determinants by pushing towards a
level of abstraction where the explanation of human actions can only be in
terms of the metaphysical operation of fate and destiny."[5] I think that Hill
rightly identifies an important trend—an unwillingness to grapple with
messy political issues—and he certainly is correct in noting a simplistic

tone in some other Irish-themed political motion pictures, though one can find that inclination amply manifested in the work of indigenous as well as foreign filmmakers. In either case, *Odd Man Out* established the pattern—a detailed examination of an individual caught up in large political events— that would continue in Irish political films for nearly fifty years.

The narrative presents Johnny McQueen as a tortured figure, a victim who still retains the traits of a victimizer. *Odd Man Out,* without highlighting causal forces, foregrounds the complexity of the impulse toward physical force linking the individual and the community inextricably. Violence remains the key to the film, but it resists a dichotomous explanation. Rather, though it dominates behavior, it functions outside clear moral guidelines. However, because the motion picture resists exploring the political context in which it is set, it can do no more than presage the issues that will dominate a film like *Michael Collins.*

In numerous instances viewers see that violent behavior affects Johnny deeply, yet rather than coming to any understanding of the condition the narrative gives itself over to despair. In the end Johnny and Kathleen Sullivan (Kathleen Ryan), who joins him as he attempts to flee, commit themselves to physical force as fully as do the British troops who eventually shoot them down. Understanding *Odd Man Out* does not mean privileging the brutality of one side or one group of individuals over another. Quite the contrary, it demands a comprehension of the acceptance of violence by strikingly different characters without in turn endorsing their approach.

In this fashion, *Odd Man Out* implicitly requires consideration of the environment from which Johnny emerged. The film may not address social and political questions as directly as Hill wishes, but it nevertheless raises questions about them through the need to comprehend Johnny's motives. Irish history, with all its contradictions, becomes the unvoiced topic of the film. For another forty years, however, that approach would stand as an exception to the narrative inclinations of many of the less imaginatively ambitious films that followed *Odd Man Out.*[6]

Certainly, filmmakers bear direct responsibility for this reductiveness. Time and again in their work evasion remains an issue. In a range of motion pictures—English, American, and Irish—made from the 1950s through the 1980s directors focus on the strain and conflict felt by people

willingly or unwillingly drawn into violent political action, and use sentimentality to deflect attention from the political circumstances that inform
their actions. The sympathies of the films vary, but the sense of the single
character trapped by fate, as John Hill has noted, turns motion pictures
in this genre into melodramas. In the few instances that take a broader
political point of view, one often finds the theme compromised by a single
perspective—Brits behaving badly or psychotics in the paramilitaries. All
of it makes political identity as stereotypical a trait as the stage Irishness of
eighteenth- and nineteenth-century dramas.

One sees the pattern of intense examinations of individual impulses
and the relative lack of concern for broader political motivations amply
illustrated in the 1959 film *Shake Hands with the Devil*. During the War
of Independence a young Irish American, Kerry O'Shea (Don Murray),
is going to medical school in Dublin. A friend and fellow student, Paddy
Nolan (Ray McAnally), is involved with the IRA. One night, Kerry and
Paddy are caught in a cross fire between British soldiers and IRA fight-
ers. Paddy is wounded while attending to a fallen IRA man. Kerry takes
his friend to the home of an IRA sympathizer, and Paddy asks to have
Sean Lenihan (James Cagney), one of their medical school teachers,
brought in to treat him. The narrative quickly reveals that Lenihan is an
IRA commander. He cannot save Paddy's life, and Kerry, whose passport
had fallen from his pocket during the incident, must go on the run. When
Lady Fitzhugh (Sybil Thorndike), an IRA sympathizer, is arrested, the IRA
kidnaps Jennifer Curtis (Dana Wynter), the daughter of the military gover-
nor, Sir Anthony Fielding (Clive Morton). To redress past wrongs, the IRA
ambushes Colonel Smithson (Christopher Rhodes), leader of the Black
and Tans, but when a truce is declared shortly after Lady Fitzhugh dies in
custody, Lenihan decides, despite news of a peace treaty negotiated in London, to go ahead with previous plans to kill Mrs. Curtis. Kerry has fallen in
love with her, and defends her, killing Lenihan.

Like any number of films in this genre, *Shake Hands with the Devil*
depends on sharp psychological differences to make its points, and, like
a number of films already critiqued, romanticism produces reductive perspectives in the narrative, denigrating without analyzing ideological points
of view. The love between Kerry and Jennifer both contrasts and condemns

the fanaticism of Lenihan. Their attraction shows that higher human emotions can overcome political differences, but such a representation too easily degenerates into simplistic sentimentality. Further, the disparity between love and brutality quickly forecloses the complicated question of how politically inspired violence threatens the humanity of the perpetrators. Lenihan is puritanical and sexually repressed, whereas Kerry takes a humanitarian view, advocating tolerance and forgiveness. There is no effort made to explore the area between such positions and certainly no attempt to examine the attitudes of the occupying British.

At the same time, *Shake Hands with the Devil*, from its title onward, sporadically suggests complexity and even ambivalence in a range of its characters. It certainly does not go as far in its exploration of violence as later films such as *Michael Collins*, nor does it engage the contrasting political positions with any level of sophistication. However, in scenes like the one in which a Collins-like figure called only the General (Michael Redgrave) makes clear that no one can leave the IRA alive, *Shake Hands with the Devil* rejects any impulse to mythologize the fight for independence.

An even less psychologically complex film, *A Terrible Beauty*, appeared a year later. The narrative focuses on the ambivalence that Dermot O'Neill (Robert Mitchum) feels as a member of an IRA unit operating against the British in rural Derry during World War II. The women in the story disapprove of the violence, while the men believe it is necessary. The IRA alliance with Nazi Germany undermines its moral authority, and the organization's unwillingness to attempt to free one of their own (Richard Harris) captured by the British causes Dermot to break with them and turn informer. In the end he flees to England with his girlfriend, Neeve (Anne Heywood).

A Terrible Beauty takes up many of the same issues examined in *Odd Man Out*. However, it fails to engage any at more than a superficial level. The film portrays the IRA as little more than gangsters, and it gives no real consideration to the problem of allying oneself with a regime like the Nazis. In the end, like *Shake Hands with the Devil*, it relies on a love interest to facilitate plot resolution.

Over the next twenty years, filmmakers made relatively little reference to political conditions, either retrospective or contemporary. (*Ryan's Daughter*, the 1970 film set during the War of Independence, is arguably a rural romance rather than a political motion picture.) Then, a decade after the civil rights struggle in the North had begun, the topic of political violence returned to the Irish cinema, but initial examinations blunted its ideological aspects. In 1979 *The Long Good Friday* chronicles the struggles of a London mobster (Bob Hoskins) with the IRA, and in Neil Jordan's 1982 directing debut, *Angel*, Stephen Rea portrays a musician determined to take revenge against Loyalist paramilitaries who in fact behave as little more than extortionists and murders. In both instances, the motion pictures presented the antagonists as involved in something more like gangland wars than political conflicts. From the mid-1980s, however, a number of films began to engage the complexities of Irish political attitudes in a way that had not previously been considered. The most successful of these motion pictures highlight the conflicted natures of their protagonists, and all inextricably link a political identity with the violence or threat of violence associated with colonialism.

Pat Murphy's *Anne Devlin*, one of several motion pictures discussed here that have been mentioned in the Introduction, appeared in 1984, and it challenged a great many of the verities that had characterized previous political films. The story focuses on the travails of the title character (Brid Brennan), a member of a Catholic family of republican activists. *Anne Devlin* shows how their nationalist activity brings them into association with Robert Emmet (Bosco Hogan), an upper-class Protestant determined to revive the revolutionary spirit that had been suppressed by Irish defeat in the Rising of 1798. To provide cover for the plotters, Anne goes to Emmet's home to pose as a servant, and is soon treated as such. The British quickly put down Emmet's rebellion of 1803, and Anne is incarcerated for a period long after Emmet's execution and the freeing of other prisoners.

Anne Devlin broadens the usual scope of political films by deftly examining how Irish conceptions of class and gender undermine the lofty principles of political equality. The narrative does not attempt to impose anachronistic perspectives on the central characters. Rather, it challenges us to reconcile Anne's compromised status both as a prisoner and as a woman with the ideals articulated by characters in the film and of viewers who come to the motion picture with expectations about the nature of Emmet and the other conspirators.

Anne Devlin: Robert Emmet (Bosco Hogan) and Anne (Brid Brennan). Courtesy of Pat Murphy.

The point is not simply to discredit men but rather to cause viewers to consider the complexity and contradictions that informed even the most idealistic political gestures. Indeed, a full understanding of Anne's character requires interpreters to sustain a sense of the revolutionary ideas that gave her strength in tension with her awareness of the profound contradictions that arose from the behavior the men who carried out the revolution. This dual perspective illuminates incidents such as her willingness to endure the insensitivity of her fellow partisans and her determination to remain silent in the face of brutal interrogation even after Emmet has urged her to be forthcoming. *Anne Devlin* very clearly illustrates the impact of political beliefs on Irish identity, but it also sets up implicitly the necessary presence of countervailing attitudes in the form of a colonial presence and masculine intransigence to vivify those beliefs. As noted in the Introduction, Murphy's *Maeve,* made three years earlier, considers many of the

Maeve: Maeve (Mary Jackson), her mother (Trudy Kelly), and her sister (Brid Brennan) on the Giant's Causeway. Courtesy of Pat Murphy.

same issues, but gives emphasis to the domestic rather than the political perspective.

In the same year, Pat O'Connor made *Cal,* a motion picture set in contemporary Belfast that focuses on the life of the title character, the nineteen-year-old Catholic Cal MacCluskie (John Lynch), a young man marginally involved with the republican movement as the reluctant driver in an IRA killing of a Royal Ulster Constabulary man. Cal lives with his father, Shamie (Donal McCann), in a housing development that is now largely Protestant. Loyalists harass them, but the two refuse to move until they are burned out. Subsequently, Cal, who has been working, coincidentally, at the farm owned by the parents of the man for whose murder he is an accessory, begins to squat in one of the outbuildings rather than return to the city every night. Cal eventually becomes emotionally and physically involved with the dead man's widow, Marcella Morton (Helen Mirren), who knows nothing of Cal's political connections. His IRA friends try to draw him into another IRA plot. When they are killed, Cal escapes, confesses to Marcella his part in her husband's murder, and then is apprehended by the authorities.

In contrast to *Anne Devlin,* a film in which a sophisticated if unvoiced sense of political commitment overshadows everything, *Cal* highlights the consequences that come from ideological ambivalence. At the same time, it too makes a powerful statement about how physical force informs Irish identity. Its narrative constructs contrasting societies—loyalist, Republican, and those Protestants and Catholics who feel no great allegiance to sectarian designations—living side by side. As in many films in this category, appreciation of the motion picture does not necessitate a choice between political principles. Indeed, the fully committed ideologues—both Catholic and Protestant—lack real character definition. It is, rather, figures like Cal and Marcella, individuals uneasy with any absolute political position, who demand our attention to the range of alternatives that they choose to countenance. In this fashion, comprehending the dynamics that propel the action of the movie requires one to hold the diverse views in suspension, seeing each as part of a chaotic universe without privileging or denying any.

Mike Leigh's *Four Days in July* also appeared in 1984, and it presents an equally powerful if profoundly detached examination of the impact of political violence on ordinary Belfast residents. The film follows the parallel lives of a Catholic family and a Protestant family from the tenth through the thirteenth of July. Both wives (Paula Hamilton and Brid Brennan) are pregnant, and they both give birth on the twelfth, coincidental with the date, widely celebrated by Protestants in the North, of the Battle of the Boyne, the July 12, 1690, which marks defeat of the forces of James II by those of William III. Billy (Charles Lawson), the edgy husband in the Protestant family, serves in the army, and the narrative follows him on patrol, at Orange Order parades, and with his wife at a loyalist bonfire. Eugene (Des McAleer), the Catholic husband, has been wounded three times in separate paramilitary attacks, and is now disabled. Although he takes a much gentler approach to his wife, he remains as paternalistic as Billy. The film ends in the maternity hospital with the women in adjacent beds realizing the religion of the other just through the names they have given their children: Billy and Máiréad.

Like *Cal, Four Days in July* is set in the North, but it offers a subtler though no less powerful manifestation of the corroding effect that sectarian violence has on human behavior. There is no clearly defined villain in Leigh's film, and violence is all referential, rather than overt. As with *Cal,* one can detect signs of victimization in many of the individuals, but to label them as victims reduces their natures to slogans. *Four Days in July* captures the humanity, the flaws as well as the strengths, of all of the characters, and they wonderfully convey the amalgamation of feelings and the complexity of identities engendered by the struggles in the North.

Despite some rather melodramatic political films that followed—*Fools of Fortune* made in 1990 and *The Last September* in 1999 bracket the era—the 1990s produced a range of important examinations of the individual's role in political violence. *Hidden Agenda* (1990) follows the frustrations of an American lawyer, Ingrid Jessner (Frances McDormand), trying to learn the truth about the death of her peace-activist lover. *High Boot Benny* (1993) questions the possibility of anyone remaining aloof in a violent political climate. *In the Name of the Father* (1993) and *Some Mother's Son* (1995) examine the effect of political incarceration on both those inside and those outside prison, whereas *Nothing Personal* (1995), *The Boxer* (1997), *Divorcing Jack* (1997), and *Resurrection Man* (1998) look at the degeneration into sadism and the progressive alienation from genuine ideological commitment as inevitable consequences of prolonged political struggle. In every instance, narratives avoid didacticism without ignoring the appalling costs of British colonialism by explicitly undermining either-or approaches to understanding the accounts that they present. Despite the brutal conditions in which characters in these films exist, the narratives retain the ability to see the contradictions informing individual lives—killing to achieve peace being the most obvious.

The motion picture *Bloody Sunday* (2000) further illustrates the complexity of this process even as it underscores the difficulties that arise when dealing with highly charged events. It is clearly an imaginative enactment of the horrific brutality that took place on January 30, 1972, in Derry during a civil rights march when British troops opened fire on the crowd, killing fourteen people and wounding thirteen more. Well-known actors take the roles of real and fictional characters. The story line follows the actual events of the day, and its narration places full blame for the dreadful slaughter on the British paratrooper unit that fired on unarmed civilians. (The 2004 film *Omagh* assumes a similar role in chronicling the responsibility of renegade IRA members for the horrific killing of innocent people.) Despite its opinionated slant, *Bloody Sunday* bases its narrative on eyewitness accounts, and follows the widely accepted chronology of events.

This approach raises the same issue discussed in the previous chapter's assessment of *The Magdalene Sisters:* how does one engage fictional accounts of actual events? Labeling *Bloody Sunday* as a historical representation opens it to charges of propagandizing. Judging this motion picture strictly as a imagined work runs the risk of trivializing the tremendous emotional impact of the actual events on the response that viewers make to this film.[7] As with other categories considered in this study, a central feature of any sophisticated analysis remains the ability to eschew closure and sustain multiple perspectives.

In that case *Omagh* succeeds where *Bloody Sunday* does not in presenting an aesthetically complex political motion picture. With its detailed examination of the terrible psychological toll that the bombing took on survivors and on the families of the victims, *Omagh* foregrounds the complex and contradictory attitudes to which brutal political violence gives rise. *Bloody Sunday* shows the horrific events, but goes no further in analyzing them than noting how they spurred IRA recruitment. Like the abuses presented in *The Magdalene Sisters,* the horrific events that these films chronicle demand further attention. However, any director who chooses to present them through a fictional narrative has the responsibility to protect their integrity from charges of propaganda.

As I will note below in the examination of *Michael Collins,* filmmakers can certainly present aesthetically rewarding political films. The key element to achieving this goal remains complexity. A simple recapitulation of received ideas stands as insufficient response to charges of didacticism. Such motion pictures must explore multiple perspectives to develop identity and engage a full range of interpretive possibilities.

The post–World War II films that I have surveyed make diverse statements about an individual's moral responsibility over involvement in political violence. However, they grow out of the same general assumption, presenting physical force as a corrosive element that inevitably corrupts those individuals who engage in it. This contention may well form the basis of effective narratives, but if taken no further it also runs the risk of over-simplifying key elements under consideration in an already narrow topic of discourse. In only a few cases do these films explore the broader causes of political unrest, and universally they require an imperial opponent—the British or their representatives—to validate attitudes and actions. As the presence of the British recedes, particularly in films focusing on sectarian violence, the function of political beliefs (as opposed to labels) as a source of identity becomes less clear without necessarily offering the interpretive alternatives that would increase imaginative engagement.

Over the decades that have passed since the founding of the Free State, the measure of political and nationalist ambivalence touched on in the earliest motion pictures has moved to the foreground of the narra-tive, displacing the enthusiasm and idealism derived from the struggle for an independent Ireland. This evolution becomes particularly evident in films produced after World War II, when politically themed motion pic-tures, from *Odd Man Out* through *Omagh,* turned their attention to gritty and ambivalent accounts of the civil rights struggles and the paramilitary and military brutality in the North, often bringing an exhausted or jaded tone to dominate the discourse. As the political environment of Ireland has changed, options for cinematic development have narrowed. In con-sequence, imaginatively successfully motion pictures dealing with Irish politics must resist the impulse to resolve themselves into predictable plots that tell a dated story turning on the application of unrestrained violence. At the same time, the more rigorously filmmakers pursue a complex vision of political attitudes, the less uniquely Irish they seem. This condition is sharply illustrated in Neil Jordan's *Michael Collins.*

A Paradigmatic Reading: *Michael Collins*

Like many of its predecessors, Neil Jordan's film *Michael Collins* (1996) looks at politics by examining the impact that the use of physical force has on individuals.[8] However, it also takes a more ambitious narrative approach, engaging the question of when if ever bloodshed becomes a justifiable political strategy. At the same time, it denies the stability that would come from a simplistic resolution of the question, and instead it deftly juxtaposes conflicting views and parallel behavior to render exclusionary interpretations of its environment ineffectual. In the process, *Michael Collins* foregrounds multiplicity as the basis for understanding the social context of the narrative, and it links an engagement of the full features of that context to the most effective interpretive approach to any film in this category.

This open divergence from the conventional form of didactic ideological exhortations produced rapid and often hostile critical reactions to Jordan's depictions not simply of Collins, Éamon de Valera, other Irish republicans, and of course the British but also of the historical events that shaped these men and to a degree they shaped in return. Such responses did not merely underscore the ambiguity characterizing central issues of the film. They highlighted the interpretive problems—particularly those issues that derived from a commitment to cause-and-effect linear thinking—that any viewer must negotiate in sorting through impressions created by the narrative of violent political response. Therefore, I would like to invert the normal order of evaluation by first looking at selected responses to *Michael Collins* and then examining the work itself.

Public events to some degree justify this interpretive reversal, for even before its initial screening *Michael Collins* evoked strong reactions. In the film diary kept during the production, Jordan frequently notes the growing excitement in Ireland inspired by the film, as social and political issues that had been assiduously avoided for decades became a matter of cultural concern and public debate. At one point Jordan portentously signals his sense of the extratextual discourse when he laments (one hopes ironically), "My problem now is how to make a film that won't feel like a national institution."[9]

Whatever the film's final cultural status, Jordan certainly experienced the response that commonly certifies a truly Irish social success, begrudging criticisms from those individuals who felt a proprietary interest in his subject. Pedants railed against the historical anachronisms that ran throughout Jordan's depiction of the War of Independence and the Civil War. Indeed, as Jordan himself noted, Irish historians Roy Foster, Ruth Dudley Edwards, and Tom Garvin raised the issue of factual inaccuracies even before *Michael Collins* had been completed and, more significantly, before any of them had seen it.[10] These individuals and other critics of the film's verisimilitude pointed out, among other things, that Ned Broy, the Collins agent inside Dublin Castle, did not die in 1920 but lived well past midcentury as a civil servant in the Irish government. Commentators noted that the British did not use an armored car in the actual Croake Park massacre. They asserted that the car bomb employed to blow up the Royal Irish Constabulary detectives from Belfast was not a method used by Collins's men, and indeed would not have worked on automobiles of the period. And they reminded any of us who might have forgotten that Harry Boland was shot north of Dublin in a hotel in Skerries and not near the city center in the River Liffey and that he died in a hospital and not at the scene.

This approach was not the only one taken by critics intent on dismissing the film. Certain Irish writers objected to what they saw as Jordan's epic pretensions, and chafed at the film's apparent hagiographic representation of Collins. Divisions between families going back generations resurfaced as pundits teased out divergent attitudes about the Civil War. On the other hand, voices in the English press fumed over images of Republican triumphalism that they detected throughout the film. They denounced *Michael Collins* as IRA propaganda, concerned with little more than foregrounding British atrocities in a distorted representation of Anglo-Irish relations.

Glen Newey's review of the film, appearing in the *Times Literary Supplement,* illustrates just how these two positions can be combined in a coordinated, vitriolic assault. Newey called his article "Both Gangster and Gandhi Agency Without Blame: The Significant Omissions of *Michael Collins*," a title emblematic of the carping and patronizing tones that characterize the entire essay.[11] Newey's review blends a concern for minutia with a tendency toward breezy generalization. It leads to a highly idiosyncratic assessment of what the film supposedly does and does not accomplish. Like many similar approaches, the article comes down to a series of cavils on the theme "what's wrong with the Irish."

My point in noting this tendency is not so much to refute individual observations as to raise questions about the relevance of unconsciously subjective critical approaches (as opposed to self-consciously subjective ones) to the motion picture that Jordan has made. Emblematic of the worst sort of linear criticism, the observations outlined above both ignore the central historical issues explored by *Michael Collins* and divert attention from more sophisticated readings. Jordan's film diary makes it quite clear that he was aware of the inaccuracies, anachronisms, and fictional license he employed in his movie. Although he does not try to defend deviations from historical facts, he presents reasoned and logical explanations for telling the story of the film as he did. His assertions do not so much justify cultural intentionality, as his critics imply, as underscore the diverse modes of perceiving his topic.

More significantly, attacks on *Michael Collins* as political propaganda seek to validate a reductive position based on polemics every bit as insidious as the ones they dismiss. In fact, ideological ambivalences are far more common in the film than are dogmatic disquisitions. As Elizabeth Cullingford has noted, the IRA can hardly have been pleased with the film's glorification of Collins, the man who in their eyes betrayed Ireland by his support of the Treaty of 1921. Conversely, modern-day Republicans can feel little empathy for Eamon de Valera, the person who systematically hunted down his IRA comrades once he came to power in the government.[12]

All these points raise the legitimate question of what, if anything, the film does say about history. Luke Gibbons makes a good start at answering that question. Writing an essay that appeared in the same journal, and in fact immediately after the Cullingford piece, he deftly dismisses efforts to sentimentalize or demonize historical and cultural representations. Instead, Gibbons emphasizes the impact of Jordan's portrayal of Collins as the pragmatic revolutionary figure. Gibbons asserts that the Collins character "is not a romantic at all, but is a realist, a man of facts, figures, and details." Gibbons sees this realism most graphically demonstrated in the film's brutal representation of events of the War of Independence and the Civil War, and centers these depictions in the broader context of a commentary on the imperial frame of mind: "Jordan's film launches a preemptive strike against those who would seek to remove violence from the prose of everyday life under colonialism."[13]

I agree with Gibbons's assessment of the representation of savagery in the film, and I think it possible to take his thesis a step further to examine the way that *Michael Collins* foregrounds the function of physical force (without necessarily justifying its use) even as it underscores the difficulty in assigning political responsibility for its implementation. More significantly, the film takes up the question of violence as an endemic feature of an Irish political identity. With this notion in mind, it seems important to me to expand the scope of the examination beyond an imperialist context.

Certainly, the colonial atmosphere surrounds events in the first half of the film, but by the midpoint of *Michael Collins* one sees the emphasis on the cause of Ireland's troubles shifted from a thousand years of English exploitation to the clash between the followers of Eamon de Valera for an uncompromised resolution and the judgment of Collins and others like him that a political solution could come only incrementally. Simply assigning blame to the English for the violence of the Civil War, a postcolonial legacy, uses reductionism to avoid the more complex issues of the contradictory impulses impelling the action forward. Consequently, a full examination of *Michael Collins*'s historical impact—and by extension of any politically oriented Irish-themed motion picture—of necessity must address the duality of this narrative.

First, let me say, however, that any interpretation of the film grounded on assumptions relating to Third World struggles against colonizing powers, especially in terms of the violence that such struggles beget, runs the risk of forwarding a reductive perspective every bit as limited as Newey's critique. *Michael Collins,* echoing the views of many contemporary Irish, rejects derivative postcolonial impulses in favor of a more complex assessment of the legacy of the relationship between the colonizers and the colonized. Despite its willingness to show the depravities of British behavior, the film proves equally assiduous at showing the ruthlessness of Collins's men. Privileging colonialism as an explanation for behavior becomes simply a symptom of the impulse to impose a linear perspective. Collins, in contrast, embraces duality as he balances violent confrontation, ordering the attack on the Four Courts, with tolerant accommodation, and journeying to Cork to find a way to end hostilities.

Of all the films mentioned in this chapter, *Michael Collins* offers the most plausible assessment of the political features of Irish identity. Although the surrender of the forces at the General Post Office (GPO) near the opening of the film seems to endorse the view of physical force as the key to understanding the origins of modern Ireland, the actual beginning of *Michael Collins* sets a very different tone. In the bifurcated scene that brackets the film, Joe O'Reilly (Ian Hart) begins a speech that he will conclude at the end of the film. He is telling Kitty Kiernan (Julia Roberts) of Collins's death in language that underscores the image of Collins as mediator with no mention of violence. "You've got to think of him. The way he was . . . [He got the British out of here]. . . . Life is possible. He made it possible." The film ends with the conclusion of that speech with Joe telling Kitty that Collins would want her to carry on. "And if he saw you now, do you know what he'd say, Kitty? Get up off the parliamentary side of your arse and get a bit of colour in your face."[14] Whereas the expulsion of the British came only after a violent confrontation, O'Reilly's remarks emphasize a different approach is necessary if one hopes to sustain those accomplishments. Joe encourages Kitty to come to grips with Collins's death by making a practical response to matters. He notably says nothing about revenge or retribution. Rather, he suggests the kind of pragmatism that Collins had advocated over the course of the narrative.

A series of mirror scenes on either end of the film underscore that flexibility in Collins, showing him not so much as a peacemaker or as a fanatic but rather as the man of the moment, able to adapt to changing conditions without the encumbrance of historical and emotional baggage, in essence a man whose identity remains malleable, even mutable. When Collins is addressing a rural crowd early in the film after his recent release from an English prison, he does not openly advocate a violent response to the British, but rather emphasizes the weapon that the Irish people possess is a Gandhi-like "right of refusal." Within a few scenes, he is instructing rural irregulars on the best way to attack a police barracks. Near the end of the film, Collins speaks to another rural crowd, advocating treaty ratification as a means of preserving the peace achieved by the War of Independence. Shortly thereafter, Collins orders the assault on the Four Courts against the antitreaty forces who have rejected the results of the referendum on the peace process.

The point is that Collins is neither adverse nor prone to violence. To understand his nature one must understand his complicated relationship to his environment. Collins is a man who sees in multiple perspectives and continually seeks to find equilibrium for these points of view. His squad of assassins is called the "Twelve Apostles," mixing blasphemy and righteousness. He chides himself for "putting a gun in young Vinny Byrne's hand," yet exhorts all of his men to kill efficiently so as not to waste bullets. Violence is certainly an element of Collins's nature, but it cannot be gauged linearly, for he shows the ability simultaneously to immerse and to detach himself from it.

Even apparently unambiguous representations of Collins as the hard man prove muted on closer examination. Although the film opens with a gun in his hand in the GPO and ends with him returning fire during the ambush at Beal na Mblath, more often than not a more complex image emerges. Most of his efforts direct rather than participate in fighting, and even in the midst of action, he generally eschews weapons. The final engagement of the War of Independence portrayed on the screen is the Customs House assault that Collins had opposed. At no point during the battle does he carry a gun, and indeed near its conclusion he watches helplessly as the Black and Tans summarily execute one of his lieutenants. In his last meeting with Harry Boland, seeking to avert a civil war, a young IRA man points a pistol at Collins, who unflinchingly stands ready to be shot but who does not respond with physical force. (It is Harry who knocks the man down.) During the scenes of the Civil War, Collins is shown as increasingly withdrawn from acts of violence even as his responsibility in their creation increases, to the point that he berates the Free State soldier of the army he commands who has shot Boland.

A memorable exchange between Collins and Harry Boland midway through the film alerts viewers to the complexity of the use of physical force. When Boland speaks admiringly of Collins's capacity for mayhem, the latter resists the implication that he takes any of these events on with enthusiasm: "I want peace and quiet. I want it so much I'd die for it." As he elaborates on his motivations, Collins seems to be caught up in circularity: "I hate [the English] for making hate necessary, and I'll do what I can to end it." At first glance, this statement seems a postcolonial gesture, placing responsibility on the colonizer for conditioning brutality in the colonized. In fact, the discussion underscores the inherent contradictions in supposedly moral individuals taking up physical force, and it suggests the inadequacy of exclusionary thinking in comprehending these antinomies.

The absence of the British in the second half of the motion picture does little to abate the impulse for savage conflicts, as the confrontations themselves, though graphically portrayed, seem to be increasingly futile, even as they underscore the efforts of both sides to impose their sense of the Irish political identity. Large-scale engagements, from the final moments in the GPO to the street fighting of the Civil War, lead only to carnage. Furthermore, selective violence produces no more satisfactory effects. Early on, with the executions at Kilmainham Jail of the leaders of the Rising, the film has established the ineffectuality of such actions. Consequently, the murders of the G-men or the Cairo Gang, whatever short-term success they might generate, have already been shown to be the wrong approach to any lasting solution to Ireland's troubles.

Although the narrative makes the influence of British colonialism on the violent actions of Collins and others evident early in the film, one cannot explain the continuing propensity to resort to physical force that brought on the Civil War simply by invoking the legacy of imperialism. *Michael Collins* does not deny the impact of imperialism on the Irish psyche, but its narrative goes well beyond simplistic suggestions that it explains all of the ills depicted. Jordan's film offers ample alternatives to physical force, and suggests that those men who apply it have made a conscious decision to do so rather than have been impelled into that course of action by incontrovertible forces.

The scene in which the British forces surrender Dublin Castle underscores this view. Collins, now in the uniform of the newly recognized Irish Army, arrives late to the ceremony and takes an open, easy approach to the transaction. The British commanding officer, with a hat adorned in the ridiculous plumes made obsolete by World War I, cannot hide his bitterness over the retrenchment of imperialism. In ill-disguised resentment, he chides Collins for his tardy appearance. "You're seven minutes late, Mr. Collins." Collins replies with aplomb: "You've kept us waiting seven hundred years. You can have your seven minutes." A few moments later, as the Union Jack is lowered, Collins makes a more telling, if less obvious, observation: "So that's what all the bother was about." With this muted irony,

Collins refuses to give a ceremonial event the significance of closure, and instead suggests to the British officer, and to the viewers, that a more profound continuity and complexity characterize Irish history.

Time and again, the narrative avoids representations that would enforce the impression that a single simple condition shaped the events in the War of Independence. In this respect, Newey's *Times Literary Supplement* article, a piece punctuated by ill-concealed contempt for the Irish position, rightly challenges one area where the narrative does not sustain this approach, the suppression of Collins's nationalistic views. His attitudes certainly would have been much more apparent had there been a detailed examination of the treaty negotiations or any mention of his gun running to the North after the partition or of his view that the partition itself was only a temporary condition that would be swept aside later. Indeed, the rabid nationalism and intransigence of Collins's opponents are always emphasized, and they are set in contrast with Collins's apparent inclinations toward peace and accommodation.[15]

In the Neil Jordan film, Collins asserts himself as a larger-than-life figure, the man who seems to stand above politics and even nationalism and wishes only peace for his country. Luke Gibbons has called the film "a rehabilitation of the tarnished legacy of the Free State," and from certain Irish perspectives that representation may be a quite accurate assessment of its impact, though of course others would see it as closer to a travesty.[16] However, the melioration of Jordan's narrative has a broader effect on an international audience, without the sophisticated sense of difference that would characterize the nuanced response of an Irish viewer.

It offers not so much an Irish history lesson as a commentary on physical force. Emphasis on factual inaccuracies imposes on the film a misconception of its aims. Like *The Informer* and *Guests of the Nation*, *Michael Collins* shows the toll that the pursuit of change through violence takes on individuals, but it also explores the way political beliefs impel the course of action. Neither vilifying nor glorifying such behavior, the film instead challenges viewers to reconcile the inherent antinomies.

This challenge leads to questions that inform not only interpretations of *Michael Collins* and other political films but all of the Irish-themed motion pictures under consideration in this study. Who determines Irishness, and how does one apply it to understanding film narratives? What stability exists in the concept of Irishness, and how readily can different viewers understand its features? To what degree do current demographics and attitudes challenge even retrospective representations of Irish identity?

These interrogations bring this study back to the concept of identity with which it began. Whatever one might say about the choices made in the portrayal of Collins in Jordan's film, he seems undeniably Irish. At the same time, the resistance of the narrative to imposing closure makes the elements of that identity and the weight given to each feature of his nature subject to the oscillating perspectives of any number of filmgoers. That is to say, elements that inform Collins's communal nature manifest themselves in a highly nuanced and individualized fashion. What viewers see as his Irishness resonates very differently from person to person. No point of view is inherently privileged, and every perspective, including associations with more universalized tendencies, can potentially make a valid contribution to a full understanding of Collins's nature, and in consequence the uniqueness of his Irish nature becomes both insistent and occluded.

As one moves from *Michael Collins* to political films to Irish-themed motion pictures, the same epistemological conditions obtain. At every level, subjective observations are placed under the stress of generalized applications, and pluralistic responses render conventional approaches inadequate. As a result, those viewers seeking the fullest possible comprehension of works in the field need to turn to hermeneutic models that more closely resemble their way of thinking: nonlinear.

This approach does not mean ignoring all previous work on cinema in Ireland. Rather, it underscores the need to acknowledge both the interpretive value of applying a concept of Irishness to the films under consideration here and the increasingly complex mutability of manifestations of that identity. Given the range and diversity of the cultural institutions, outlined over the course of this study, shaping the features of identity, the most effective approach to understanding this condition as manifested in Irish-themed motion pictures involves the nonexclusionary multiplicity sustained by analyses that reject cause-and-effect thinking.

Appendixes

Notes

Bibliography

Index

Appendix A

The Subjectivity of Irishness

In a postmodern world, the elements of a contemporary national character—those features that go beyond the geographic boundaries of states to reflect the seeming psychological cohesiveness of a nation—prove increasingly difficult to identify in any objective fashion, not simply in First World countries but anywhere across the globe. On the one hand, studies increasingly delineate concepts of nation and nationalism steeped in individuality. At the same time, national identity remains a crucial feature of interpretation, for insistent cultural, social, geographic, and economic factors continue to inform representations of local behavior and attitudes. In Ireland scholars keep striving to categorize and trace the effects of dominant communal features that exert specific influences on individuals.[1] As with broader studies of nation and nationalism, what becomes problematic for delineating the Irish character is deciding the significance of these diverse elements from person to person and gauging their cumulative effect on a national identity.

As an island nation, populated through oscillating phases of invasion and amalgamation, dependent until very recently on a complicated, agriculturally based, preindustrial economic system, Irish society possesses clearly evolved, defining features that exert measurable influence. At the same time, these crucial elements manifest a variability that resists rigid delineation. Indeed, they have such a high sensitivity to change that they seem perpetually under threat of erasure.[2] Popular markers used to measure Irishness have come to inform Irish character without clearly defining it. The result, predictably, is often highly skewed and widely diverse conjectures on identity.

Even a cursory survey of attitudes about Irishness makes clear how every impression remains infused with subjectivity. Denis Donoghue sums up this dilemma in a commentary on what he infers to be Seamus Deane's critique of essentialism in the concept of Irishness: "Indeed, I am not sure that Deane or anyone else could indicate the point at which an acceptable degree of self-consciousness can be distinguished from a vain 'essentialism.' The attempt to correlate essentialism with myth, and to urge that the sentiment that accommodates them should be rebuked by the more astringent sentiment that respects existence and history, is fruitless. It only requires a further degree of irony to drive the second sentiment at the first."[3] The sinuous elegance of Donoghue's prose underscores my point about subjectivity. Once one has teased out the essence of his remarks, one sees that he does not relinquish his interest in Irish identity but instead, in language appropriately elusive, acknowledges its slipperiness. (The title of the work in which this quotation appears, *We Irish*, plays with the idea of essentialism even as his observations go on to undercut it.)

A range of other Irish commentators, both generalists and specialists, echo this ambivalence about the specific nature of Irishness. Luke Gibbons asserts the instability of concepts of nationhood by asserting that "disintegration and fragmentation were always part of [Irish] history." Colin Coulter focuses attention on present conditions in an assessment of how a relatively specific economic phenomenon exerts a reductive influence on delineations of Irishness: "In a remarkably short space of time, the notion of the 'Celtic Tiger' would come to operate as a widely recognized and understood master signifier for a very particular and essentially hegemonic reading of the nature of contemporary Irish society."[4] Essays in the volume edited by Coulter and Steve Coleman go on to chronicle the disparate impact, divided along class lines, of the economic boom of the 1990s, making clear the deceptiveness of a broad view of Ireland based on recent prosperity.

Eamonn Slater even more bluntly articulates this concept of fragmentation in his introduction to a collection of essays on contemporary Irishness. "All the processes which have promoted and ushered in modern society have broken a magic spell: the spell of simply belonging to a very definite and familiar social world, a world which we take for granted."[5]

Linking alienation and modernity is by no means original with Slater; more significant is the range of perspectives this connection presumes as a consequence.

Along these lines but in a more anecdotal style than any of the other references, *Being Irish: Personal Reflections on Irish Identity Today,* edited by Paddy Logue, offers the views of one hundred contributors writing short essays on the topic. What stands out is not the subjectivity of these reflections, which one would expect, but the addition of a striking number of contributions from people who are not native Irish—including Tony Blair, Andrew Greeley, Tom Hayden, immigrants living in Ireland, and individuals residing around the world—who have a sense of themselves as Irish. Without affirming or denying the validity of all of these figures seeing themselves as Irish, one is still struck by the diverse perception of national character to which the inclusion of so many individuals who actually are citizens of other countries attests.

More academically oriented and thematically focused studies take a remarkably similar tone. Indeed, Richard Kearney echoes this concept in a rigorous examination of the changing posture of Ireland and the United Kingdom: "When one speaks of the 'Irish Community' today, one refers not merely to inhabitants of a state, but to an international group of expatriates and a subnational network or regional communities."[6] Although Kearney's analysis lays out a forthright agenda for engaging concepts about Northern Ireland, it also takes up the way diverse cultural efforts lead to a "subversion of fixed identities." All this scrutiny simultaneously suggests a very broad concept of Irishness, with people from all over the world claiming that characteristic, and a highly individualized sense of the term, as it varies from person to person.

In citing this range of opinions I intend simply to highlight the inherent subjectivity of the concept of Irishness and the range of features one might invoke to discern it. As evidenced by these views, the dichotomies commonly applied—church versus secular, provincial versus metropolitan, Republican versus Unionist, and numerous other polarities—no longer provide a stable foundation for understanding the parameters within which a national identity exists. Indeed, David McWilliams has recently suggested, in his book on the segment of contemporary Irish just immersing themselves in adulthood whom he calls the pope's children, that economic and social growth over the past few decades has radically changed even these seemingly dependable reference points for identity:

> The Old Irish Dream—which was mother's milk to their parents and previous generations—was of Catholicism, nationalism, community, chastity, the Brits, the six counties, the Irish language, the famine, the underdog, getting a good job in the bank and the glamour of Grace Kelly. Things were offered up, sacrificed in this life for fulfillment in the next. This has been replaced by a New Irish Dream.
>
> The New Irish Dream can be best summed up by "I wanna trade up." I want the biggest fridge, the best holiday, the newest car, the loudest sound system, the healthiest food, the best yoga posture, the most holistic world-view, the most talked about wedding and the best sex with as many part-ners, in as many positions as possible. I want it all and I want it now. I want to measure, compare and out-perform. I want to be recognized, appreci-ated and loved. I wanna be number 1 and no one is going to stop me.
>
> The Old Irish Dream was about us, ours and them. The New Irish Dream is about me, mine and yours. The New Irish Dream speaks in the possessive case.[7]

McWilliams's talent for imagery and his rhythmic contrasts between Old and New Irish Dreams may tempt one to see this fragmentation in Irish society as a recent phenomenon, but the cultural, economic, and psycho-logical changes of the past twenty-five years that McWilliams chronicles only highlight an ambivalence and idiosyncrasy that have long been part of Irish identity.

Even when the bifurcated perspectives of institutions and relation-ships mentioned above occupied important positions within the Irish identity, conventional modes of analyzing them led many commenta-tors into a zero-sum game. A critic could not examine one element in a binary set without damaging the integrity of the other, for to pursue a linear approach to finding a characteristic or characteristics common to all often reductively requires ignoring a range of very plausible features that do not meet the test of universality. On the other hand, as Leopold Bloom learns in the passage from *Ulysses* quoted as an epigraph to the

Introduction, to incorporate diverse criteria for identity often provokes seeming contradictions.

What trips up Leopold Bloom, as it has entangled so many others who address the subject, is his commitment to either-or thinking. The inherent exclusiveness of cause-and-effect analysis produces the dilemma presented above. In coming to a sense of Irishness, one needs an approach that sustains multiple, even contradictory, conditions, though one that also accommodates traditional perceptions. The social institutions that the modernists sought to demolish nearly a century ago and that for the past fifty years postmodernists have been claiming no longer exist—the family, the church, and the nation—have been and remain shaping features of Ireland's national character, even as their prominence has markedly declined and perceptions of each have diversified. Historical events also insistently persist in informing identity, though the relevance of particular aspects of Irish history continues to be debated. None of these observations rebuts the existence of Irishness, but they clearly complicate its delineation. At a time when Polish is the second most common language heard on Dublin streets, one needs to understand the pluralism that informs contemporary Irish society before coming to any specific conclusions about identity.

The nation's colonial and postcolonial traumas as well as its economic struggles (reflected in massive immigration) and triumphs (seen in rampant materialism) have produced well-documented attitudes and patterns of behavior. They reflect an Irish sense of self in which traditional and homogeneous attitudes coexist with a sophisticated cosmopolitanism. Realizing this fact, however, is not enough to demarcate Irishness, for individuals respond to these elements in diverse and often contradictory fashions. This mutability makes it tricky to apply the concept of nation as a critical tool in examinations of regional filmmaking, while at the same time the proliferation of the topic makes it necessary to engage.

Appendix B

The Irish Infrastructure

From the mid-1980s Irish film criticism began to develop a clearly defined theoretic nature when Kevin Rockett, Luke Gibbons, and John Hill brought out the first academic book-length analysis of Irish film, *Cinema and Ireland*. In three freestanding essays, the book announces topics (historical evolution, political debate, and the conflict of romanticism and realism) and the format (formal, thematic examinations) that will dominate discussions of Irish film for the next three decades.

About the same time, several publishing initiatives provided platforms for an ongoing dialogue on contemporary film in Ireland and abroad. Beginning in 1990, *Film West,* publishing in Galway, offered a strong forum for opinions. Unfortunately, after forty-one issues, the journal went out of existence in 2001. More positively, *Film Base News,* founded in 1987 and renamed *Film Ireland* in 1992, celebrated its one hundredth issue in 2004 and continues to appear every two months. As the film journal of record in Ireland, it remains an important source for industry news, theoretical speculation, and timely reviews of works relating to the Irish motion picture industry.

Additional support for critical and creative development came with the Irish Film Institute's opening in 1992. Its film archive serves as an invaluable scholarly resource, and its screening facilities continually offer a range of important cinematic works. A year later the reestablishment of the Irish Film Board offered a renewal of backing, though at times controversial, for independent projects.[1] During the same period Dublin City College, the Dun Laoghaire Institute of Art and Design, University College–Dublin, and other academic venues began to provide professional training.

From the opposite side of the process, a growing economy produced an increase in disposable income for filmgoers and fostered boom times for the Irish cinema. Between 1980 and 1998 cinema attendance in Ireland rose by nearly one-third, from 9.5 million people per year to 12.5 million.[2] Lance Pettitt lists thirty-six feature-length commercial Irish dramas that appeared in the '90s—a sharp jump from the preceding decades—and Ruth Barton, in her catalog of top-grossing Irish films from 1993 to 2001, adds two dozen more titles to Pettitt's compilation.[3] The current decade has shown no abatement in production.

The growth in both of these areas accentuates the challenges facing individuals wishing to discuss an Irish cinema. If one undertakes the examination of Irish films, one needs to pursue inclusiveness, an impulse often at odds with academic protocols. Avant-garde or art-house films remain perfectly legitimate forms for Irish filmmakers to pursue. However, the study of nationally affiliated films demands consideration of films seen by and appealing to a significant portion of the nation and not simply to coterie constituencies. (See Appendix D for further discussion.)

Appendix C

The Migration of Talent

From the silent era when members of the Abbey Theatre went to the United States to perform in feature-length films, Irish cinema talent has migrated overseas. In recent decades, however, there has been more than the occasional shifting of actors such as Barry Fitzgerald or Maureen O'Hara or directors such as Rex Ingram. A vast repositioning of talent across the Atlantic has been under way for a number of years, but a very different condition now obtains. The shifting goes in both directions between the United States and Ireland, and the movements are generally temporary rather than permanent. In the process actors and directors slip their nationality on and off, which gives students of film a unique opportunity to access the function of national identity.

Irish film has not been hurt by actors relocating back and forth between Dublin and Hollywood. Fionnula Flanagan can make *Divine Secrets of the Ya-Ya Sisterhood* and have a home in Los Angeles without compromising her ability to turn in powerful performances in Irish films. Colm Meaney can travel on the *Starship Enterprise*. Brendan Gleeson can take the role of a backwoods Maine sheriff *(Lake Placid)*. Stephen Rea can perform the acts of a deranged torturer in New York *(In Dreams)*. And Liam Neeson can be a German industrialist *(Schindler's List)*, an American sexologist *(Kinsey)*, and a Jedi knight *(The Phantom Menace)*. None of these roles undermines the credentials as an Irish artist of the actor who assumed it.

The real erosion of an Irish film identity comes in the effect that directors feel and in the projects that they undertake (or fail to undertake). Neil Jordan stands as the prime example of one struggling to sustain the schizophrenic identity of an American and an Irish director. Two-thirds of the films he has directed have no Irish identity, and from *The Miracle* onward his Irish films are continually fighting against ingestion into a larger American ethos. Jim Sheridan's evolution has been slower but as definitive. After a straightforward biopic, *My Left Foot*, he moved from rural period dramas to political works—*The Field, Into the West, In the Name of the Father,* and *The Boxer. In America,* despite having an emigrant Irish family at its center, is unabashedly American. And his latest—*Get Rich or Die Tryin'*— examines the black American underclass. Its proposed follow-up, *Emerald City,* is about Irish gangs in New York City's Hell's Kitchen. My point is not that these directors do not have a perfect right to make any sort of film they wish. Rather, I feel that exposure to Hollywood has blunted their abilities to bring Irish identity into their work.

The long-term effect of this process remains to be seen. For now, it serves to underscore a central point of my study: a growing internationalization obtains within the Irish film industry, and that condition makes the assertion of Irishness an even more fragile endeavor than it was in the past.

Appendix D

Popular Attitudes in Irish Audiences

One must recognize that the "commercial market" itself dictates the nature of Irish films and that the imperative to address the needs of a "commercial market" increasingly informed by multinational cultural values presents the greatest challenge to the continued existence of the Irish motion picture. At present, popular tastes simply do not favor joint productions; they demonstrate a yen for nonindigenous movies. Recent figures from the film licensing board show that the vast majority of films approved for screening in the Irish Republic are American. Figures from the film censor's office on proportion of foreign, particularly American, to Irish films licensed to be shown are particularly revealing. From 1997 to October 2005, 1,755 films were submitted for licensing. Of that number, 54 percent were American. An additional 14 percent were American and some country other than Ireland. Further, 21 percent were films from other countries. Only 6 percent were Irish films, and the remainder were Irish and some other country or countries.[1] These films are imported because distributors judge them to be the ones audiences are most likely to come to see. Clearly, Hollywood-style films appeal to the Irish, and no Irish filmmaker can hope to succeed financially by ignoring that attitude.

Appendix E

Cross-Cultural Filmmaking

As an alternative simply to a xenophobic response to foreign influence, Brian McIlroy has turned to the work of scholars of Third World cinema, like Hamid Naficy, to gain insights into the impact of Hollywood on Irish filmmaking.[1] Naficy has tried to come to terms with cross-cultural borrowing over a range of societies, writing a book-length study examining the phenomenon of exiled Third World filmmakers incorporating Western techniques and concepts into nationalist projects. Naficy's concern for those individuals working in the Western filmmaking tradition with a strong nationalist perspective, a condition he identifies as "accented cinema," provides a good starting point for understanding identity-oriented film. This approach acknowledges the technical presence of Hollywood filmmaking while asserting the psychological, spiritual, and cultural dominance of the native ethos. At the same time, because they generally work outside their countries of origin, these men and women do not duplicate the experiences of indigenous filmmakers.

Certainly, one cannot apply this view to Irish-themed films with complete accuracy. Third World filmmakers can balance technical borrowings with thematic independence more easily because their cultures stand as distinct from the First World from which Hollywood emerges. Ireland has a Western culture, and so has difficulty setting itself apart from the First World. Globalization, promoting what Richard Kearney calls a postnationalist society, has made these distinctions even more difficult to enforce as the Irish move toward a more cosmopolitan worldview. In light of what this

239

appendix has already discussed, this trend only increases the obstacles to the formation of a national cinema.

Nonetheless, Naficy introduces the possibility of comprehending Irish-themed films outside the narrow restraints of previous approaches. His accented cinema acknowledges the both-and qualities that permeate films of exiles, and suggests an alternative approach to conventional methods. Perhaps most significantly, Naficy acknowledges the imperative need to negotiate the vexed relationship between national and international impulses.

Notes

Preface: What's the Point?

1. Lance Pettitt, *Screening Ireland: Film and Television Representation;* Martin McLoone, *Irish Film: The Emergence of a Contemporary Cinema;* Ruth Barton, *Irish National Cinema.*

2. *Irish themed* stands as a term I will use throughout this study. Seeing films as Irish themed rather than as part of an Irish cinema gives one the flexibility needed to incorporate aspects of Irish society into an interpretation without succumbing to rigid categorization. It encompasses the work of both indigenous and nonindigenous filmmakers, and it distinguishes between any films made in Ireland and films that demand an understanding of an Irish ethos for interpretation.

3. Alan Williams, introduction to *Film and Nationalism,* ed. Alan Williams, 1.

4. Theoretical physicists, albeit working on a grander scale, use the term *Theory of Everything* to denote efforts to find a unified explanation of all phenomena. Paradoxically, acknowledging an incomplete understanding of ultimate causes enhances opportunities for understanding. Observations function at the broadest imaginable level of aesthetic perception. The viewer does not automatically exclude any response because it does not fit an already determined pattern of criticism, nor is any response privileged because it complements a particular linear reading. For examples of how physicists approach the problem, see Jack Cohen and Ian Stewart, *The Collapse of Chaos: Discovering Simplicity in a Complex World,* 11, 377–90. A more detailed and esoteric articulation of this concept appears in James Lovelock, *The Ages of Gaia.*

5. I have discussed the prevalence and the limitations of traditional linear-film interpretations in "The Chaos and Complexity of Classic Hollywood Cinema." Although in this study I will not draw on explicit images from chaos and complexity theory as metaphors in my analysis, I will pursue the advantages of using nonlinear logic in film interpretation.

6. See, for example, Chris Barker, *The SAGE Dictionary of Cultural Studies,* 22–25; Peter Brooker, *A Concise Glossary of Cultural Theory;* Jacques Derrida, "Structure, Sign, and Play in the Discourse of the Human Sciences"; Clifford Geertz, *The Interpretation of Cultures: Selected Essays;* Hugh J. Silverman, ed., *Questioning Foundations: Truth/Subjectivity/Culture;* and H. C. Triandis, *The Analysis of Subjective Culture.*

7. Like so many critical terms, *genre* has acquired a range of denotations, not always positive. Most specifically, a number of critics see it disparagingly as a simplistic and rigid categorization best suited to commercial Hollywood films. A series of essays collected by Brian McIlroy, *Genre and Cinema: Ireland and Transnationalism,* shows the limitations of such reductive thinking, especially for studies of Irish-themed films. In particular, see McIlroy's introduction, 1–8; Christine Gledhill's "Genre and Nation," 11–25; Dervila Layden's "Discovering and Uncovering Genre in Irish Cinema," 27–44; and my "Is Californication a Mortal Sin? The Influence of Classic Hollywood Cinema on Indigenous Irish Film," 61–75.

8. One finds an excellent, sardonic elaboration of these contrasting class attitudes in the RTÉ series *Paths to Freedom,* a mocumentary-style comedy that examines the lives of a middle-class physician and a working-class layabout in the twelve months following their release from Mountjoy Prisons.

9. Two exceptions to this trend, released in 2007, *Garage* and *Small Engine Repair,* illustrate respectively the rich narrative possibilities of a rural film and the plotline dangers of a work that overextends its uniqueness. I will touch on both in Chapter 4.

10. Harvey O'Brien's recent book, *The Real Ireland: The Evolution of Ireland in Documentary Film,* offers a good overview of the interpretive options open to viewers of documentaries. It also underscores the difficulties for both readers and critics not in Ireland to engage in any detail this topic.

11. Chapter 1 underscores how leading Irish film critics consistently use thematic criteria in delineating national cinema. Although my study aims to do more than just respond to their ideas, I also understand the need to address directly the opinions that they have articulated. A thematic approach has proved to be the best strategy for such engagement.

Introduction: The State of Irish Film

1. For an excellent assessment of the impact of these issues and other critiques of nationhood on the concept of national cinema, stressing the fabricated implications of the term, see Susan Hayward, "Framing National Cinema."

2. Ernest Gellner, *Nations and Nationalism,* esp. 19–38.

3. Benedict Anderson, *Imagined Communities: Reflections on the Origin and Spread of Nationalism,* 19, 6–7.

4. See Anthony D. Smith, *The Ethnic Origins of Nations.*

5. See in particular a collection of essays that Homi Bhabha edited, *Nation and Narration,* and *The Location of Culture.*

6. Homi Bhabha, "Narrating the Nation," introduction to *Nation and Narration,* edited by Bhabha, 1.

7. Williams, introduction to *Film and Nationalism,* edited by Williams, 3; emphasis in the original.

8. See Valentina Vitali and Paul Willemen, introduction to *Theorising National Cinema*, edited by Valentina Vitali and Paul Willemen, 1–14.

9. Ibid., 4.

10. Ibid., 2, 3, 4.

11. Ibid., 7.

12. Fernando Solanas and Octavio Gettino, "Towards a Third Cinema," in *Movies and Methods: An Anthology*, edited by Bill Nichols, 46–64.

13. Ibid., 57, 52; emphasis in the original. This concept has direct relevance to efforts to view Ireland from the perspective of a Third Cinema. Even before the Celtic Tiger, there was strong opposition to the designation of Ireland as a Third World country. See, for example, Thérèse Caherty, ed., *Is Ireland a Third World Country?* Luke Gibbons neatly captures the source of this ambivalent Irish attitude by saying that "Ireland is a First World country, but with a Third World memory" (*Transformations in Irish Culture,* 3).

14. Homi Bhabha, "The Commitment to Theory," in *Questions of Third Cinema*, edited by Jim Pines and Paul Willemen, 111–32.

15. Paul Willemen, "The Third Cinema Question: Notes and Reflections." This essay is reprinted as the introduction to Pines and Willemen, *Questions of Third Cinema.*

16. At the same time, Ashish Rajadhyaksha, in an essay titled "Debating the Third Cinema," which also appears in *Questions of Third Cinema*, edited by Pines and Willemen, 170–78, examines the issue from a strongly articulated Third World position. Though he does not specifically set out to affirm a link between Third Cinema and Third World cinema through the arguments he makes and the examples he uses, Rajadhyaksha illustrates how difficult it is to dissociate the two concepts.

17. Julianne Burton, "Marginal Cinemas and Mainstream Critical Theory," 10.

18. Michael Chanan, "The Changing Geography of Third Cinema," 377.

19. Stephen Crofts, "Reconceptualizing National Cinemas," 50; emphasis in the original.

20. Ibid.; emphasis in the original.

21. Andrew Higson, "The Concept of National Cinema," 36–37.

22. Ibid., 42; emphasis in the original.

23. Hayward, "Framing National Cinema," 89, 93 (quote); emphasis in the original.

24. Philip French, "Is There a European Cinema?" in *Border Crossing: Film in Ireland, Britain, and Europe*, edited by John Hill, Martin McLoone, and Paul Hainsworth, 35.

25. For further details, see Brian McIlroy, *Irish Cinema: An Illustrated History*, 5–9; and Arthur Flynn, *The Story of Irish Film*, 13–18.

26. McIlroy, *Irish Cinema*, 9; Kevin Rockett, *The Irish Filmography: Fiction Films, 1896 to 1996*, 1.

27. For detailed enumerations of specific efforts, see Rockett, *Irish Filmography.*

28. The best source for background information on the film remains Des MacHale, *The Complete Guide to "The Quiet Man."*

29. A great many film texts have invoked the term *classic Hollywood cinema* in a variety of contexts. To clarify my approach, allow me to offer the following definition. In my view, it describes an approach to filmmaking organized around a highly regularized narrative arrangement, one that devotes all its attention to efforts to resolve a central problem. As a result, all relevant thematic elements—such as characterization, subplots, or setting— remain dependent on and defined by their relations to that central problem. *The Wizard of Oz*, highlighting the efforts of Dorothy Gale to find the means to return to Kansas, exemplifies this approach. The film defines Dorothy in terms of her desire to go home. It subordinates the concerns of other characters—the Tin Man, the Scarecrow, the Cowardly Lion—to the imperative of helping Dorothy. And even the setting, the kingdom of Oz, gathers significance because it is the home of the man, the Wizard, who presumably can facilitate Dorothy's return to her home.

30. Luke Gibbons has noted several points in *The Quiet Man* where Ford employs this technique (Kevin Rockett, Luke Gibbons, and John Hill, *Cinema and Ireland*, 225–26).

31. As Luke Gibbons notes, "Communal brawling, excessive drunkenness, garrulousness, singing and dancing, aversion to discipline and the law, irreverence towards death" were the traits that nationalist reformers continually sought to efface from "the lower orders" (*"The Quiet Man,"* 15). Overall, Gibbons sees the film as much less caustic than I do. His emphasis on the pastoral elements in *The Quiet Man* offers an engaging reading, and his view of Sean Thornton's eventual integration into the society of Innisfree remains quite sound. However, I see additional complex features in the narrative that play against these elements. Ford takes this emphasis on the pastoral and the impulse for acceptance into the community a step further. He emphasizes the corrupting effect of that amalgamation, highlighting the infectious nature of the darker attributes of communal identity for a *naïf* like Thornton. For detailed analysis of this structure, particularly as it compares and contrasts with Gibbons's views, see my "The Myth of Hidden Ireland: The Corrosive Effect of *The Quiet Man*."

32. See Fidelma Farley, *"This Other Eden."*

33. Also like *The Quiet Man*, *This Other Eden* is essentially an outsider's view. Although the supporting cast stands as essentially Irish, the leading man, Leslie Phillips, is English, and the leading lady, Audrey Dalton, though born in Ireland, had been trained in England and had come back after establishing herself as an actor in Hollywood. Further, the director, Muriel Box, was English, with no other experience in Irish film.

34. Barton, *Irish National Cinema*, 78–79.

35. McLoone defines the term as "the first period of independent film-making in Ireland from the mid-1970s to 1987. . . . In this period a group of both young and more experienced film-makers began to explore the contradictions of a changing society in a form of culture (the fiction film) in which there was little in the way of national tradition or precedence" (*Irish Film*, 131).

36. The filmography of John Ford offers examples of the contrasting impulse, using distinct groups synecdochically. Despite the unique circumstances in each of his westerns,

characters are represented and judged according to generalized American values. The portrayal of Ethan Edwards in *The Searchers* generates such great power because even in his alienated role, he cannot escape or deny the force of national values.

37. Though Anne is enlisted to portray a servant to give domestic credibility to the house where Robert Emmet plans his rebellion, Irish men soon come to see and treat her as if she actually were one.

38. Kevin Rockett, "Aspects of the Los Angelesation of Ireland," 22. For an alternative perspective, see Appendix E.

39. For an impressive study of this condition from its inception to the present, see Ruth Barton, *Acting Irish in Hollywood: From Fitzgerald to Farrell*.

40. Thomas Elsaesser, "Chronicle of a Death Retold," 166. The experience of Liz Gill, writer and director of *Goldfish Memory*, illustrates this point quite well. Simply finding funding for even a low-budget film is a tremendous challenge, and it places a great deal of pressure for financial success on the production crew. If one feels that Irish audiences are looking for a sophisticated, cosmopolitan approach to romantic comedy, then retelling the national narrative seems far less important. Indeed, given the struggles that such filmmakers go through to secure financial backing for their projects, it would be arrogant for any film critic to prescribe the approach that a director should take.

1. What Is to Be Done?

1. Rockett, Gibbons, and Hill, *Cinema and Ireland*, xiv; McIlroy, *Irish Cinema*, viii; Rockett, *Irish Filmography*, i.

2. Anthony Kirby and James MacKillop, "Selected Filmography of Irish and Irish-Related Feature Films," 182; Pettitt, *Screening Ireland*, 29, 30.

3. McLoone, *Irish Film*, 128.

4. Barton, *Irish National Cinema*, 4–5.

5. *How Harry Became a Tree* (2001), a film I will examine in detail in Chapter 4, illustrates how tricky it is to engage the cultural mutability of plotlines and characterizations. In this film, a Serbian director, Goran Paskaljevic, films a Chinese story adapted to an Irish setting using prominent Irish actors in the leading roles—Colm Meaney, Adrian Dunbar, and Cillian Murphy. With rampant cultural borrowing informing every element of the movie's structure, what national perspective can an interpreter legitimately bring to bear?

6. Dudley Andrew, "The Theater of Irish Cinema," 26.

7. For more on Kenneth Burke's approach, see his *Grammar of Motives*.

8. Quoted in Rockett, Gibbons, and Hill, *Cinema and Ireland*, 38. The volume contains an excellent account, written by Rockett, of the development of indigenous films from the silent era to the early 1980s (3–144). It is particularly good in its discussions of the dominance of British and American releases in Irish movie houses.

9. Martin McLoone, "Reimagining the Nation: Themes and Issues in Irish Cinema."

10. The film goes on to engage the issue of creativity in contemporary Irish arts without imposing simplistic explanations. Its central character, Timmy (Brian O'Byrne), lives in a world that has the very attributes proscribed by the de Brie speech. At the same time, he has difficulty discerning the difference between the material world that surrounds him and the imaginative world that he evokes. With delightful self-consciousness, the narrative invokes and then parodies images from Hitchcock's *Psycho* and then elaborates on them in Timmy's troubled exchanges with his psychiatrist (Ian Richardson), overall underscoring the issues of identity in an artistic work.

11. Imagine you are attending a public lecture, listening to a noted authority on a topic with which you have a great deal of familiarity. As the man drones on, taking a long time to say very little, you note a number of things: the banality of his argument, the pedantry of his delivery, an ensemble that suggests he dressed in his closet with the light out, and the poor personal hygiene of the person sitting next to you. You also wonder if you remembered to mail the letter that you left in your front hallway, and remind yourself to call your mother to wish her a happy birthday. If, consequently, someone asked you what the talk was like, giving the linear answer—"disappointing"—would hardly encompass your full sense of the experience.

12. As I noted in the Preface, in a number of film analyses throughout this study, I will provide detailed summaries of the motion pictures under consideration. I understand that doing so will create a measure of redundancy for those individuals familiar with the films, but my hope is that it will increase the accessibility of my argument for readers, particularly outside Ireland, who have not had the opportunity to view selected movies.

13. Hugh Linehan, "Myth, Mammon, and Mediocrity: The Trouble with Recent Irish Cinema," 46.

14. Hugh Linehan, "The Story So Far."

15. Harvey O'Brien, http://homepage.eircom.net/~obrienh/.

16. Neil Jackson, "Kirk Jones," 170.

17. McLoone, *Irish Film*, 59.

18. Ruth Barton touches on a similar element in analyzing a scene from *Hear My Song*, a film that I must admit I never saw as anything but a stereotypical representation until I read Barton's comments ("From History to Heritage: Some Recent Developments in Irish Cinema," 51).

19. For a sample of some of the critiques of the film, see Elizabeth Cullingford, "The Reception of *Michael Collins*"; Luke Gibbons, "Demisting the Screen: Neil Jordan's *Michael Collins*"; and Glen Newey, "Both Gangster and Gandhi Agency Without Blame: The Significant Omissions of *Michael Collins*." I will refer to these essays in greater detail in Chapter 6.

20. McLoone, *Irish Film*, 128. This categorization reflects an expansion of a list that McLoone offered in an essay in *Border Crossing*, edited by Hill, McLoone, and Hainsworth, 157–58.

21. For similar approaches, albeit along linear lines, see Ruth Barton, "Kitsch as Authenticity: Irish Cinema and the Challenge of Romanticism"; and Luke Gibbons, "Romanticism, Realism, and Irish Cinema."

2. Latent Metrosexuality: The Erasure of Irish Identity in Middle-Class Cinema

1. For a good overview of conditions during this period, see Mary Daly, *The Slow Failure: Population Decline and Independent Ireland, 1920–1973*.

2. For a good survey of this development, see G. Honor Fagan, "Globalization, Identity, and 'Ireland.'"

3. See, for example, Michael Mays, "Irish Identity in an Age of Globalisation."

4. For a statistical analysis of Irish views regarding national identity, see Thomas C. Davis, "The Irish and Their Nation: A Survey of Recent Attitudes."

5. The *Daily Mirror (Eire Edition)*, December 13, 2004, 4, reported the average total gross annual household income for Ireland for 2004 at EUR 49,000, whereas the poverty level was set at EUR 9,680.

6. In contrast, U.S. filmmakers have proved adept at conveying images of the American middle class from the screwball comedies of the 1930s onward.

7. The phrase comes from a letter from James Joyce to his publisher, Grant Richards, describing the effect of the stories in *Dubliners* (*Letters of James Joyce*, 64).

8. *Images* (1972) was an earlier motion picture filmed in Ireland, focusing on middle-class lives. Directed by Robert Altman, it also deals with marital discord, but the narrative almost exclusively examines the internal struggles and ultimately the psychological breakdown of Cathryn (Susannah York), with little real attention given to the impact of the environment that surrounds her.

9. The significance of the name Ailsa itself creates problematic issues. It seems to come from Scots, Ailsa Craig, a rocky inlet in the Clyde estuary. Its English equivalent could be Elizabeth or possibly Alistair. This name, like the name of the baby's mother, Campbell, serves to blur sexual identity.

10. For an examination of contemporary sexual attitudes among Dublin women, using the opening of an Ann Summers branch on O'Connell Street as a benchmark, see Karen Sugrue, "Sex in the City."

3. Urban Legends: The Survival of Working-Class Films

1. See Hilary Tover, "Sociology in Ireland: Intimations of Post-modernity."

2. See, for example, Kieran Allen, *The Celtic Tiger: The Myth of Social Partnership in Ireland*, for a detailed analysis of the economic impact on the working class. See also Proinnsias Breathnach, "Social Polarization in the Post-Ford Informational Economy: Ireland in International Context"; as well as Roy Foster, "'Changed Utterly'? Transformation and Continuity

in Late-Twentieth-Century Ireland." For a view of the lifestyle changes experienced by the middle class, see David McWilliams, *The Pope's Children: Ireland's New Elite*, referenced in Appendix A.

3. Allen, *Celtic Tiger*, 71.

4. Michael Cronin endorses this passage as underscoring the uniqueness of the working-class environment of the film when he says, "The statement can only make sense in terms of the experience of *specific* kinds of Dubliners who are united by social exclusion" (*The Barrytown Trilogy*, 22; emphasis in the original).

5. As a rule of thumb, any film that gratuitously introduces a midget into the narrative announces its inherent weakness.

4. Down on the Farm: The Calcification of Irish Rural Drama

1. In contrast, the world of the urban middle class did not so much erode as metamorphosize.

2. For a clear sense of the mores of rural Ireland through the 1960s, see Conrad M. Arensberg and Solon T. Kimbal, *Family and Community in Ireland*.

3. One sees the same phenomenon in American westerns, where a number of second-rate efforts, particularly in the 1950s, earned the derisive nickname "oaters."

4. Elsewhere, I have examined in greater detail the parallels between *The Quiet Man* and two rural films from the 1970s, *Poitín* and *Reefer and the Model*. See "Is Californication a Mortal Sin?"

5. *Traveller* is one of a series of films, including *Into the West*, *Trojan Eddie*, and *Pavee Lackeen*, that deal with this marginalized community. Arguably, they form a category in their own right. In my approach, however, I have chosen to examine each in the context of a larger grouping.

6. On a personal note, I first saw *Traveller* at the Irish Film Institute. The print provided to me had French subtitles. Despite my weak grasp of that language, they were an invaluable aid to understanding the dialogue.

7. Although *December Bride* remains an underappreciated film, Lance Pettitt has written a wonderful introduction to it as part of the Cork University Press series Ireland into Film. See particularly pp. 5–8, in which Pettitt outlines the cultural context from which O'Sullivan's film emerged.

8. Although Martin McLoone sees in *December Bride* ironic references to *The Quiet Man* (*Irish Film*, 209–10), his argument does more to establish the influence of Ford's film. See also Pettitt, *December Bride*, 44–45, for a reasoned response to this claim.

9. Ruth Barton, *Jim Sheridan: Framing the Nation*, 40–41.

10. Cathal Black's *Love and Rage*, released in 2000, may at first glance seem a thematic exception to this trend. Set on Achill Island at the turn of the last century and based on a true story, it recounts the escapades of James Lynchehaun (Daniel Craig). He charms the

divorced woman in the Big House, Agnes MacDonnell (Greta Scacchi), seduces her, persuades her to employ him as her land agent, and proceeds to disrupt the household. In the end she drives him off. He returns for a final confrontation, and it is unclear if she actually kills him. *Love and Rage* has beautiful cinematography and a riveting story line, though critical responses to the performances of the actors were mixed. Whether one agrees with these assessments or not, the fact remains that engaging narratives of rural Ireland depend on the tension of rival political, religious, or cultural positions to provide a cohesive plot. Presenting a narrative with few indications of what forces motivate its characters goes beyond fostering multiplicity to producing arbitrariness.

11. Ruth Barton gives a detailed assessment of Pierce Brosnan's acting in *Acting Irish in Hollywood*, 198–99.

12. A further element of the production might provide some additional evidence of the erasure of Irishness. The director, Goran Paskaljevic, is Serbian, shooting his first English-language film. (He did have an earlier motion picture, *Twilight Time* [1982], filmed in Yugoslavia in Serbo-Croatian with some English dialogue.) This fact in itself does not preclude the creation of an Irish-themed work. John Ford has shown that a nonindigenous director can make a rural Irish-themed film. Likewise, many of the narratives in Irish films have archetypal echoes of situations explored in many national literatures. In every instance, however, a sense of specific communal values defines the identity of the film. In contrast, Sergio Leone's spaghetti westerns fail to qualify for a place in the genre because, despite the presence of American actors in the leading roles, these movies never grasp the fundamental American myths that animate them. Indeed, with their international casts, individual actors often delivered their lines in their native languages and had the dialogue dubbed into English during the editing process.

5. Suffer the Little Children: Reconstructions of the Family

1. For an example of how subjective, even to a professional educator, this concept can be, see Bernie Purcell, *For Our Own Good: Childcare Issues in Ireland*. For a view of how Irish children define Irishness, see Fionnuala Waldron and Susan Pike, "What Does It Mean to Be Irish? Children's Construction of National Identity."

2. Diarmaid Ferriter, "Suffer Little Children? The Historical Validity of Memoirs of Irish Childhood." For a specific example of a good memoir, see Bernadette Fahy, *Freedom of Angels*.

3. Clair Willis, "Women, Domesticity, and the Family: Recent Feminist Work in Irish Cultural Studies"; Leo Tolstoy, *Anna Karenina*, 1.

4. The 1956 film *Jacqueline*, which takes place in Belfast during Elizabeth II's coronation week, can hardly be seen as the exception that proves the rule. Based on the Catherine Cookson novel *A Good Man*, which was set in England, the film rarely moves beyond the outlines of a prescriptive domestic comedy. Scenes from the Belfast shipyards attempt to

enforce a geographic Irishness, but stereotypical characters and a predictable plot truncate any gesture toward cultural uniqueness, much less an examination of an Irish childhood. Indeed, the vitriolic attacks on the Irishness of *Waking Ned Devine*, recounted in Chapter 1, seem far more applicable to this film.

5. Even ordinary language highlights this condition of isolation. In fact, the boys' accents make the dialogue so difficult to follow that, according to Kevin Rockett, the British version of the film supplied English subtitles (*Irish Filmography*, 28).

6. The reconciliation, even celebration, of an out-of-wedlock pregnancy that one sees in *The Snapper*, a film discussed in Chapter 3, is so unusual as to be aberrant. A much harsher view generally obtains in Irish-themed films. This notion also reflects a condition not specifically examined in the study but implied through references to multiple perspectives: the malleability of specific motion pictures when cataloged. I identified *The Snapper* as a working-class film to emphasize a key feature of identity: the transition of Dessie, Sharon's father, from a conventional, intolerant patriarch to a caring, supportive parent. The film would produce a different reading with emphasis on Sharon, and in fact the most effective interpretation would hold both views, and the views of subordinate characters, in tension with one another.

7. Pettitt, *Screening Ireland*, 270–71.

8. This point is not to say that any Irish-themed film dealing with social issues inevitably becomes tedious, though indeed many have. A number of motion pictures have explored the experiences of children in institutions with diverse results. These movies form an extension of the previous category, examining how institutions acting in loco parentis exert a kind of tyranny unique to Irish experiences. The subjects of these films are hardly surprising. In a country where religion in general and Catholicism in particular exert a dominant influence on daily life, motion pictures examining the world of childhood can take advantage of definitive cultural markers to establish their Irishness. Tracing the growth—emotional, spiritual, and physical—of a child in Ireland involves an engagement with stages of religious development particular to the Irish experience. Further, the close association of the Roman Catholic Church and national education, a tie going back to the early nineteenth century, offers the possibility for uniquely Irish films. Because of the connection with religion, education, and care for homeless children, I will examine films about children in state institutions such as *Lamb*, *Our Boys*, and *The Magdalene Sisters* in the next chapter.

9. Neil Jordan's 2005 film, *Breakfast on Pluto*, an adaptation of another Patrick McCabe novel, pursues the same issues. That motion picture, however, lacks the force and complexity of *The Butcher Boy*. Although Jordan does not shy away from gritty representations of the rent-boy sexuality of male prostitution, overall the film considerably modifies the harshness of McCabe's book, exemplified in the decision to give the central character, Patrick Braden, the nickname "Kitten" rather than "Pussy," his soubriquet in the fictional work. As a consequence, Patrick Braden seems more eccentric than wounded, and a surprisingly optimistic tone infuses the film's conclusion.

10. For an examination of how the film represents Irish identity in terms of its relation to Hollywood cinema, especially westerns, see Gretchen Bisplinghoff, "Irish Images: Constructs of Film Space/Time." Bisplinghoff's close reading focuses on the marginalized status of the Traveller community.

6. In the Name of the Father: Images of Religious Beliefs

1. See Tom Inglis, "Religion, Identity, State, and Society."

2. For details on the early stages of this process, see Emmet Larkin, *The Roman Catholic Church and the Emergence of the Modern Irish Political System, 1874–1878.*

3. For an excellent overview of Catholicism in Ireland since the founding of the Free State, see Tom Inglis, *Moral Monopoly: The Rise and Fall of the Catholic Church in Modern Ireland.* See also Louise Fuller, *Irish Catholicism since 1950: The Undoing of a Culture.*

4. See Patrick Murray, *Oracles of God: The Roman Catholic Church and Irish Politics, 1922–37;* and John Cooney, *John Charles McQuaid: Ruler of Catholic Ireland.*

5. Inglis, "Religion, Identity, State, and Society," 62.

6. Ibid., 73. He does not, however, cite a source for these figures.

7. Curiously, in contrast to Ireland's relative lack of interest in religious-themed motion pictures, Catholic films have enjoyed a long-standing popularity in the more secularized environment of the United States. From the tough ghetto priests in 1930s films such as *Angels with Dirty Faces* and *Boys' Town;* to hagiographies including *The Song of Bernadette* (1943); to clerical buddy pictures, the Bing Crosby–Barry Fitzgerald films of the mid-1940s, *Going My Way* and *The Bells of St. Mary's;* to a celebration of individual faith, including *On the Waterfront* (1954), *The Nun's Story* (1959), *Heaven Knows, Mr. Allison* (1957), *Francis of Assisi* (1961), *The Cardinal* (1963), and *A Man for All Seasons* (1966); to an interrogation of the structure of the church, such as *True Confessions* (1981), *The Assisi Underground* (1985), *The Mission* (1986), *The Last Temptation of Christ* (1988), *Black Robe* (1991), *The Passion of the Christ* (2004), and *The Da Vinci Code* (2006), Hollywood has shown a fascination for the church, its institutions and beliefs, and the people who make up its hierarchy. Irish filmmakers have seemed more reticent to take up the topic, and have proved to be far less sentimental when they do.

8. James M. Smith is less overtly critical of the film in his essay "*The Magdalene Sisters:* Evidence, Testimony . . . Action?" However, he does note the didacticism that I find reductive.

9. As Peter Mullan himself admitted in a September 16, 2002, interview in the *Manchester Guardian,* he undertook his project after seeing the 1998 Channel 4 documentary directed by Stephen Humphries, *Sex in a Cold Climate,* which dealt with the excesses of the Magdalene homes and powerfully affected him. Two years earlier, Louis Lentin, with funding from RTÉ, directed *Dear Daughter,* a documentary about a woman who grew up in the Sisters of Mercy orphanage in Goldenbridge, Dublin. In 1999 RTÉ aired a three-part documentary, *States of Fear,* directed by Mary Raftery, that elaborated on abuses in Irish industrial

schools. That point in turns begs the question: why present a fictionalized version of such incidents when acclaimed factual accounts already exist?

10. Leanne McCormick, "Sinister Sisters? The Portrayal of Ireland's Magdalene Asylums in Popular Culture."

11. Kevin Rockett, in *Irish Filmography*, translates *Budawanny* as meaning "monk's penis" (38). In the title and subtitle of Father Conor's novel the crude pun also suggests a complicity that becomes more apparent when the companion film, *A Bishop's Story*, appears.

12. Nonetheless, it is important to note significant cinematographic differences between the two films. Bob Quinn shot *Budawanny* as a silent film on 16mm stock; in black-and-white, sepia, and color; in English; with synchronized sound. *The Bishop's Story*, on the other hand, is on 35mm film stock that uses the island footage from *Budawanny* (which Quinn blew up to 35mm, making it very grainy). Quinn makes these images sepia-toned rather than black-and-white, has dialogue in Irish (which had to be rerecorded and dubbed over the images), and now has the Irish-language dialogue translated not by subtitles but by silent-movie-style intertitles. The evocation of another era stands out clearly, but the genius of the gesture lies in Quinn's implicit invitation to find in these nuanced images new meaning for the reiterated narrative.

7. The Struggle for Independence in Irish Political Films

1. Of course, nationalism and political beliefs are not synonymous entities. However, Irish-themed films often elide the distinctions between the two. Indeed, the near-universal articulation in these motion pictures of nationalism through diverse political perspectives indicates the fragmented point of view that the cinema imposes on national identity.

2. For an examination of these evolving ideologies, see Liam O'Dowd, "Republicanism, Nationalism, and Unionism: Changing Contexts, Cultures, and Ideologies."

3. In the Preface, I note the range of views regarding Ireland's status as a First or Third World nation. Whatever one's position on that issue, one cannot deny its condition as a postcolonial country. However, scholars continue to debate what that condition specifically entails. See, for example, Colin Coulter and Steve Coleman, eds., *The End of Irish History: Critical Reflections on the Celtic Tiger;* Desmond Fennell, *The Revision of Irish Nationalism;* Richard Kearney, *Postnationalist Ireland: Politics, Culture, Philosophy;* and Michel Peillon and Eamonn Slater, eds., *Encounters with Modern Ireland: A Sociological Chronicle, 1995–1996.*

4. John Hill, "Images of Violence," 149.

5. Ibid., 150 (emphasis in the original), 158.

6. Dai Vaughan, in *"Odd Man Out"*, a very thorough formal analysis of the film, reaches a slightly different conclusion. Through careful study of mise-en-scène, Vaughan emphasizes the near-existential representation of the major characters and what he sees as the de-emphasis of the political context from which they emerge.

7. Indeed, in the context of events surrounding the 1972 killings, the term *fiction* takes on mutable characteristics, for one might legitimately ask whether *Bloody Sunday* is any more

fictional than the Widgery report, the British government's account of the official investigation of events that found no member of the armed forces at fault for the deaths of fourteen peaceful protesters.

8. Ken Loach's 2006 film, *The Wind That Shakes the Barley*, covers much the same political ground as *Michael Collins*, albeit with some key differences. It focuses on a flying column operating in West Cork rather than on the urban warfare in Dublin, and it privileges the Die Hard point of view rather than the Free Staters'. However, Loach's own sympathies and melodramatic tendencies make his motion picture a far more simplistic effort. He gives attention to important events, including rural fighting, and issues, such as the impact of socialism on opposition to the British, but he has no interest in going beyond representations that offer viewers few imaginative choices and instead promote passive acquiescence.

9. Neil Jordan, *"Michael Collins": Film Diary and Screenplay,* 17.

10. Ibid., 63.

11. Newey, "Both Gangster and Gandhi," 20.

12. Cullingford, "Reception of *Michael Collins.*"

13. Gibbons, "Demisting the Screen," 16.

14. Jordan, *"Michael Collins,"* 71, 165. Bracketed lines are in the film but not in the shooting script.

15. This emphasis is by no means accidental, since Jordan used the Tim Pat Coogan biography of Michael Collins, a book that gives a very different picture of Collins's nationalism and his views on the status of the North, as the basis of his film, and Coogan makes these attitudes clear.

16. Luke Gibbons, "Engendering the State: Narrative, Allegory, and *Michael Collins,*" 269.

Appendix A: The Subjectivity of Irishness

1. For a sociologist's analysis of the formation of contemporary Irish identity, see Markus Kornprobst, "Episteme, Nation-Builders, and National Identity: The Re-construction of Irishness."

2. Brendan Bradshaw highlights the disruptive impact of violence on Irish culture, lamenting how "seared as the record is by successive waves of conquest and colonization, by bloody waves and uprisings, by traumatic dislocations, by lethal racial antagonisms, and indeed, by its own nineteenth-century version of the holocaust" ("Nationalism and Historical Scholarship in Modern Ireland," 338).

3. Denis Donoghue, *We Irish,* 9. In his typically breezy fashion, Donoghue fails to identify precisely the source of his paraphrase of Seamus Deane, further blurring distinctions between subjectivity and objectivity.

4. Gibbons, *Transformations in Irish Culture,* 6; Colin Coulter, introduction to *End of Irish History,* edited by Coulter and Coleman, 4.

5. Eamonn Slater, "Becoming an Irish *Flâneur*," in *Encounters with Modern Ireland*, edited by Peillon and Slater, 5.

6. Kearney, *Postnationalist Ireland*, 99. One finds a less sweeping reassessment in Fennell, *Revision of Irish Nationalism*.

7. McWilliams, *Pope's Children*, 53–54.

Appendix B: The Irish Infrastructure

1. For a detailed account of the Film Board revival and other political developments, see Barton, *Irish National Cinema*, 104–12.

2. Pettitt, *Screening Ireland*, 285.

3. Ibid., 286; Barton, *Irish National Cinema*, 191–92.

Appendix D: Popular Attitudes in Irish Audiences

1. These figures come from e-mails sent to me by the film censor's office. Ratings for these films roughly paralleled one another, so it was not the case of distributors importing a particular sort of foreign film.

Appendix E: Cross-Cultural Filmmaking

1. See Hamid Naficy, *An Accented Cinema: Exilic and Diasporic Filmmaking;* and Brian McIlroy, "Exodus, Arrival, and Return: The Generic Discourse of Irish Diasporic and Exilic Narrative Films."

Bibliography

Allen, Kieran. *The Celtic Tiger: The Myth of Social Partnership in Ireland*. Manchester: Manchester Univ. Press, 2000.

Anderson, Benedict. *Imagined Communities: Reflections on the Origin and Spread of Nationalism*. 1983. Reprint, London and New York: Verso, 1991.

Andrew, Dudley. "The Theater of Irish Cinema." *Yale Journal of Criticism* 15, no. 1 (2002): 23–58.

Arensberg, Conrad M., and Solon T. Kimbal. *Family and Community in Ireland*. 2d ed. Cambridge: Harvard Univ. Press, 1968.

Barker, Chris. *The SAGE Dictionary of Cultural Studies*. London: SAGE Publications, 2004.

Barthes, Roland. *S/Z*. Translated by Richard Miller. New York: Hill and Wang, 1974.

Barton, Ruth. *Acting Irish in Hollywood: From Fitzgerald to Farrell*. Dublin and Portland, Ore.: Irish Academic Press, 2006.

———. "From History to Heritage: Some Recent Developments in Irish Cinema." *Irish Review* 21 (1997): 41–56.

———. *Irish National Cinema*. London and New York: Routledge, 2004.

———. *Jim Sheridan: Framing the Nation*. Dublin: Liffey Press, 2002.

———. "Kitsch as Authenticity: Irish Cinema and the Challenge of Romanticism." *Irish Studies Review* 9, no. 2 (2001): 193–202.

Bhabha, Homi. *The Location of Culture*. New York: Routledge, 1994.

———, ed. *Nation and Narration*. New York: Routledge and Kegan Paul, 1990.

Billig, Michael. *Banal Nationalism*. London: SAGE Publications, 1995.

Bisplinghoff, Gretchen. "Irish Images: Constructs of Film Space/Time." *Critical Studies* 14, no. 1 (2000): 74–87.

Bradshaw, Brendan. "Nationalism and Historical Scholarship in Modern Ireland." *Irish Historical Studies* 25, no. 104 (Nov. 1989): 329–51.

Breathnach, Proinnsias. "Social Polarization in the Post-Ford Informational Economy: Ireland in International Context." *Irish Journal of Sociology* 11, no. 1 (2001): 3–22.

Brooker, Peter. *A Concise Glossary of Cultural Theory*. New York: Oxford Univ. Press, 1999.

Burke, Kenneth. *A Grammar of Motives*. New York: Random House, 1969.

Burton, Julianne. "Marginal Cinemas and Mainstream Critical Theory." *Screen* 26, nos. 3–4 (May–Aug. 1985): 2–21.

Caherty, Thérèse, ed. *Is Ireland a Third World Country?* Belfast: Beyond the Pale Publications, 1992.

Chanan, Michael. "The Changing Geography of Third Cinema." *Screen* 38, no. 4 (Winter 1997): 372–88.

Cohen, Jack, and Ian Stewart. *The Collapse of Chaos: Discovering Simplicity in a Complex World*. New York: Viking, 1994.

Cooney, John. *John Charles McQuaid: Ruler of Catholic Ireland*. Dublin: O'Brien Press, 1999.

Coulter, Colin, and Steve Coleman, eds. *The End of Irish History: Critical Reflections on the Celtic Tiger*. Manchester: Manchester Univ. Press, 2003.

Crofts, Stephen. "Reconceptualizing National Cinemas." *Quarterly Review of Film and Video* 14, no. 3 (1993): 49–50.

Cronin, Michael. *The Barrytown Trilogy*. Cork: Cork Univ. Press, 2006.

Cullingford, Elizabeth. "The Reception of *Michael Collins*." *Irish Literary Supplement* 16 (Spring 1997): 17–18.

Daly, Mary. *The Slow Failure: Population Decline and Independent Ireland, 1920–1973*. Madison: Univ. of Wisconsin Press, 2006.

Davis, Thomas C. "The Irish and Their Nation: A Survey of Recent Attitudes." *Global Review of Ethnopolitics* 2, no. 2 (Jan. 2003): 17–36.

Derrida, Jacques. "Structure, Sign, and Play in the Discourse of the Human Sciences." In *Knowledge and Post-modernism in Historical Perspective*, edited by Joyce Appleby. New York: Routledge, 1996.

Donoghue, Denis. *We Irish*. Berkeley and Los Angeles: Univ. of California Press, 1988.

Dowling, William C. "John Ford's Festive Comedy: Ireland Imagined in *The Quiet Man*." *Eire-Ireland* 34, nos. 3–4 (1999): 190–211.

Elsaesser, Thomas. "Chronicle of a Death Retold." *Monthly Film Bulletin* 54, no. 641 (June 1987): 162–73.

Fagan, G. Honor. "Globalization, Identity, and 'Ireland.'" In *Globalization and National Identities,* edited by Paul Kennedy and Catherine J. Danks, 113–23. New York: Palgrave, 2001.

Fahy, Bernadette. *Freedom of Angels.* Dublin: O'Brien Press, 1999.

Farley, Fidelma. *"This Other Eden."* Cork: Cork Univ. Press, 2001.

Fennell, Desmond. *The Revision of Irish Nationalism.* Dublin: Open Air, 1989.

Ferriter, Diarmaid. "Suffer Little Children? The Historical Validity of Memoirs of Irish Childhood." In *Childhood and Its Discontents,* edited by Joseph Dunne and James Kelly, 69–106. Dublin: Liffey Press, 2002.

Finn, Eugene. "From the Ex-Country." *Film Ireland* 100 (Sept.–Oct. 2004): 22–24.

Flynn, Arthur. *The Story of Irish Film.* Blackrock: Currach Press, 2005.

Foster, Roy. "'Changed Utterly'? Transformation and Continuity in Late-Twentieth-Century Ireland." *Historical Research* 80 (2007): 419–41.

Fuller, Louise. *Irish Catholicism since 1950: The Undoing of a Culture.* Dublin: Gill and Macmillan, 2004.

Gabriel, Teshome. *Third Cinema in the Third World: The Aesthetics of Liberation.* Ann Arbor: UMI Research Press, 1982.

Geertz, Clifford. *The Interpretation of Cultures: Selected Essays.* New York: Basic Books, 1973.

Gellner, Ernest. *Nation and Nationalism.* Oxford: Blackwell, 1983.

Gellner, Ernest, and Anthony D. Smith. "The Nation: Real or Imagined? The Warwick Debates on Nationalism." *Nation and Nationalism* 2, no. 3 (1996): 357–70.

Gibbons, Luke. "Demisting the Screen: Neil Jordan's *Michael Collins.*" *Irish Literary Supplement* 16 (Spring 1997): 16.

———. "Engendering the State: Narrative, Allegory, and *Michael Collins.*" *Eire-Ireland* 31 (Fall–Winter 1996): 261–69.

———. *"The Quiet Man."* Cork: Cork Univ. Press, 2000.

———. "Romanticism, Realism, and Irish Cinema." In *Cinema and Ireland,* by Kevin Rockett, Luke Gibbons, and John Hill, 194–257. Syracuse: Syracuse Univ. Press, 1988.

———. *Transformations in Irish Culture.* Cork: Cork Univ. Press, 1996.

Gill, Liz. "Low Future." *Film Ireland* 103 (Mar.–Apr. 2005): 16.

———. "Where to Now?" *Film Ireland* 104 (May–June 2005): 16.

Gillespie, Michael Patrick. *The Aesthetics of Chaos: Nonlinear Thinking and Contemporary Literary Criticism.* Gainesville: Univ. Press of Florida, 2003.

———."Is Californication a Mortal Sin? The Influence of Classic Hollywood Cinema on Indigenous Irish Film." In *Genre and Cinema: Ireland and Transnationalism,* edited by Brian McIlroy, 61–75. New York and London: Routledge, 2007.

———. "The Chaos and Complexity of Classic Hollywood Cinema." *Nonlinear Dynamics, Psychology, and Life Science* 10, no. 1 (Jan. 2006): 123–41.

———. "The Myth of Hidden Ireland: The Corrosive Effect of *The Quiet Man.*" *New Hibernia Review* 6 (Summer 2002): 18–32.

Griffin, Joe. "The Golden Bowl." *Film Ireland* 94 (Sept.–Oct. 2003): 30–31.

Hayward, Susan. "Framing National Cinema." In *Cinema and Nation,* edited by Mette Hjort and Scott MacKenzie, 88–102. London and New York: Routledge, 2000.

Higson, Andrew. "The Concept of National Cinema." *Screen* 30, no. 4 (Autumn 1989): 36–46.

Hill, John. "Images of Violence." In *Cinema and Ireland,* by Kevin Rockett, Luke Gibbons, and John Hill, 147–93. Syracuse: Syracuse Univ. Press, 1988.

Hill, John, Martin McLoone, and Paul Hainsworth, eds. *Border Crossing: Film in Ireland, Britain, and Europe.* Belfast: Institute of Irish Studies in Association with the Univ. of Ulster and the British Film Institute, 1994.

Hjort, Mette, and Scott MacKenzie, eds. *Cinema and Nation.* London and New York: Routledge, 2000.

Hughes, Art J. "Advancing the Language: Irish in the Twenty-first Century." *New Hibernia Review* 5, no. 1 (2001): 101–26.

Inglis, Tom. *Moral Monopoly: The Rise and Fall of the Catholic Church in Modern Ireland.* Dublin: Univ. College–Dublin Press, 1998.

———. "Religion, Identity, State, and Society." In *The Cambridge Companion to Modern Irish Culture,* edited by Joe Cleary and Claire Connolly, 59–77. Cambridge: Cambridge Univ. Press, 2005.

Iser, Wolfgang. *The Act of Reading: A Theory of Aesthetic Response.* Baltimore: Johns Hopkins Univ. Press, 1978.

Jackson, Neil. "Kirk Jones." In *Contemporary British and Irish Film Directors,* 170. London and New York: Wallflower, 2001.

Jauss, Hans Walter. *Towards an Aesthetic of Reception.* Translated by Timothy Bahti. Minneapolis: Univ. of Minnesota Press, 1982.

Jordan, Neil. *"Michael Collins": Film Diary and Screenplay.* London: Vintage, 1996.

Joyce, James. *Letters of James Joyce.* Vol. 1. Edited by Stuart Gilbert. New York: Viking Press, 1957.

———. *Ulysses.* New York: Random House, 1986.

Kearney, Richard. *Postnationalist Ireland: Politics, Culture, Philosophy.* London: Routledge, 1997.

Kiberd, Declan. *Inventing Ireland.* Cambridge: Harvard Univ. Press, 1995.

Kirby, Anthony, and James MacKillop. "Selected Filmography of Irish and Irish-Related Feature Films." In *Contemporary Irish Cinema: From "The Quiet Man" to "Dancing at Lughnasa,"* edited by James MacKillop, 182–231. Syracuse: Syracuse Univ. Press, 1999.

Kornprobst, Markus. "Episteme, Nation-Builders, and National Identity: The Reconstruction of Irishness." *Nations and Nationalism* 11, no. 3 (2005): 403–21.

Larkin, Emmet. *The Roman Catholic Church and the Emergence of the Modern Irish Political System, 1874–1878.* Dublin: Four Courts Press, 1996.

Linehan, Hugh. "Myth, Mammon, and Mediocrity: The Trouble with Recent Irish Cinema." *Cineaste* 24, nos. 2–3 (1999): 46–49.

———. "The Story So Far." *Film Ireland* (Oct.–Nov. 1994): 28–30.

Logue, Paddy, ed. *Being Irish: Personal Reflections on Irish Identity Today.* Dublin: Oak Tree Press, 2000.

Lovelock, James. *The Ages of Gaia.* New York: W. W. Norton, 1988.

MacHale, Des. *The Complete Guide to "The Quiet Man."* Belfast: Appletree Press, 2000.

MacKillop, James. "The Quiet Man Speaks." In *Contemporary Irish Cinema: From "The Quiet Man" to "Dancing at Lughnasa,"* edited by James MacKillop, 169–81. Syracuse: Syracuse Univ. Press, 1999.

Mays, Michael. "Irish Identity in an Age of Globalisation." *Irish Studies Review* 13 (2005): 3–12.

McCormick, Leanne. "Sinister Sisters? The Portrayal of Ireland's Magdalene Asylums in Popular Culture." *Cultural and Social History* 2, no. 3 (2005): 373–79.

McIlroy, Brian. "Exodus, Arrival, and Return: The Generic Discourse of Irish Diasporic and Exilic Narrative Films." In *Keeping It Real: Irish Film and Television,* edited by Ruth Barton and Harvey O'Brien, 69–77. New York and London: Wallflower Press, 2004.

———. *Irish Cinema: An Illustrated History.* Dublin: Anna Livia Press, 1988.

———, ed. *Genre and Cinema: Ireland and Transnationalism.* New York and London: Routledge, 2007.

McLoone, Martin. *Irish Film: The Emergence of a Contemporary Cinema.* London: British Film Institute, 2000.

———. "National Cinema and Cultural Identity: Ireland and Europe." In *Border Crossing: Film in Ireland, Britain, and Europe,* edited by John Hill, Martin

McLoone, and Paul Hainsworth, 146–73. Belfast: Institute of Irish Studies in Association with the Univ. of Ulster and the British Film Institute, 1994.

———. "Reimagining the Nation: Themes and Issues in Irish Cinema." *Cineaste* 24, nos. 2–3 (1999): 28–34.

McNee, Gerry. *In the Footsteps of "The Quiet Man."* Edinburgh: Mainstream Publishing, 1990.

McWilliams, David. *The Pope's Children: Ireland's New Elite.* Dublin: Gill and Macmillan, 2005.

Murray, Patrick. *Oracles of God: The Roman Catholic Church and Irish Politics, 1922–37.* Dublin: Univ. College–Dublin Press, 2000.

Naficy, Hamid. *An Accented Cinema: Exilic and Diasporic Filmmaking.* Princeton: Princeton Univ. Press, 2001.

Newey, Glen. "Both Gangster and Gandhi Agency Without Blame: The Significant Omissions of *Michael Collins.*" *Times Literary Supplement,* Nov. 15, 1996, 20.

Nichols, Bill, ed. *Movies and Methods: An Anthology.* Berkeley and Los Angeles: Univ. of California Press, 1976.

O'Brien, Harvey. *The Real Ireland: The Evolution of Ireland in Documentary Film.* Manchester: Manchester Univ. Press, 2004.

O'Dowd, Liam. "Republicanism, Nationalism, and Unionism: Changing Contexts, Cultures, and Ideologies." In *The Cambridge Companion to Modern Irish Culture,* edited by Joe Cleary and Claire Connolly, 78–95. Cambridge: Cambridge Univ. Press, 2005.

O'Hearn, Dennis. "Globalization, 'New Tigers,' and the End of the Developmental State? The Case of the Celtic Tiger." *Politics and Society* 28, no. 1 (Mar. 2000): 67–92.

Peillon, Michel, and Eamonn Slater, eds. *Encounters with Modern Ireland: A Sociological Chronicle, 1995–1996.* Dublin: Institute of Public Administration, 1998.

Pettitt, Lance. *December Bride.* Cork: Cork Univ. Press, 2001.

———. *Screening Ireland: Film and Television Representation.* Manchester: Manchester Univ. Press, 2000.

Pines, Jim, and Paul Willemen, eds. *Questions of Third Cinema.* London: British Film Institute, 1989.

Pittock, Murray G. H. *Celtic Identity and the British Image.* Manchester: Manchester Univ. Press, 1999.

Purcell, Bernie. *For Our Own Good: Childcare Issues in Ireland.* Wilton, Cork: Collins Press, 2001.

Rockett, Kevin. "Aspects of the Los Angelesation of Ireland." *Irish Communication Review* 1 (1991): 22–30.

———. "Culture, Industry, and Irish Cinema." In *Border Crossing: Film in Ireland, Britain, and Europe,* edited by John Hill, Martin McLoone, and Paul Hainsworth, 126–39. Belfast: Institute of Irish Studies in Association with the Univ. of Ulster and the British Film Institute, 1994.

———. *The Irish Filmography: Fiction Films, 1896 to 1996.* Dublin: Red Mountain Media, 1996.

Rockett, Kevin, Luke Gibbons, and John Hill. *Cinema and Ireland.* Syracuse: Syracuse Univ. Press, 1988.

Said, Edward. *Orientalism.* New York: Pantheon Books, 1978.

Silverman, Hugh J., ed. *Questioning Foundations: Truth/Subjectivity/Culture.* New York: Routledge, 1993.

Smith, Anthony D. *The Ethnic Origins of Nations.* Oxford: Basil Blackwell, 1986.

Smith, James M. "*The Magdalene Sisters:* Evidence, Testimony . . . Action?" *Signs: Journal of Women in Culture and Society* 32, no. 2 (2007): 431–58.

Sugrue, Karen. "Sex in the City." In *Ireland Unbound: A Turn of the Century Chronicle,* edited by Mary P. Corcoran and Michel Peillon, 51–62. Dublin: Institute of Public Administration, 2002.

Tolstoy, Leo. *Anna Karenina.* Edited by George Gibian. Norton Critical Edition. New York: W. W. Norton, 1970.

Tover, Hilary. "Sociology in Ireland: Intimations of Post-modernity." *Irish Journal of Sociology* 10, no. 2 (2001): 77–85.

Triandis, H. C. *The Analysis of Subjective Culture.* New York: Wiley, 1972.

Vaughan, Dai. "*Odd Man Out.*" London: British Film Institute, 1995.

Vitali, Valentina, and Paul Willemen, eds. *Theorising National Cinema.* London: British Film Institute, 2006.

Waldron, Fionnuala, and Susan Pike. "What Does It Mean to Be Irish? Children's Construction of National Identity." *Irish Educational Studies* 25, no. 2 (June 2006): 231–51.

Willemen, Paul. "The Third Cinema Question: Notes and Reflections." *Framework* 34 (1987): 4–38.

Williams, Alan. Introduction to *Film and Nationalism,* edited by Alan Williams. New Brunswick: Rutgers Univ. Press, 2002.

Wills, Clair. "Women, Domesticity, and the Family: Recent Feminist Work in Irish Cultural Studies." *Cultural Studies* 15, no. 1 (2001): 33–57.

Woods, Mark. "Response from BSÉ/IFB." *Film Ireland* 103 (Mar.–Apr. 2005): 17.

Index

Italic page number denotes illustration.